REALISM AND COMPLEXITY IN SOCIAL SCIENCE

Realism and Complexity in Social Science is an argument for a new approach to investigating the social world, that of complex realism. Complex realism brings together a number of strands of thought, in scientific realism, complexity science, probability theory and social research methodology.

It proposes that the reality of the social world is that it is probabilistic, yet there exists enough invariance to make the discovery and explanation of social objects and causal mechanisms possible. This forms the basis for the development of a complex realist foundation for social research, that utilises a number of new and novel approaches to investigation, alongside the more traditional corpus of quantitative and qualitative methods. Research examples are drawn from research in sociology, epidemiology, criminology, social policy and human geography.

The book assumes no prior knowledge of realism, probability or complexity and in the early chapters, the reader is introduced to these concepts and the arguments against them. Although the book is grounded in philosophical reasoning, this is in a direct and accessible style that will appeal both to social researchers with a methodological interest and philosophers with an interest in social investigation.

Malcolm Williams is a Professor and Co-Director of the Q-Step Centre, at Cardiff University.

Complexity in Social Science

This interdisciplinary series encourages social scientists to embrace a complex systems approach to studying the social world. A complexity approach to the social world has expanded across the disciplines since its emergence in the mid-to-late 1990s, and this can only continue as disciplines continue to change, data continue to diversify, and governance and responses to global social issues continue to challenge all involved. Covering a broad range of topics from big data and time, globalisation and health, cities and inequality, and methodological applications, to more theoretical or philosophical approaches, this series responds to these challenges of complexity in the social sciences – with an emphasis on critical dialogue around, and application of these ideas in, a variety of social arenas as well as social policy.

The series will publish research monographs and edited collections between 60,000 and 90,000 words that include a range of philosophical, methodological and disciplinary approaches, which enrich and develop the field of social complexity and push it forward in new directions.

David Byrne is Emeritus Professor at the School of Applied Social Sciences, Durham University, UK.

Brian Castellani is a Professor in Sociology and Head of the Complexity in Health and Infrastructure Group, Kent State University, USA. He is also an Adjunct Professor of Psychiatry, Northeastern Ohio Medical University.

Emma Uprichard is an Associate Professor and Deputy Director at the Centre for Interdisciplinary Methodologies, University of Warwick, UK. She is also the co-director of the Nuffield, ESRC, HEFCE funded Warwick Q-Step Centre.

Lasse Gerrits is Professor of Urban Planning at the Institute for Housing and Urban Development Studies at the Erasmus University of Rotterdam (The Netherlands).

Books:

The Defiance of Global Commitment
A Complex Social Psychology
Brian Castellani

Emotions, Embodied Cognition and the Adaptive Unconscious
A Complex Topography of the Social Making of Things
John A. Smith

Realism and Complexity in Social Science
Malcolm Williams

For more information about the series, please visit: https://www.routledge.com/Complexity-in-Social-Science/book-series/CISS

REALISM AND COMPLEXITY IN SOCIAL SCIENCE

Malcolm Williams

LONDON AND NEW YORK

First published 2021
by Routledge
2 Park Square, Milton Park, Abingdon, Oxon OX14 4RN

and by Routledge
52 Vanderbilt Avenue, New York, NY 10017

Routledge is an imprint of the Taylor & Francis Group, an informa business

British Library Cataloguing-in-Publication Data
A catalogue record for this book is available from the British Library

Library of Congress Cataloging-in-Publication Data
A catalog record has been requested for this book

ISBN: 978-1-138-33561-5 (hbk)
ISBN: 978-1-138-33555-4 (pbk)
ISBN: 978-0-429-44370-1 (ebk)

Typeset in Bembo
by KnowledgeWorks Global Ltd.

This book is dedicated to a superb methodologist and good friend, the late W Paul Vogt.

Contents

Note about Author *viii*
Series editors' preface *ix*

1 Introduction: Knowing the social world – challenges and possibilities 1

2 Realism and its discontents 14

3 Complexity, probability and necessity in the social world 37

4 Causes and complexity 55

5 Representation and reality 81

6 Theory choice – verification, falsification and inference 102

7 Objective knowledge 124

8 Mechanisms 146

9 A methodological toolkit: From micro complexity to macro explanation 168

10 A manifesto for complex realism 196

References *207*
Index *222*

Note about author

Malcolm Williams is a Professor at Cardiff University where he teaches philosophy and methodology of the social sciences. He is a sort of sociologist, but not a proper one and his interests lie at the boundaries of disciplines – sociology, geography, statistics, social policy and philosophy of science. Over the years he has conducted research on homelessness, living alone, counterurbanisation and the barriers to learning quantitative methods in social science. This suggests he is either eclectic, or has a low boredom threshold! His favourite areas to work on are more philosophical and methodological and include probability, representation, objectivity/subjectivity and how these play out in realism and complexity, which is of course what the current book is about! He has published several books in philosophy and methodology, most recently *Key Concepts in the Philosophy of Social Research* (Sage 2016) and *Objectivity and Subjectivity in Social Research* (with Gayle Letherby and John Scott, Sage 2013).

https://www.cardiff.ac.uk/people/view/38062-williams-malcolm.

Series editors' preface

Does the study of social complexity feature a naturally-given epistemology and ontology? Arguably not (yet) but not many scholars seem to be acutely aware of this, so there is still a considerable mountain to be conquered. Since at least the 1990s, Malcolm Williams, Professor at the School of Social Sciences at Cardiff University (UK), has been at the forefront of climbing this philosophical mountain. The current book is the latest edition to the journey, some parts summary, others a rethinking of previous climbs; and still others entirely new climbs altogether.

Still, a topic as broad and vague as social complexity comes with a rather steep ascent; and so is not so easily climbed. Questions about the nature of reality are not new of course. For as long as people have thought about what makes the world tick, they have asked questions about what of this world can be known and how it can be known. The advent of the complexity sciences gave momentum to explore these questions in new directions. Williams recounts how he himself walked into this territory in response to the still-popular but ultimately false dichotomy between the school of thought that believes that social reality can be measured, assessed, and known directly and without further consideration – all you can see you see is reality – and those who adhere to the school of thought that such an endeavor is simply impossible, and that one is limited to discussions of perceptions of reality – nothing you see is real. It is between those two extremes that the most interesting things happen and that is where Williams' work is positioned.

The tale of understanding social complexity is one of bewildering complexity itself. One of the most important first attempts to scale this mountain, Williams says – and we, as Editors, agree – is Reed and Harvey's 1992 paper. This paper, appropriately entitled "The New Science and the Old: Complexity and Realism in the Social Sciences", identifies and joins two important strands: insights and theories from the complexity sciences on the one hand, and the work of British philosopher Roy Bhaskar on the other. As much as these are now more often seen in tandem, this was not the case in the 1990s. The emergence of the complexity sciences may challenge mechanistic and deterministic accounts of causality, subsequently challenging modernism. However, many of its core findings still run on good old positivism. Whether it is John Holland's emergent patterns or Chris Langton's flocks of simulated birds, a lot of complexity's canon derived from mathematics converted into innovative computational models such as cellular automata and agent-based models.

In hindsight, it is not always clear how much this challenged the conventional, positivist way of doing science. However, it is evident that the complexity sciences reimagined the kind of questions science could ask, and the nature of the answers it could render. Those concepts and methods questioned established truths about the relationship between the micro and the macro, put an emphasis on the non-linear nature of those relationships and reconsidered the ways in which non-linearity impacted the objects of interest. Bhaskar's work – vast as it is – does not engage directly with that kind of complexity but his understanding and articulation of causal complexity (as evident in e.g. "A Realist Theory of Science" from 1975) comes tantalizing close to what complexity theorists were after. It took Reed and Harvey to bring these two strands together and to outline the way in which the complexity sciences could be embedded into the social sciences. Nowadays, many scholars pair Bhaskar's realism with the complexity sciences when studying social complexity.

There is one problem, however: the tandem is not as much enacted in research as it is mentioned, and by a large margin. In other words: there is a gap between what scholars say must be done to scale this mountain and what they are actually doing. In fact, addressing this gap is part of the reason the Routledge Complexity in Social Science series was created.

This is where William's current book comes in.

While the realist understanding of social complexity has often been taken to be synonymous with Bhaskar's school of thought, there is actually much more variety when it comes to realism. Certainly, Bhaskar's work is undeniably important and has a real impact on the field. But it is also opaque in places, which may lead to misunderstandings and a disconnect between what is written and how it is enacted in research practice. In this book, Williams sets out to reconcile ideas from the complexity sciences with those about realism – and not just Bhaskar's work – to articulate a *complex realism* that merges the two strands more fully. Importantly, this is not (critical) realism with complexity theory added as rhetoric. Rather, it is true advance where the properties of both strands are brought into a real dialogue. A manifesto full of concrete ideas and starting points for researchers comes out on the other end of the process.

Why is this book needed right now? Now that the initial hype seems to have calmed down, we believe that the complexity sciences as used within the social domain has arrived at an important cross-road in its climb – a bifurcation point, if pardon the pun – where things may either die out *or* advance sufficiently to continue the climb. This book, and this entire book series in fact, aims to contribute to that advance by outlining the progress made since the 1990s and by showing how to move from there. The future trajectories cover a wide range of topics, including from our series innovations in research methods (Haynes' book), a recasting of our relationship with ecological and biological systems (the book by Smith and Jenks), and a complexity-based explanation of the deep tensions and real anger driving contemporary global society (Castellani's book). Williams' book provides a much-needed epistemological and ontological underpinning for such endeavors.

Importantly, he does much more than the merging of and elaboration of arguments. Williams provides concrete focal points for any social scientist wanting to do research in a complexity-informed manner, no matter whether they wish to compare a small number of qualitative case studies using QCA or carry out a quantitative cluster analysis. However, the utility of the book – for lack of better word – extends beyond the work of social scientists. The study of social complexity saw an influx of natural scientists, a trend arguably reinforced by the advent of so-called big data and automated data processing. Technically skillful but sometimes less well-versed in social theory and methods, they may find this book a perfect accompaniment to their ventures. Williams shows that there is much more depth to causality, the nature of social objects and the possibilities and limitations to prediction than is often assumed in those realms. The book will also be a fascinating reading for social scientists not directly engaged with social complexity. His discussion shows how complexity is relevant for any social scientist, not only to those that subscribe to the complexity turn. Since the book covers both theoretical considerations and practical examples, there will be enough entry points for each type of scholar.

This book is the next one in a series of important works he published over the years. In his introduction, he writes "It is not intended to be the last word on the matter". We concur that there is still much ground to cover but we are excited to see that this is new territory with ample room for new research into social complexity (plus, we did not want him to get away with the "definitive book"). There are many profound insights in this book. We welcome Williams to the book series and hope that the reader will be as inspired as we are about the book.

On behalf of the editors (Emma Uprichard, Brian Castellani and David Byrne),
Lasse Gerrits

1

Introduction

Knowing the social world – challenges and possibilities

Realism and Complexity in Social Science is a somewhat daunting title for a book, but presumably if you have got this far you are not that daunted! Nevertheless, a little reassurance may be in order. "Realism" and "Complexity" are not two separate concepts, indeed in this book I will present the case for something I describe as *Complex Realism*. Complex realism is not intended to be deep philosophy, though at least some philosophy comes into it. Rather the book is methodological in intent. If it is philosophy, then its philosophy for methodologists, not philosophers. Indeed, for my own part, whilst I have some background in philosophy of the social sciences, my life in the social sciences has always been as a researcher and teacher with a commitment to the practical value of social research. Complex realism is intended as a contribution to the building of a methodological base for a scientific social science. It is a contribution, because it is a work in progress, perhaps a small part of a bigger conversation about the value and methodological effectiveness of social science.

I'd like to begin with a bit of autobiography. This book is the product of an intellectual journey over the last 20 years or so. It all started in a book I edited, with Tim May, called *Knowing the Social World* (May and Williams 1998). In that book I wrote a chapter called "The Social World as Knowable", a brief overview of some of the philosophical and methodological issues facing us in such an endeavour, and reached an optimistic conclusion that such an endeavour is possible, because through research we can know enough of social reality to provide good enough descriptions and explanations. In that same volume some very fine scholars wrote deeper and more analytic papers than mine and these in turn came to influence my own thinking. Nevertheless, my chapter became something of a personal manifesto and over time developed into a version of what is termed "complex realism".[1]

So why does any of this matter? Surely social science and specifically social research is already quite successful in what it does? Indeed, this was precisely my own conclusion 22 years ago. I complained then that too many people were pessimistic about the possibilities of social research and went around saying why the bridge must fall down, whilst manifestly it was still standing! "Critical" had come to mean scepticism about the possibility of a science of the social. My plea was to try to understand the *success* of social science.

Whilst I was then finding my way towards a version of realism, my priority was to argue the case for a scientific social science. My main concern then, was that a powerful discourse held that a science of the social world was not possible. Later I wrote a book called *Science and Social Science* (Williams 2000a), in which I argued that whilst social science is a socially constructed enterprise (as indeed are the natural sciences), it is capable of discovering enough of *reality*, to produce socially useful descriptions and explanations. This book and subsequent thinking, expressed in several journal articles, eventually led me to complex realism. During this journey, much has happened in the practice and technology of the social sciences, but also in the nature and politics of social data.

In the late 1990s, the last battles of the "science wars" were being fought. Alan Sokal had perpetrated his hoax of fooling a fairly eminent cultural journal, with postmodern leanings, into publishing a whole load of scientific nonsense, which they believed to be a postmodern defence of quantum gravity (Sokal and Bricmont 1998). The implication of the hoax being that the whole of social science was either pseudo-scientific, or riddled with anti-scientific postmodernist mumbo-jumbo. This was certainly not the case, and there was plenty of good rigorous social science being done. But there were those, let's call them the "humanists",[2] who cried "foul" about the hoax, not because they defended scientific social science, but rather because they believed that a science of the social was not possible, that it was superficial and possibly politically conservative. In *Science and Social Science*, I tried to understand the reasons for this opposition. They were complex, partly the result of an anti-science culture that went back to opposition to the Vietnam War, nuclear arms and nuclear power (Williams 2000a: Chapter 4). Partly, in the UK and other European countries, there emerged a body of thinking that had a methodological antipathy towards "positivism", with its origins in the *methodenstreit* dispute of the 19th century (Manicas 1987: 124–126). This included Wittgenstinian and linguistic sympathies of thinkers, such as Peter Winch (Winch 1990 [1958]) poststructuralists, postmodernists and some feminists.[3]

Although the opposition to science in social science was, I maintained, methodologically based largely on a straw-person, one had to concede that scientific social science, as practised, was often grounded in a rather narrow and outdated conception of value free measurement and a reification of statistical methods. Such a similar position had been advanced by Aaron Cicourel as long ago as 1964 (Cicourel 1964). In particular, there existed (and perhaps still exists) a somewhat unthinking and naïve view that one could directly "measure" social reality. An example will suffice for now (and I will say more about this particular example later in the book) when measuring ethnicity it was the assumption that one was measuring something that had a direct correspondence between the measure and the lived reality, when in fact the concept of ethnicity and its measurement were each relative to time and place. These measures then become variables in a linear model, within which the relationship between a dependent variable and one or more independent variables is analysed and the strength of the statistical relationships is calculated. The assumption of linearity, that changes in what is caused are proportionate to changes in what is doing the causing, hugely over-simplified the complexity of social life. In causal analysis, this approach reaches its apotheosis. It's not that there is anything wrong with the analysis techniques and I will mount a limited defence of causal analysis towards the end of this book, what is wrong is rather the belief that such models are sufficient in themselves to accurately explain social reality.

In the UK, at least, opposition to scientific social science has declined, though recent evidence indicates that UK sociology, in particular, whilst mostly not anti-science, remains primarily concerned with micro-methods of interpretation and critique (Brookfield 2017, Williams et al 2017). Meanwhile quantitative research and methods, have in recent years, undergone a renaissance as a result of Economic and Social Research Council (ESRC) support for "investments", such as the *Millennium Cohort Study*[4] and *Understanding Society* panel studies.[5] Further large-scale investment, in teaching and learning quantitative methods, has come through the Q-Step programme, a £19 million investment intended to bring about a "step change" in the teaching of quantitative methods.[6]

In the two decades since *Science and Social Science* was published, the methodological landscape has changed. In terms of technique, quantitative researchers have largely changed with it. In 1998, techniques such as factor analysis, logistic regression and log linear analysis, were at the cutting edge, but just as importantly these techniques tested most computers to their limit and other than SPSS, researchers had recourse to clunky and slow applications, such as GLIM.[7] (Healy 1988). Now, even undergraduates can be capable of using structural equation modelling and multi-level models and are often introduced to advanced applications such as STATA, R and Python. Despite these important developments in statistical techniques, programming and fast computing, what might be called "the culture of analysis" remains positivistic in the ways I sketched out above. But the terms of engagement and the data landscape have changed. Although, despite warnings of its decline (Savage and Burrows 2007), the social survey continues to be a major form of data collection, particularly through large-scale panel studies, but the way data are collected is changing. Face-to-face interviews are becoming rarer, whilst internet surveys have become widespread and are increasingly used by polling companies and social researchers (Fricker 2016). These latter methods provide access to large samples, and reduce the problem of non-response, but equally they introduce a major problem of non-representative sampling. Other difficulties for traditional survey methods include the ubiquity of mobile phones, fewer people with access to fixed landline phones, survey fatigue and the difficulties in recruiting participants through home visits and street surveys.

Meanwhile the digital revolution has facilitated internet research and this has given rise to new forms of data collection that can automatically record the transactions, both economic and social of everyday life. These include cookies, which collect browsing data, shopping transaction data, via the internet or physical retail outlets and social communication through Facebook, Twitter, WhatsApp, etc. These data, are not the few hundred or even thousand data points of traditional data collection, but can be millions of data points. The availability of these kinds of data may not spell the end of survey research, but may topple it from its pre-eminent place as a major social research tool (Savage and Burrows 2007). In the last couple of decades, a new term has entered language, to describe this and other very large datasets – big data.

Methodologically, what is important, is that "big data" is itself very different to survey data and requires a different approach to thinking about it and analysing it. Sample surveys are variable-based, that is they record the number of cases (which are a sample of a wider population) that can be attributed to a value on a particular variable, whereas transactional data and new social media data begins with the case and then explores its characteristics and compares millions of cases with each other in an enormous matrix, made possible through the massive growth in computational power in the last few years.

Meanwhile, a considerable amount of social research is still "qualitative" in character and whilst there have been important technological advances, particularly in analysis, the traditional corpus of qualitative methods has been less changed or challenged by the above. Some researchers have critically considered the relationship of "big data" to qualitative research and have cautiously embraced the possibility of the latter contributing qualitative questions about actions, reasons and perceptions (Mills 2017). Yet, in much of qualitative research there has been "resistance" to the digital/big data revolution, seeing it as "neo-positivist" or "metric-mania" (Lather and St. Pierre 2013: 609).

This fairly brief sketch of change over the last two decades, is the socio-methodological backdrop to this book. There are challenges of the social organisation, the politics and the technical capabilities of social research. They are important, but underlying these are deeper philosophical challenges, represented by the continued adherence of many social researchers to those monolithic paradigms of humanism and positivism. In the former case, the risk is that in disciplines, such as sociology (particularly in the UK), the eschewal of science and quantitative methods will lead to self-indulgent, inward looking irrelevance. In the second case, a failure to engage with "big data", in particular, will cede the ground to "data scientists", who are technically adept, but often lacking in social science theorising or imagination. The result, in this case, is the answering of trivial questions, or analyses solely in pursuit of profit or ideology.

Complexity

It is against this background of disciplinary and methodological change and challenge (and indeed to some extent stasis), that complex realism has developed. As far as I know, the term was first used by Reed and Harvey in 1992 and again by David Byrne in 2004. Its intellectual parents are realism, a philosophy that has been around for about 2000 years and complexity science, a new kid on the block for around 30 years. Readers may be more familiar with its forebear, "chaos theory".

Complexity is, in many ways an unfortunate word, implying head-scratching difficulty of comprehension. People use it, in everyday speech, interchangeably with "complicated". But as Paul Cilliers (1998: 3) shows through illustration, complicated can have more components, ingredients and possibilities than complex! He compares a jumbo jet to mayonnaise.

A jumbo jet has (and I'm guessing) millions of components, but these are known, can be assembled, disassembled, replaced and so on. An assembled jumbo jet is the sum of its parts. It is stable and predictable (well, at least most of the time). A mayonnaise, on the other hand, has only two essential ingredients – egg yolks and oil. The result is an emulsion that is more than the sum of its parts, it is emergent and cannot be disassembled. Though to get that emulsion, some skill is required. Egg yolks and oil must be at the appropriate temperature, the yolks must be well beaten and the oil added very slowly, initially. For the beginner, a positive outcome is far from certain! A jumbo jet is complicated, but a mayonnaise is complex!

Moreover, a jumbo -jet, once assembled will be the sum of its parts, but the humble mayonnaise, with just two essential ingredients, if correctly made, produces an emulsion that is more than the sum of its parts. In the vocabulary of complexity, the egg yolks and oil, when whisked correctly have emergent properties. Whisked incorrectly, they remain just egg yolks and oil!

Complexity is non-linear (more of that later), its components might be known, but they interact in unpredictable ways. The interactions may be simple, but the outcomes great.

In fact, social reality often combines the jumbo- jet type characteristics with mayonnaise-type characteristics. That is, there will be relatively fixed orderly elements combined with indeterminate, random or stochastic elements. Often interactions will be simple, but produce complex outcomes (and indeed vice versa). An acceptance that social reality is complex, in the way I describe, has huge consequences for the two central tenets of science, explanation and prediction. And, assuming we want to do scientific social science, the way we think about complexity and explanation and complexity and prediction has important consequences for our methodological thinking.

The claim of complexity in the social and physical worlds is an ontological one – it says "the world is like this", that reality itself is complex, not merely complex to understand. It is, in itself, a realist claim and one that might be said to lend substance to realist claims about reality.

Realism

Realism, is a philosophy that accords with a common sense understanding of the world, that the world is not our dream, but is real. And moreover, that reality is not simply that which we perceive, but extends to those things we cannot immediately perceive. Bernard Russell (2009[1912] Chapter 2), used the analogy of his cat being fed in the morning and again in the evening and the inference that follows, that the cat continued to exist in the intervening period, even though Russell did not see him.

That realism became elevated to a philosophy, is because at a philosophical level, it has been challenged and those challenges can be summed as saying "but *how* do you know this?" It is this "how" question that realist philosophy of science has attempted to answer, through philosophical counter argument, through the history of science and through empirical closure – evidence. The claim of realist science and I think it is fair to say, most natural scientists are intuitive realists, that the methods of science can get beyond the immediate apparent data, to provide deeper level explanations of the world. One defence of realism, that captures this well and it is that, if realism were wrong then it would render the accretion of knowledge about the world as a miracle!

Realism itself also takes many forms and it is not unfair to say that one may be "somewhat realist". Philosophically, one might be an empirical realist claiming that we can have knowledge of the existence and nature of material objects in space and time, or a transcendental realist who claims that the existence and nature of objects is independent of our knowledge of them. Realists who support the first view are not so distant from empiricists, who maintain we can only have knowledge of those things which we experience, the difference being only that they accord a reality to those objects whereas a true empiricist would not take a view either way. Often, in both natural and social science, this "empirical realism" is the default position for practitioners and is sometimes (perhaps unfairly) described by its realist critics as naïve realism.

From critical realism to complex realism

Empirical and transcendental forms of realism are far from absent in social science, although historically the existence of a self-aware realism can be dated to the 1960s. The "classic" work of Marx and Durkheim has been reinterpreted as "realist", *aprés la lettre*, (Keat and Urry 1982[1975]: 126, Nye and Ashworth 1971), but probably the first social science methodologists to embrace realism was Donald Campbell (Campbell 1973, 1984). He used the term "critical realism", later to be taken up by Roy Bhaskar and his followers. The term "critical" for Campbell reflected the Popperian view of the scientific community being methodologically self-critical and he coined the phrase, the "experimenting society". As in Popper's case, he believed social progress would be achieved through social experiment and it was the job of social researchers to assist in this.

> The experimenting society will be one which will vigorously try out proposed solutions to recurrent problems, which will make hard-headed and multidimensional evaluations of the outcomes, and which will move on to try other alternatives when evaluation shows one reform to have been ineffective or harmful.
>
> Campbell 1991: 223

Campbell's realism finds its modern expression in the "realist evaluation" movement, pioneered by Ray Pawson and Nick Tilley (Pawson and Tilley 1997). I will refer to the work of Pawson and his colleagues at various points in this book, for it is this strand of realism that at least partially informs the approach I take here.

The "Bhaskar" version of critical realism has, however, been the most influential, in recent years. In this case the "critical" element means something quite different to that of Campbell's version and refers to the "critical stance" of privileged knowledge, said to derive from the methodology of this version of realism. As with most other versions of realism, it seeks truth, but it is claimed that the acquisition of such truth provides emancipation. This element of (this version of) critical realism has affinity with Marxism and even standpoint feminism (Harding 1996, Hartsock 1998) and has its roots in the Enlightenment critique of the *Ancien Regime* (Hammersley 2002: 33). It is also controversial, because it harnesses the power of social research for change, by introducing a value premise of need. But, as Martyn Hammersley argues, it does not always follow that the existence of need means that need should be fulfilled (op cit: 46–47). Although this aspect of critical realism is controversial and is often rejected on the grounds that science cannot logically derive an "ought" from an "is", my grounds for rejecting it is that science should not *try* to derive an ought from an is! I'll come back to that in Chapter 8.

There are two difficulties in describing critical realism. The first is that much of it has a rather inaccessible architecture of neologisms and concepts that often, unfortunately, give it the air of a cult. This is especially so of the latter work of Bhaskar himself. Secondly there are many versions, or interpretations of it. Joseph Maxwell, embraces a broad definition of critical realism as incorporating versions such as: experimental, subtle, emergent, natural, multi-perspectival (Maxwell 2012: 4–5). Some aspects are shared by all or most versions, for example, an emphasis on ontology, as opposed to epistemology, the importance of dispositional characteristics, the importance of causation, the existence of mechanisms and the desire to find a correspondence between theoretical statements and reality. All of which are key components in this book.

There are, however, other aspects of Bhaskarian critical realism, in addition to its "emanicipatory" character, that I am troubled by, matters I will consider in this book: for example, the confusion about "natural necessity" and the indifference towards probability and quantitative methods.[8] The latter, I think, is an unintended consequence of the critique of positivism, but nevertheless has meant that realism has had very limited impact upon the one area of social enquiry that is explicitly scientific – that of quantitative methods, which is a pity because critical realism is an avowedly scientific philosophy and methodology.

The realism I am advocating in this book is not an amended critical realism with the added ingredient of complexity. Many critical realists would be the first to defend complexity, but critical realism plus complexity is not enough. Rather, the core principle of complex realism, is for me, that of probability, not in the usual and commonplace use of the word – the probability of it raining, of contracting a disease, etc., when these are expressed as our estimations of what might happen, but rather as probability as the fundamental characteristic of the social world and much of the physical world. Put it another way, my claim is that events, in the social world are never socially determined and therefore are always probabilistic. That, in my view, is the real character of social reality. Complexity is probability.

In this and in other aspects of methodology, whilst critical realism has many valuable insights, there are (as they say) other brands available. In philosophy of the natural sciences, other kinds of realism have been presented, critiqued and further developed over time. Some are fully throated realism, others coyly so. But this eclecticism and the debates about realism, in the natural sciences can provide useful insights. And, although critical realism has predominated, there have been (and increasingly so) other realist voices in social science, including the aforementioned evaluation realism of Ray Pawson and his followers, the "local" realisms of Dan Little (Little 2009) and Uskali Maki (2005). Each of these has something useful to say and will appear later in this book, as will the insights of "non realists" such as Nancy Cartwright and Bas van Fraassen and implicit realists, such as John Goldthorpe.

Synthesis and hypothesis

The Complex realism, I describe and argue for here, is the attempt to provide the beginnings of a philosophical and methodological basis for a moderate scientific social science. It is not intended to be the last word on the matter. I am not proposing a fully formed philosophy or methodology. My goals are twofold. Firstly, I want to synthesise a number of ideas that have come from realist and non-realist thinkers, from complexity and from empirical social science. The list of thinkers, or researchers whose ideas I have plundered here is eclectic and include Karl Popper, Roy Bhaskar, Max Weber, Nancy Cartwright, Ian Hacking, Ray Pawson, David Byrne, Helen Longino, Robert Nozick, Nancy Cartwright, Wendy Dyer and Brian Castellani.

I also want to synthesise a number of my own ideas that I have developed over the last couple of decades. It's an eclectic mix and a work in progress. Indeed, in the Table 1.1, I indicate the origins of the ideas in each chapter, in my own previous work. Mostly, these publications develop the specific ideas in some depth. Nevertheless, you may reasonably ask, why trouble us with work in progress, an unfinished product? My answer is twofold. Firstly, science itself (and I include social science) is always unfinished. Science is a human conversation with reality and in social science, it is a conversation with social reality – in effect, ourselves. In these conversations we uncover error, we learn new things and we make proposals about what we think the world is like. The conversations will not end, whilst there is still science.

Secondly, in the spirit of Karl Popper's remark "I may be wrong and you may be right, and by an effort, we may get nearer to the truth" (Popper 1966: 225), the arguments and observations in this book are offered as hypotheses that might be tested through rational discussion, or empirical operationalisation. Over time, there have been many things I have revised my views on and a few to which my commitment has grown firmer. In the first case, for example, I have relaxed my views about what constitutes realism, in order to account for and permit an eclectic methodology. For some to the point of apostasy (Norrie 2011)! In the second case … well, that's for you, the reader, to judge and possibly suggest some better ways to get nearer to the truth! So, I invite you to think of complex realism as a hypothesis, one that may be partially or completely refuted, at least in the form in which it is presented here!

Summary of the chapters

Although the book is called Realism and Complexity in Social Science, the anchoring philosophy is that of realism and it is the character of social reality that it is complex – at least that is what I contend. So, in **Chapter 2**, I begin by taking on one of the biggest questions in philosophy, that of the nature of reality, and specifically, social reality! I do not claim to have resolved the philosophical issues here, my task is mostly a descriptive one of views advanced, and a basis on which we might move from metaphysical assertions, to methodology. But realism is contested, in the natural and social sciences by empiricism, and specifically its alias in social science – positivism. Here I sketch out some of the challenges to scientific versions of realism that need to be addressed for realism to be credible. But in the social sciences, there is another and often more pressing challenge, that of epistemological relativism, that has its intellectual home in postmodern and linguistically prioritised humanism. It is a double challenge to social science, because not only does it challenge realism from the philosophical perspective of idealism, it challenges social science as a scientific project. Three things emerge from this chapter: that social reality is *complex*, that realism must address the issue of causality and that reality itself can only ever be represented, rather than accessed directly. The first of these is the topic of **Chapter 3**. Complexity approaches are

TABLE 1.1 Published works that are the basis of the chapters

Note: This does not include applied or empirical work referred to in the text. Some works below are relevant to more than one chapter, but the principal chapter to which they refer is cited.

Chapter 2: Realism and its discontents	Williams, M. (1998) The Social World as Knowable in May, T. and Williams, M. (eds.) *Knowing the Social World*. Buckingham: Open University Press. pp 5–21. Williams, M. and Dyer, W. (2004) Realism and Probability in Carter, B. and New, C. (eds.) *Making Realism Work*. London: Routledge. pp 67–86.
Chapter 3: Complexity, contingency and necessity in the social world	Williams, M. (1999) Single case probabilities and the social world: The application of Popper's propensity interpretation, *Journal for the Theory of Social Behavior,* 29(2), 187–201. Williams, M. (2001) Complexity, probability and causation: Implications for homelessness research, *Journal of Social Issues,* 1(2), http://www.whb.co.uk/socialissues/ Williams, M. and Dyer, W. (2009) Single case probabilities in Ragin, C. and Byrne, D. (eds.) *Case Based Methods*. London: Sage. Williams, M. and Dyer, W. (2017) "Complex realism in social research". *Methodological Innovations Online*. https://doi.org/10.1177/2059799116683564
Chapter 4: Causes and complexity	Williams, M. (2009) Social objects, causality and contingent realism, *Journal for the Theory of Social Behavior,* 39(1), 1–18. Williams, M. (2011) Contingent realism – abandoning necessity, *Social Epistemology,* 25(1), 37–56. Williams, M. (2000a) *Science and Social Science: An Introduction*. London: Routledge.
Chapter 5: Representation and reality	Williams, M. (2003a) The problem of representation: Realism and operationalism in survey research, *Sociological Research On Line,* 8(1), http://www.socresonline.org.uk/8/1/williams.html
Chapter 6: Theory choice – verification, falsification and inference	Williams, M. (2000a) *Science and Social Science: An Introduction*. London: Routledge.
Chapter 7: Objective knowledge	Williams, M. (2005a) Situated objectivity, *Journal for the Theory of Social Behavior,* 35(1), 99–120. Williams, M. (2006) Can scientists be objective?, *Social Epistemology,* 20(2), 163–180. Letherby, G., Scott, J. and Williams M. (2013) *Objectivity and Subjectivity in Social Research*. London: Sage. (Chapters four and six). Williams, M. (2015) Situated objectivity, values and realism, *European Journal of Social Theory,* 18(1), 76–92.
Chapter 8: Mechanisms	Williams, M. (2014) Probability and models in Edwards, P., O'Mahoney, J. and Vincent, S. (eds.) *Studying Organisations Using Critical Realism*. Oxford: Oxford University Press. Williams, M. (2019) Making up mechanisms in realist research in Emmel, N., Greenhalgh, J. Manzano, A., Monaghan, M. and Dalkin, S. (eds.) *Doing Realist Research*, London: Sage.
Chapter 9: A complex realist toolkit for social research	Williams, M. (2000b) Interpretivism and generalisation, *Sociology,* 34(2), 209–244. Payne, G. and Williams, M. (2005) Generalisation in qualitative research, *Sociology,* 39(2), 295–314.

gaining followers in the social sciences and various concepts, such as phase space, strange attractors and emergence, are taken from the natural science literature and applied to the social world. Although these are useful, my approach begins from a different starting point, that of the ontological probabilistic character of the social world, in particular, expressed through Karl Popper's single-case probability theory. My argument is that the difference between the natural and social worlds, is that in the former, there is natural necessity. Some things must happen and some things are forbidden from happening, but in the social world, all things have some probability of occurrence, however small. In practice, however, some things are very much more likely and this likelihood produces, what I have called, relative invariance. But change does occur in the social world in different ways and through different time scales. Often, that change is through complex emergence. My argument is that to explain social reality we must begin from the ontological starting point that complexity is probability and probability is real. Knowing those probabilities is part of knowing social reality.

The next chapter, **Chapter 4** extends the concept of propensities to causality and causal explanation. The word "cause" is a deceptively simple one, but in science its definition and methodological operationalisation are much more difficult. I begin this chapter by reviewing deterministic and probabilistic approaches to causality. Whilst these can work in specific domains they cannot capture the complexity of the social world, particularly that causes in the social world must take into account the beliefs and desires of agents. Following on from the previous chapter I will argue that causes are a special case of ontological probability and a realisation of dispositional properties. The realisation of causes creates the relative invariance of social objects. I conclude that causality is not a singular phenomenon and that there is a variety of different kinds of causes, which can operate in different ways. Consequently, we need a variety of methodological strategies, the purpose of which is to tell plausible causal stories! Such stories, nevertheless, imply methods in which we can "close in" on the truth. We need, therefore, to measure. But to measure what and how? That is, in effect, what **Chapter 5** is about. What I argue *against*, in this chapter is operationalism, a creed supposedly dead, but living on in the naïve belief that there can be a correspondence between what there is and what we measure, in the social world. Occasionally, there is, but crucially representation is inevitable. Mostly we cannot directly measure the social world, but rather this must be mediated through theory and context. I continue with the question of theory in **Chapter 6**, by initially sketching out some of the issues of theory choice, in the philosophy of science. From this I propose a realist methodological framework that combines middle-range theory, inference, with what I have termed "reflexive falibilism". Both Chapters 5 and 6 attempt to bridge the methodological gap between an ontology of complex realism and social research methods. But there is a further important issue in such an endeavour, that of how social scientists can know the social world objectively, when they are both "part of what they study", and that our theories and methods themselves are social constructions. In **Chapter 7**

I argue for a situated version of objectivity, that is nevertheless grounded in the relative invariance of the social world, and that relies on the transcending values of truth, purpose and the differentiation of social objects. I adopt Karl Popper's "third world of knowledge" as an ontological anchor for situated objectivity. **Chapter 8** takes up further some of the themes of Chapters 3 and 4 in a discussion of what a complex mechanism might consist of and how we may know it. Consistent with Chapter 5, I argue that we can only know mechanisms under a description, but we can know them enough to achieve empirical adequacy.

Throughout this book I have attempted to anchor my theoretical or methodological claims in research examples. Many of these come from my own research in homelessness, counterurbanisation and the measurement of ethnicity, but in **Chapter 9**, I have used the analogy of the complex realist "methodological toolkit" to illustrate how we might combine a range of methods with complex realist thinking. Consequently, I have taken a few "non realist" examples and rationally reconstructed them along realist lines, but also I have introduced some examples of research that began from complex realist thinking. Finally, **Chapter 10**, is both a summary of the foregoing arguments, but also a polemical manifesto for a complex realism.

Acknowledgements

Apart from the people mentioned above whose ideas I have plundered, many people have assisted, influenced or encouraged me in the writing of this book. Some, such as Ray Pawson, David Byrne, Wendy Dyer and Brian Castellani have been both intellectual influences on the book as well as good colleagues and friends. Amongst the many other friends and colleagues I would like to thank for inspiration, challenge, advice and support are Dick Wiggins, Tim May, Ros Edwards, Will Baker, Luke Sloan, Charlotte Brookfield, Martyn Hammersley, Geoff Payne, John Scott, Gayle Letherby, Emma Uprichard and the late Paul Vogt.

My thanks to Brian Castellani and his co-authors for permission to reproduce the figures in Chapter 9.

Notes

1 I settled on this term as a result of conversations with David Byrne and Brian Castellani. I have in the past referred to it variously as "contingent realism" and contextual realism", but complex realism is a termed embraced by others and I see my efforts here as part of a broader interpretation of realism in social science.
2 In using this term, it is not my intent to impugn the very rigorous work of scholars in the humanities, nor to deny the importance of humanist perspectives in social science. Rather it is a shorthand for the broad category of "critique", which Luke Sloan, Charlotte Brookfield and I contrasted to "analytic" to describe non-scientific and scientific social science (Williams et al 2018).
3 I will discuss this further in Chapter 2.
4 https://cls.ucl.ac.uk/cls-studies/millennium-cohort-study/ Accessed 24/06/20.

5 https://www.understandingsociety.ac.uk/ Accessed 24/06/20.
6 https://www.nuffieldfoundation.org/students-teachers/q-step Accessed 24/06/20.
7 GLIM was the first statistical software package to allow the fitting of various kinds of linear models. Though it was cutting-edge at the time, it was far from user-friendly by today's standards. It was joked that GLIM stood for a glib user manual and a grim application! Though it can't have been too bad – I carried on using it for years after it was superseded!
8 In this book, it is not my intention to enter into a debate with critical realism. I have, to an extent, done this elsewhere, in respect of necessity and probability (see Williams 2011).

2

Realism and its discontents

Someone once remarked – and I forget who, the only problem for realism is reality. Realism is, in essence, a common-sense position that there is a real world out there, even if we can't experience it. As I observed in the Introduction, realism only becomes a problem for philosophers and scientists, because a case against it has been well argued, and it is one that challenges the common sense position as a basis for doing science. As social science realists, we encounter two species of argument, whereas natural science realists must deal only with one. The first set of arguments, faced by realists in both the natural and social sciences, comes from within the philosophy of science itself. Broadly speaking, these arguments are located in the empiricist or positivist tradition and have at their core a metaphysical disagreement about reality and our possible knowledge of it. Realism, in social science, must face the same issues, but because the social world is seen to have some quite different characteristics to the physical world, it attracts criticism from a different quarter, that of the idealist tradition. The upshot of this, is that whilst realism, of one kind or another, is the default position of many natural scientists, this is far from the case in the social sciences.

This chapter does some basic groundwork outlining some broad characteristics of realism and comparing it to its rival philosophies, in terms of the challenges they present to its basic tenets. The first part of the chapter is concerned with realism as a philosophy of science, where the key challenge is from empiricism and the second part of the chapter focusses more specifically on the challenges that realism faces in social science.

I'm going to begin this chapter, perhaps bravely or foolishly, talking about reality. I say bravely or foolishly, because this matter is at the very heart of philosophy and entire careers have been built around this. Yet, before we can assess the case for and against realism, in natural or social science and build the case for complex realism, we need to think a bit about what we mean by "reality".

Reality and social reality

Let us begin with physical reality. Prior to the mid-18th century, realism was, at least to its advocates, fairly straightforward. It was the proposition that physical objects exist independently of their being perceived. At a common sense level, this makes perfect sense and we can extend the argument to encompass things like light waves, electricity and the wind and indeed the relations between these kinds of things can be expressed in physical laws. But there are two kinds of problem here:

The first problem, is that all of our descriptions are necessarily representations, by definition we cannot know, what Kant called "noumena", the thing in itself (Körner 1955: 94). This not a problem at an everyday level, in terms of assumptions about the continued existence of things we cannot see. This was the point of Bertrand Russell's cat story in the Introduction. Yet, it gets problematic when it comes to things that are real for the scientist. Scientists, historically, have treated things like phlogiston or ethers as real, only to later discover they were fictions of their own creation. The intended "real" in science, is inevitably what is theorised as such. This has important implications, because it means scientists' access to reality must be indirect, through the mediation of theories, which they hope, represent reality. Furthermore, such theories often cannot be tested by simple observation, nor can they usually be tested through one or two observations. The confirmation of the existence of the Higgs boson, in 2012, was the result of both multiple observations of particles through the use of sophisticated instruments and the complicated predictions of a whole body of theory, developed over time (Lederman and Hill 2013). Moreover, this theoretical development was far from linear and involved error and blind alleys. But this is the way of science. As G.A. Miller said, science is both an error exterminator and error breeder (Miller 1921).

The second problem relates to the material–mental relationship. In essence it is this: that we require mental concepts to describe the material world and to argue for its existence, or indeed that only it exists, so whether or not the mental (and by implication, of course, the social) is reducible to the material, there is something, that maybe masquerades as the mental, to be explained (Margolis 2006: 208). What we can mean by "material" is in itself not straightforward. In the 19th century, the material was solid matter, forms of energy such as light and sound were excluded. But nowadays, the picture is very much more complicated and matter itself is a higher level property that supervenes on characteristics at the sub-atomic level. At this level, matter and energy can display characteristics of both waves and particles so we must talk of "states", rather than "matter" as before.[1] So even if we do not know what the mental is, we do know that it has physical origins and moreover in itself, apart from electro-chemical stimulus in the brain, it is incapable of operationalisation without the physical. My words on the screen may have originated as thoughts, but are mediated through my own complex physiology and electro-mechanical and digital workings of a computer.

Social reality

We turn now to social reality. The theory–representation issue is of the same logical kind for the social scientist, as the natural scientist. But there are three particular problems in conceiving of a social reality. The first is that of supervenience (Seager 2000: 480–482, Le Boutillier 2001, 2003). The social world is more complex than the physical world, because its higher-level properties supervene on a smaller number of lower-level physical properties. This is *not* to say that social properties are reducible to particular physical properties, but they depend on lower level physical properties. Take for example, illness. There are, a massive array of different kinds of physiological and psychological illness, that can manifest themselves in many different ways. Illness is complex, but the myriad of micro, meso[2] and macro social relationships in regimes of healthcare is exponentially more complex than the number of possible illnesses. Investigating and treating illness and caring for patients presents the challenges of complex biology, but additionally the even more complex social relationships. So, any concept of social reality and it follows, its investigation, will inevitably be more complex than that of the physical world, even though it is only concerned with the social life of one species. The social relations of illness can be said to supervene on its physical properties, but those social relations may take many different forms.

The second problem is the assumption that the natural scientist can separate the physical world from her ability to know it. In the past, scientific realism has been the view that there is a mind independent reality, to which scientific theories refer. Only a solipsist would say that physical reality was wholly mind dependent. There is, demonstrably, something beyond "us", however, much this is mediated through our theories and observations. There can be no such separation when we conceive of social reality, because social reality is ultimately mind dependent. A social scientist, suggesting a theory of a particular aspect of social reality, is mind dependent theorising of mind dependent states. Analogously, in the physical world, this would be like liquids, in turbulence flows, being self-aware!

The third problem, follows from this and it is that of self-awareness and consequent feedback loops. Leaving aside the problem of quantum indeterminateness (Healey 1993), an observation of a phenomenon, say, the detection or measurement of a small electric currents, using a galvanometer, will not cause any major change in that current. But, the very act of observation of people, either directly or through the proxy of an instrument, such as a questionnaire, will directly impact on the mental states and quite possibly on the beliefs and behaviour of those people. The social scientist, in "measuring" the social world will change the ecology of that world to a degree and in ways she cannot accurately know. Moreover, the problem is not just with what the social scientist does in her investigations, social behaviour in wider society is changed by awareness of new information. Propagandists over the centuries have been well aware of this. Consequently, a body of theory about aspects of social reality may be more or less correct at time *t1*, but as a result of social externalities, not described by the theory, but as a result of new information leading to unexpected actions, the theory becomes wrong at time *t2*. Whereas an awareness of gravity does not lead to a need to reformulate the law describing it, because it has changed!

This kind of feedback in the social world is born, of and entails, an enormous complexity of inter-relationships of mental states such as beliefs, intentions and desires and that of language and action. Indeed, it is these things that, along with the problems of mind-dependency and self-awareness, have led many to reject the possibility of social scientific realism. Many, of course, reject the possibility of realism *tout court*, but a few philosophers of science, notably Rom Harré (Harré 2002) are realists about the physical world, but are, in effect, anti-realists about the social world.

Social and physical reality

Social science realism depends on what might be called "ontological naturalism". It is a position that holds that there is no disjuncture between the natural and social worlds, that they are not separate kinds of things. Aside from the important fact that the social world supervenes on the physical world, the causal interactions between the physical and social are both constant and transformative and indeed one could extend my illness example to illustrate this point. We constantly change the state of the physical world, purely by existing in it. By the 21st century, the complexity of human social organisation has dramatically changed the physical world, not just for humans but also for virtually every other species. But it too changes the social world by making forms of social organisation possible, as the result of the existence or exploitation of resources, such as oil, water, sunshine. The social and physical world interact and whilst we can talk of things, such as institutions, customs laws and so on as, social, virtually every referent to the social entail physical properties. Even that most "social" of social constructions, social class, is to a large extent grounded in the distribution of physical resources.

I think there is simple useful heuristic to describe these relationships. There are three broad ontological "kinds":

Physical structures and properties that we do not yet know, but through our discoveries of previous unknown structures and properties we can surmise that they exist. These unknowns have no social properties, until they become known.

Physical structures and properties that we know of and to one extent or another, we interact with. These may be a feature, such as a mountain we name, climb, or revere as sacred. Our actual interaction with them, physical or social may be minimal, even trivial. Or other things we manipulate or make: a motor car, a computer or a spoon that is physical, but made by humans and is part of our quotidian social interaction.

Finally, there are social structures or properties that have only a social existence (though may utilise objects from the physical world as tools, tokens or more recently artificial intelligence). These may be a greeting, a contract, a ritual, money, a law.

Throughout the foregoing, despite my suggesting some difficulties, there is nevertheless an implicit assumption that there is a reality, whatever difficulties we may face in knowing it. Realism rises to the challenge, meeting some of these difficulties with arguments that circumvent them or reconstruct them to make a virtue of the difficulties. However, realism's rival philosophical positions are sceptical of such strategies and construct epistemologies that either sceptically ignore "reality" or use the term in a very limited way.

In the next section, I will sketch out both realism and its rival epistemologies to act as a reference point for the following discussion of the challenges to realism. The descriptions are brief, because their further characteristics will emerge in the critical discussion which follows.

Realism and its rivals

Realism

The core metaphysical claim of realism is the view that there is an actually existing world that is independent of our perceptions of it. Scientific realism can be said to operationalise this metaphysical claim through a number of further constituent claims that make it a theoretically and empirically adequate strategy for science. As I noted in the introduction, here are many different variants of scientific realism[3] and I have touched upon some of these in this book. Indeed, in this book, I advocate a particular version, that of complex realism. However, all versions of scientific realism share some core characteristics.

Although we cannot ever say we "know" that world, our methods of investigation can provide knowledge of parts of that world that we cannot necessarily observe and scientific explanation is therefore possible. This requires us to theorise beyond that which we can observe, either with our senses or our instruments. Alexander Bird (1998: 121–122) provides a nice example from 18th century chemistry. It was known that elements react together in fixed proportions to produce compounds. Carbon and hydrogen combine in fixed proportions to produce methane, oxygen and hydrogen in differing proportions to produce nitrous or nitric oxide. John Dalton had proposed that particular atoms are associated with each element and in the right proportions bind together to produce clusters of the atoms of the elements as molecules. Dalton's atomic hypothesis was controversial, because he moved from observation to theorising the existence of a process of combining of things we could not see – atoms. We know now that Dalton's atomic hypothesis is broadly correct and was empirically confirmed.

Moreover, this was the route to further theoretical propositions about atoms themselves and further empirical confirmations. As with other scientific developments, this was not simple march towards the truth and along the way to our present knowledge, many theories were proposed and empirically disposed of. Realism accepts this, but also that this process of theory proposal and confirmation or refutation, leads us to close in on the empirical truth of the matter. It thus follows that if a theory is confirmed, then it must be wholly or partially true. As I said in the Introduction, realists maintain, that if that were not the case, then science and epistemic progress in science, would be a miracle. Moreover, and considering the Dalton example, if theories about unobservables were not proposed, realists would claim that there would be no structural direction to investigation and all we would end up with would be a whole lot of unrelated observations.

The second characteristic is a belief in causes. As with realism itself, cause–effect relationships, where an effect follows a cause in time and we can reason that A was responsible for B, is common sense. If I find a hole in my pocket and my money has gone, I will probably reason the presence of the hole caused the loss of my money, rather than goblins stealing it from me. However, our data in science will often demonstrate the association of two events contiguous in time, but they may or may not be causally related. However, scientists need to demonstrate causal connections (as with Dalton example) to provide explanations. Very rarely, in science or social science, will a scientist be content with saying A caused B, without invoking, C, D, E, etc. In social science, A, C, D, E may be independent variables in a regression model and between them they may statistically explain a large proportion of the variance in that model, but they are still only "associated" together. So, realists will bring a theoretical component to provide a plausible explanation as to why they are associated. This is not just "made up", but usually based on empirical confirmation of previous associations of such kind, in known circumstances. All realists will view causes as broader and deeper than simply A caused B and many will use the language of mechanisms to propose a way in which causes are arrayed and linked. It might be said that realists tell a "causal story". That we end up with causal stories, will be my conclusion in Chapter 4.

The third characteristic is that things or people are "dispositional", or that they have "causal powers", or "tendencies".[4] Salt has the disposition of solubility and can be dissolved in water. A police officer has the disposition of arresting powers. Salt may not be dissolved and a police officer may not arrest, but when these dispositions are realised, then they are realised as part of a causal process. I will have more to say about dispositions, also in Chapter 4.

Empiricism

The core doctrine of empiricism is one of the simplest, but also most influential in philosophy. It is that all of our knowledge of the external world comes from the interaction of our five senses with the world. Though in more recent times, empiricists allow that such observation might be conducted through the proxy of instrumentation. The most famous iteration of empiricism, certainly in philosophy of science, was logical empiricism, or more usually known as logical positivism (Philips 1987: 36–48) and more recently it has taken a more sophisticated form in instrumentalism and in social science, causal analysis (more of these later). Its more sophisticated versions might be said to meet realism at the border and certainly my own version of realism is far from dismissive of all aspects of empiricism. However, let us look at some of the core or founding elements of it.

Empiricism is essentially a sceptical doctrine that aims to eliminate metaphysical speculation from science. David Hume, one of its founding fathers, did not deny that that there were causes, but rather that we cannot observe them, only the constant conjunction of events. He illustrated his argument with the example of billiard balls. In his example, all we see is one ball hitting the other and the second ball moving. To say that a cause was present requires us to infer beyond what we observe, that if a billiard ball is hit by another and moves that the first caused the second to move.

Whilst this may seem pedantic, there are plenty of examples where one event follows another, but the first did not cause the second. Eating your breakfast before leaving home is a common association, but there is no causal connection.

Empiricism, at its purist, will therefore say that we can only talk of constant conjunctions, or regular associations, rather than causes. There is no necessary association between the events. Any necessary connections must be assumed, as Hume maintained such assumptions are psychological not ontological. The scepticism lies not in a denial of a connection, but in our knowledge of it. The Humean proof for this sceptical stand lies in the principle of contradiction, that it would be logically possible for an alternative outcome to take place (Harré and Madden 1975: 44). There is no necessity in the variables themselves that must produce a link, because a counterfactual would be equally logically possible. It would be logically possible for (say) increased prosperity to follow unemployment. This principle arises from the problem of induction, that although we informally assume from our experience that B follows A, the world can change and often does in that B does not follow A at a later time.

Although Hume raised the problem of induction (sometimes called Hume's problem, Popper 1959a: 27), that we are psychologically dependent upon regular patterns and indeed that such regularity is readily apparent, empiricist method is actually reliant on the principle of induction, most particularly in science, through probability. Empiricists have no problem in recognising regularities, expressed as probabilities, but for the "purists", these can never amount to causal claims.

Idealism

Idealism incorporates a wide range of doctrines in philosophy. They have in common the view that the external world is a creation of mind. It does not mean that idealists necessarily deny the existence of a "real" world, but rather that we can never directly perceive it. We can think of idealism in two ways. Firstly, as an opposing ontology to materialism, a belief that the world consists only of "ideas", what is sometimes called mental monism, associated with philosophy of George Berkeley, and secondly a broad range of philosophical positions that prioritise ideas to one extent or another.

The first of these positions, though logically sound, is rarely advanced by modern philosophers of science and is of interest to us only because a version of it, constructivism, was and still is to an extent a contemporary disrupter in social science. But more of that below. Berkeley's view was, to be is to be perceived and whilst this seems counter intuitive to the modern mind, what might be called the "train example", shows that it's not entirely crazy. A person travelling on a train will be seen as stationary by fellow passengers, but moving at speed by those observing the train passing. Who is correct in their observation? This homely example is a problematic at the heart of relativity theory (speed and time are relative to the observer). It was also the impetus for operationalism and in social science the specificity of social manifestations in time and place (Williams 2003a).

The second form of idealism is much more heterogeneous and may variously emphasise mind, in the transcendental idealism of Immanuel Kant or language, in the philosophy of Ludwig Wittgenstein, thus bringing it quite close to the emphasis on experience in empiricism. Indeed, Wittgenstein's earlier work, through its emphasis on the logical relations of language[5] can be considered as empiricist. More of him and his later work below.

Kant still emphasised the characteristic of humans as mind-endowed beings, this must be done in the context of existing in a world of space and time (Körner 1955: Chapter 4), thus he admits of things that are beyond mind. Nevertheless, he also held that we can only know phenomena through mind dependent perception of it, we cannot ever know the thing in itself, what he called "noumena". Kant's "transcendental idealism" was particularly influential in the work of Max Weber. In the social world (as in the world in general), we can never grasp the essence of something, "the thing in itself", but we can hold in our minds a representation of something in the social world that may not exist in such form in reality. Weber coined the term "ideal type" to describe such representation. Ideal types are not averages, or the most desirable form of social phenomena, but a way in which an individual can reason from a shared rational faculty to a model or pure conceptual type that would exist if all agents acted perfectly rationally. Weber's methodology therefore crucially depends on rationality as the product of minds (Albrow 1990).

In many ways Kant's idealism, allowing a separation between the objects we can know (phenomena) and the objects we cannot know, or can surmise only (noumena) has resonance with scientific realism and is a long way from the epistemological relativism of linguistic or constructivist versions of idealism, which challenge the rationality of the scientific project itself, yet alone realism.

The above "primer" on the key philosophical positions may be useful to the newcomer to philosophy, but it also provides some early groundwork for my rather eclectic version of realism, which problematise at least one key aspect of that doctrine in relation to the social world, that of natural necessity and incorporates some concepts from its rival philosophies, the importance of interpretation and quantification.

Challenges to realism

Realism about what?

Realism is not a settled or straightforward approach to knowing the world. Ian Hacking, in an excellent book, which considers how scientists represent, intervene and experimentally manipulate the natural world (Hacking 1983: 27–29) considers different ways in which one can be realist. Fundamentally, he suggests there are two realisms – realism about entities and realism about theories.

Let us suppose there are "entities", things in the world that have a "real" existence. If we want to describe, measure, explain or predict these entities we must have some statements which represent them and makes claims about their properties. What must it mean to say we are realists about entities?

To say there are entities in the world, is to claim that they have distinguishing properties that are due to them, rather than descriptions of them. On its own, this is hard to sustain at anything beyond a common sense level. The anti-realist would say that these are inevitably representations or even fictions, because what is being described is subject to human description. In science, these descriptions are likely to change over time and in some cases, what was once considered real, is no longer considered so. Take for example, the "ether". From Aristotle until the late 19th century most thinkers and gradually fewer thinkers believed that space could not be empty, that there was something they called "the ether", through which electro-magnetic waves must pass, rather like ripples through water. The ether was as real as anything could be, was described explained, attributed properties and then in 1887, the Michelson–Morley experiment (Consoli and Pluchino 2018) indicated there was no such thing and indeed Einstein's theory of special relativity depended upon its non-existence! Even a well-understood concept such as velocity is problematic when examined more closely. Whist objects move, their movement is through time. Mean velocity is the measurement of how far an object moves within a specific time period. That period may be as short as can be measured, but there must be mathematical limits to this – it cannot be zero, so actually velocity is a mathematical abstraction. The issue of representation is important for social science realist methodology, in Chapter 5.

So, those who are sceptical about entities will say, how many of those things we claim as "real" now will turn out to be fictions. A metaphysical, but fairly useless defence would say, that there must be entities, otherwise we would not be conscious beings in space–time, able to talk about them! But this is an article of faith and does not take us very far.

Most "scientific" realists are realists about theories. Theories, it is said are true or false independently of what we know. Theories aim to connect what we believe is the case in the world with what the world really is.

Another way of putting this, is that theories are said to have "truth content", that the statements made in the theory correspond with the what the entity really is. Thus, the phrase "the cat sat on the mat" is true, if and only if the cat sat on the mat.[6] Of course, in science, refutations such as that of the claim to the existence of the ether, are quite rare and what is often the case, is that part of a theory is refuted through evidence and part survives, to be superseded by a new theory which can explain or predict everything the old one can, but also provides new explanations or predictions. I will return to this in Chapter 6 (and the issue of truth in Chapter 7). Occasionally, there is no theory to replace the partially refuted one, or indeed there may be several competing theories.

There are two major problems with being realist about theories. The first, summed up by Rom Harré (Harré 1986: 51) is an epistemic problem, "no human enterprise could decide whether the typical statements of scientific theories were true or false". This is a problem of induction – Hume's problem, that no amount of observations can confirm all Xs are Ys. Karl Popper (Popper 1959a) famously claimed to have solved this problem, through his principle of falsification. Whilst it is the case that we can never claim all Xs are Y, the discovery of one X is enough to falsify the prior inductive claim. More of Popper and falsification in Chapter 6, but suffice to say for the moment, this does not solve the problem, at least empirically, because of what can count as a falsification?

Evidence that confirms or refutes is itself mediated, by what counts as a measurement and how well measurement devices measure. The discovery of the Higgs boson, for example, was made possible through an interrelationship between theoretical statements and measurement technique. Consequently, what is discovered, is itself a mediated product. So, it is rarely the case in complex scientific (yet alone social scientific) investigations to straightforwardly produce a measure which discriminates between true and false theoretical statements. In many of the sciences, it is not a question of discriminating between true and false statements, but rather there is a probability of truth.

In 2012, the discovery of the Higgs boson was regarded as definitive, and whilst most physicists accept this, though not to the extent of the popular description of it as the "god particle", a minority have begun to dispute this and offer evidence which claim to refute at least the status of the discovery (https://phys.org/news/2014-11-wasnt-higgs-particle.html). So, whilst in a general sense, Popper (1989 [1963]) was right to talk of "conjectures and refutations" in science, the refutations themselves may turn out to be provisional or incomplete and themselves have the status of inductive statements.

To be a realist about entities, but an anti-realist about theories does not necessarily require a leap of faith. We can observe events and things and predict outcomes successfully, without knowing much about how or why something happens. Political pollsters, for example, can analyse a series of polls and on this basis produce quite accurate predictions of electoral success, without knowing why Party A is more favoured than Party B. What we can say, post-election, is that particular party won, in line with predictions. To be realist about entities does not commit you to an explanation of what particular entities are, but simply that there are entities that can be measured. Indeed, as we will see, newer versions of empiricism are comfortable with this position. The converse does not seem to be a tenable position. If you believe a theory is true, or partially true, if it explains and predicts with some accuracy, then the entities it describes must (more or less) exist in the form described by the theory (though see below for an interesting take on this from Bas van Fraassen). However, this could be provisional position, if one is testing more than one theory, where theory A contradicts theory B in important ways. Both cannot be true, so one must misdescribe the entity(ies) and those entities are not "real".

To sum up so far: the abiding problem for realism is that of unobservables. Critics of unobservables want to reduce the amount of metaphysical speculation in science, whereas realists find it unavoidable. Unoberservables may be postulated entities or the theories that purport to describe and explain them. By extension, measurement instruments measure those things that are theorised and if the theories are wrong, then they are measuring the wrong thing. There is no simple answer to this problem. Realists would say that observation on its own must presuppose some kind of epistemological or cognitive framework. In science, this is inevitably structured through training and experience. I have often been struck by how even a simple single regression plot can appear mysterious to inexperienced undergraduate students, but with a minimum of explanation and instruction they move quite quickly to a quite sophisticated reading of the data and a basic understanding of multiple regression. Medical colleagues tell me the same thing about CT imaging and data.

A further problem for realists and anti-realists alike, is the ontological one of what entities actually are. In physics, we are no longer talking about lumps of matter, but often forms of energy that do not have mass, but "behave" in particular ways. Although not of the same ontological category, but nevertheless leading to the same kind of measurement problem, in the social world, we have mental states, behaviour and action, all of which are subject to reflective feedback from social actors.

There have been a number of generic answers to these problems, offered from the philosophy of science, that would hold for both the physical and social worlds. I'm going to focus only on two of these, because I think they both have something valuable to say about how we think of theories. Both approaches are broadly realist about entities, but anti-realist about theories. The first of these is associated with the work of Bas van Fraassen (1980, 1985) and the second Nancy Cartwright (1983, 1989, 2004).

Bas van Fraassen and constructive empiricism

van Fraassen's constructive empiricism is a version of instrumentalism. Instrumentalism holds that theories about unobservables are true or false, even though we do not know whether they are true or false. Theories must be assessed on the basis of their explanatory adequacy and their ability to predict. It follows from this that there is agreement with realists about the success of science, but it does not really matter which theories were true or which parts of theories were true, all that matters is empirical success. In this view, theories are merely predicting instruments.

Although van Fraassen retains the empiricist principle of experience, he does not retain the empiricist scepticism about theories and would accept the claim that all explanatory or predictive statements scientific statements must be based on some kind of theoretical suppositions. Theory, then, is unavoidable. However, the crucial difference between him and the realists is that they aim to produce theories which are true about the world, whereas for van Fraassen they are assessed on the basis of their explanatory and predictive success. Indeed, van Fraassen claims that this is precisely how science works. Scientists appraise theories for their empirical adequacy. Two theories may have differing ontological content, but may be empirically equivalent. Theories, he says, should be assessed on a number of criteria: Theory A is to be preferred if its information content is greater than theory B. In other words if it explains more. The elements in a theory should each be logically consistent with each other – that is, they should not contain non-sequitors and finally (the principle of Occam's razor), a simpler theory should be preferred over a more complex one.

The concept of empirical adequacy is important and one I want to it retain for later, however, an important problem for constructive empiricism is the difficulty in determining the difference between empirically adequate statements and those which are true. If something is empirically adequate, then at least some part of that theory is true and if a theory is true, then it must be empirically adequate. van Fraassen (1980) criticises a feature of realism that I think is important and that is inference to the best explanation, a device that might be used to asses empirical adequacy. I shall return to this and van Fraassen's criticisms in Chapter 6.

Nancy Cartwright and the "dappled world"

Although Nancy Cartwright's philosophy is influenced by empiricism and has some resonance with van Fraassen's constructive empiricism, it is not "anti-realist" and, as I will contend later, there is a great deal of overlap between her work and complex realism. Cartwright, similarly to van Fraassen, draws on the empirical success of science to underwrite her philosophy, but more than that she draws on the actual practice of science, as found in the best examples of scientific discovery (Hoefer 2008: 2). Two things are central to her philosophy. Firstly, a denial of the veracity of most natural laws and secondly a "complex" view of causality.[7]

In her first book, wonderfully entitled *How the Laws of Physics Lie* (Cartwright 1983), she maintains most laws, when examined, operate only *ceteris paribus*, they are approximations, always operating within contexts. Furthermore, though fundamental laws can be adequately predictive, they nevertheless have components that are unobservable and unmeasurable. What they do, she says, is tell "causal stories", which are themselves fit for purpose. Whilst scientists will use fundamental equations, of known laws, to produce less fundamental equations in models, the models themselves will contain *ad hoc* approximations and corrections for causal disturbances. A phenomenon may be predicted by a number of models – she uses the example of "quantum damping",[8] but what is important for scientists is that there is only one causal explanation (or "causal story"). For her this is evidence that, in practice, laws are less important to scientists than establishing causes.

Though few social scientists would ever claim that there are fundamental social laws and even those who believe that there are laws (Kincaid 1996: 90–91), will accept there are not many of them and that they certainly operate *ceteris paribus*. Cartwright's scepticism about laws has a resonance for social scientists, who may develop rival theories to explain phenomena, but the models derived from these theories may end up with the same terms in them, mostly because the terms in the models are derived from the variables that are actually measured.

It is perhaps not an exaggeration to say that Cartwright is a realist about causes, but not in the way that causality is frequently treated by realists as implying a natural necessity (admittedly *ceteris paribus*). Rather, she sees causes as specific events, the presence or absence of singular causal relations in given contexts. Her strategy to isolate such causal efficacy through controls, until such time that it is clear that A causes B. Yet this is far from the claim that A causes B, in the sense of a law that must necessarily apply, but rather that A has the capacity to cause B in particular circumstances. Isolating the A -> B relationship under differing circumstances is far from straightforward. A may sometimes cause B, but not always and this will depend on the operation of other causal capacities being realised. Cartwright's examples are usually drawn from physics and economics, but it is telling that she is prepared to attribute some stable capacities to the physical world, but has doubts about whether there are stable capacities in economic life (Cartwright 1989: 170). Cartwright's "dappled world", is one of contingency, where laws operate in a piecemeal way and in at least one place she expresses the view that there may be no laws operating at all, in nature (Hoefer 2008: 10).

Finally, and consistent with both her adherence to what scientists actually do and her stance of ontological contingency, Cartwright places great emphasis on the use of models to provide viable approximations of how the world works. Although, perhaps not consciously doing so, in this, she comes close to describing what social scientists attempt to do in building statistical models. Whether this is good enough or even the equivalent of models in the natural sciences, is something we will return to later. In particular, can social science models capture the complexity and contingency that is the ontological backdrop to Cartwright's philosophy? Furthermore, if she is right about the absence of any fixed capacities in social phenomena, then where does that leave us in a quest to isolate causes, even contingent ones? Nevertheless, at this stage, it is enough to say that van Fraassen and especially Cartwright offer us a philosophy of science that attempts to bridge the differences between traditional forms of empiricism and realism.

Anti-realism in social science

The issue of anti-realism in social research is not wholly a philosophical or methodological matter, but is bound up with the history of social science. Unlike the philosophy of the natural sciences, there are few attempts to provide a scientifically based critique of realism in the philosophy of the social sciences, though there is a huge literature arguing in its favour.

"Anti-realism" tends to take two forms, what we might term "passive" anti-realism, mostly associated with quantitative research and a more active version in qualitative research. But even in the latter case, there is not much specific anti-realist critique, rather there is a very powerful constructivist anti-science discourse, that does not begin from the shared goals of prediction and explanation that underpin both realism and much anti-realism in the philosophy of the natural sciences. Thus "active" anti-realism is actually anti-science and an argument for explorations of the social world to be more like those of literature or the arts. In the following sections, I will describe both the passive and active versions of anti-realism. In the case of the first, more sympathetically, because its practices in empirical social science, need not be the baby thrown out with the empiricist bathwater! In the case of the second, though we may derive some useful insights, this is a position that I believe to be fundamentally wrong and for the most part only engaged with at all, because in certain jurisdictions (such as the UK and New Zealand) it is very powerful and in some disciplines, such as sociology, dominant (Williams et al. 2017). Nevertheless, I do not intend taking on this anti-science view in a deep or systematic way, because a defence of science in social science is not the purpose of this book, but was indeed the purpose of a book I wrote some years ago (Williams 2000a).

Quantitative methods and causal analysis

The maverick form of empiricism, in social science, reached its apotheosis in the work of George Lundberg (1963 [1947]), Paul Lazarsfeld (1993) and Stuart Dodd (1942) in the mid-20th century. Lundberg denied that it was possible to theorise, or even recognise concepts that were not measurable. Lazarsfeld was famously attacked by C. Wright Mills for his "abstracted empiricism"[9] (Mills 1959) and Dodd (1963 [1947]: 310–311) suggested a means to overcome the need for causal statements in his "pan sample", which was, in effect, a giant data matrix of every possible variable in which the researcher would seek correlations. This being achieved after extensive (several hundred hours) interviews with a panel of persons. Nowadays this is often described as data dredging! Lazarsfeld achieved justifiable admiration for the quantity and quality of his sociology, whilst in operationalism, Lundberg set social science (and especially realist social science) a challenge which remains today – how can we empirically move beyond those things which are measurable? This restates, in empirical language, the central problem of realism, that of unobservables.

US social science was and is empiricist by temperament, often mediated through the lens of pragmatism. This philosophy shares with empiricism a scepticism about theories and a "truth" is assessed on the basis of its consequences or "truth value". It was the underlying philosophy of the Chicago School and more recently provides the methodological justification for much of US mixed methods research. In some ways, it can be thought of as an "anti-philosophy", emphasising instead the practical value of findings, or the potential empirical value of choosing one explanatory theory over another. In social science, theory choice is rarely discussed and the social science manifestation of pragmatism is almost procedural in its treatment of causes. One will search in vain for extensive discussion of pragmatism as a basis for quantitative analysis, the very nature of it precludes any philosophical introspection. Even in John Brewer and Albert Hunter's justifiably acclaimed *Foundations of Multi-Method Research* (Brewer and Hunter 2006) there is no mention of pragmatism, yet the book wears it on its sleeve. Chapter 2, for example, is entitled "A Healthy Skepticism About Theory and Method". Its definition of the essential criteria for causality is worth quoting at length, for its wonderful simplicity – and dare I say it, naivety.

> To establish that one phenomenon causes another, three things must be demonstrated empirically. First, it must be shown that the two phenomena covary. Which is to say, changes (or variations) in their values must occur together more often than chance alone would lead you to expect. (If two variables no more often than chance, one variable might, of course, still be the cause of the other. But the influence of a cause so weak as to be indistinguishable from the influence of a large number of small unorganised causes, or chance, is obviously of little explanatory value.) Second, it must be shown that variations in the supposed cause (X for short) occur before variations in the supposed effect (Y, for short), since simple covariation is consistent with either the hypothesis that X caused Y or the reverse hypothesis that Y caused X. And third, it must be shown that variation in the supposed cause can bring about variation in the supposed effect even when other possible causes of Y are constant or inoperative. (In other words, to observe the influence of any one cause it is necessary to control in some fashion the influence of other causes.)
>
> Brewer and Hunter 2006: 126

The problem with this definition is not what it says, but what it implies: that variables can be simply measured, operationalised, put into a statistical model and out pops a causal explanation. We are invited to conclude that the issues are technical, not methodological or philosophical.

That there is more to a cause was admitted by one of the founders of the US causal analysis tradition, Hubert Blalock. He perhaps remains empiricist, operationalist and possibly pragmatist in spirit, but his *Causal Inference in Non Experimental Research* is a classic of social research methodology. Whilst his techniques are simply a more sophisticated version of the position quoted above, not only does he approvingly cite Mario Bunge[10] (himself no empiricist), but he has this to say of causes:

> One admits that causal thinking belongs completely on the theoretical level and that causal laws can never be demonstrated empirically. But this does not mean that it is not helpful to think causally and to develop causal models that have implications that are indirectly testable.
>
> Blalock 1961: 6

At the risk of reading to much into this quote, it nevertheless not just prefigures the position of later thinkers, such as Cartwright, but also realism.

Nevertheless, whilst the causal analysis tradition has developed in a most sophisticated way technically, it retains a theory of causality that is either simplistic, or simply "renders to Caesar" in matters of theory. Consequently, it is not a question of whether it is realist or not realist, for those working in causal analysis the question is irrelevant. In fairness, they share this characteristic with many natural scientists, in that whatever their philosophical "positioning" is, they rarely articulate it.

In US quantitative social science, there is no anti-realism, because actually there is no realism, or at least not much of it. I will return to the empirical issues raised by causal analysis in Chapter 4.

In the UK and other Anglophone countries quantitative social science, as in the US, rarely indulges in philosophical or methodological introspection. Its methods of analysis have often been US imports and these have been grafted onto a strongly empiricist tradition (from John Stuart Mill onwards) in public and social policy. If anything there is a naïve realism about the UK quantitative analysis tradition that treats measurement of phenomena as being literally true representations of that phenomena (Byrne 2002).

In the matter of realism and anti-realism in quantitative social science, one is put in mind of what Oscar Wilde wrote in *The Picture of Dorian Grey*: "There is only one thing in the world worse than being talked about, and that is not being talked about". Realism is pretty much ignored.

Mythical beasts, language and anything goes

Throughout the history of social science, there have been a number of cleavages, some more radical than others. G.H. von Wright in his paper, "Two Traditions" (von Wright 1993), makes a number of distinctions in approach, that he traces to the differences between the Aristotelean and Galilean traditions and then to that of the *methodenstreit* dispute in the 19th century. He contrasts the monistic causal approach of positivism with that of the hermeneutic tradition of understanding – of explanation versus understanding. Others have contrasted the nomothetic scientific approach, which emphasises regularity and laws, with the idiographic focusing on the particular and in studies of the social world, the individual agent (Williams 2002). This cleavage was apparent in the early days of US sociology, with a tendency for that emanating from Columbia university to broadly follow the first approach and that from Chicago following the second (Madge 1963). Subsequently, this division was reinforced by a lot of politics, both inside and outside social science. The politics can be traced to the 1960s and a growing disillusionment with science that had its origins in opposition to the Vietnam war, the anti-nuclear movement and a growing awareness of the environmental impact of the 20th century growth of science and technology. This led to an opposition of "progressive" anti-science against "reactionary" science. Anti-science became associated with the left and indeed given intellectual weight by the writings of Hannah Arendt (1958) and Herbert Marcuse (1964). At the same time, disciplines such as sociology, were seen by many on the anti-science left as potentially emancipatory and in several countries this coincided with a growth, in universities, of social science. It was reinforced by the emergence of second wave feminism, which itself regarded much of science as oppressive and androcentric (see Payne 2014 for a discussion of these developments). The new cohort of "anti-science" academics found much to complain about, from the functionalist theory of Talcott Parsons to the use of "positivist" methods to measure and explain the characteristics of society.

Meanwhile by the mid-1960s, "anti-positivism" in the philosophy of science had begun to be increasingly influential. The publication of Popper's *Logic of Scientific Discovery*, for the first time in English, in 1959, had serious implications for logical positivism (or logical empiricism), casting doubt on the possibility of an "observational language" and a "theoretical language", as distinct elements in science[11] (Carnap 2000 [1966]). Rather, Popper demonstrated how theory and observation are mutually dependent. Famously, he resurrected "Hume's Problem" of induction, maintain that theories can never be logically confirmed, only falsified.

Thomas Kuhn's reading of the history of science (Kuhn 1970 [1962]) led him to question the orthodoxy of the growth of knowledge, in science, in favour of the view that science was punctuated by epistemological revolutions. More radical still was the relativism of Paul Feyerabend (1975), whose motto "anything goes", was derived from the claim that moral and social values, along with the tacit knowledge of scientists, shaped science rather than "scientific method".

There was a symbiosis between these views and the new left politics of those entering the social sciences and a desire to do social science in a different way. The term "positivism" became a short-hand for a rejection of measurement, explanation and prediction – the goals of science, and much of social science hitherto. Positivism was (and to some extent still is) a useful mythical beast of many faceted evils (Philips 1987: 36–37).

The above potted history serves to explain why much of social science (and particularly outside of the United States), views knowledge of the social world as a non-scientific project. Mostly it is not overtly anti-realist in that it is anti-realist philosophy or methodology of science, but rather it begins from a different conception of what social reality is. The "anti-realism" is a rejection of any reality beyond that which is constructed by individuals from own experience. That this leads to a radical scepticism or, indeed, a different form of "abstracted empiricism" has not been lost on its critics (Bryman 1988: 119).

This second form of anti-realism is such because it embraces facets of idealist philosophy, constructivism and an emphasis on the ontological primacy of language.

What is often called the "lingustic turn" was much influenced by the work of Peter Winch (1990 [1958]), who in turn was influenced by the linguistic philosophy of Ludwig Wittgenstein. Wittgenstein treated language as primarily social and asks us to consider the philosophical impossibility of a "private language". The rules of such a language could only be known to (and therefore infinitely changeable) by the owner of such language and would therefore not be a language, because there would be no intelligibility for others. Winch maintained that the task of social investigation is to make intelligible the "forms of life" of a particular society (Winch 1990 [1958]: 42). The forms of life are embodied in rules which are expressed and known through language. Therefore, to understand a form of life one must understand the language. If a social "reality" is created by the rules of its language, then the different rules in a different society create different realities and it follows from this that the reality of an investigator is just another reality and there can be no privileging of an investigator account from that of the society investigated. The most radical form of this position predated Winch and can be found in the Sapir Whorf hypothesis (Whorf 1956), first suggested by Edward Sapir and developed by Benjamin Whorf (see also Mennell 1974: 41–42 for a discussion of this) which maintains that language does not simply reproduce ideas, but actually shapes the ideas themselves. In this view, Newtonian space and time are not intuitions about reality, but instead are the product of linguistically produced culture (Whorf 1956: 153).

This was where it began, but it went much further in the hands of the postmodernists in social science. Postmodernism has a plethora of intellectual influences some of which arose from the anti-establishment, anti-science movements of the 1960s, particularly the Paris "commune" of May 1968 and the existential philosophy of Heidegger, the nihilism of Nietzsche, romanticism, literary criticism, anti-scientism post Marxism and hermeneutics. To describe a unified system of thought, or movement is to describe something postmodernists reject as a "meta-narrrative". Post-modernists deny the possibility of universal explanation, it has an "incredulity toward meta-narratives" (Lyotard 1984). Thus, post-modernism epitomises both moral and epistemological relativism. In the latter case, a position quite opposite to realism.

Wittgenstein's (and later Winch's) position on language was taken much further by postmodernists, such as Jaques Derrida (1978). Derrida philosophy incorporated images into his linguistic philosophy. The "text", which may be language or visual images, are prioritised over their author. Though texts may be interpreted, these interpretations are relative and tell us nothing about reality beyond the text itself, thus the role of interpretation becomes a rhetoric of persuasion. It follows, from this rather like more radical forms of hermeneutics, historical interpretation is similarly simply one reading of a text or texts and there is no historical truth to grasp. In the writings of Jean Baudrillard (1983), this takes an ontological dimension (if indeed the concept of ontology can mean anything in postmodernism) in which he maintains we live in a world of simulacra nowadays. Whereas once, one could point to originals or copies (say a master tape, or photographic negative) the digital age has left us with an equivalence of image.

These influences found their way into social science (indeed if it could be called that anymore) and gave rise to a linguistic, relativistic and literary approach. It is exemplified in the ethnography of Clifford and Marcus (1986). Their approach is not without its sophistication (Hammersley 2008), but in essence, it questions the possibility of fidelity of any accounts of social reality. Indeed, those accounts were as constituting the realities they portrayed. Rather in the manner of Derrida (Hammersley *op cit*: 131–132), these were seen as literary processes of metaphor and narrative, as exclusion and rhetoric. It followed from this that the line between "research" and fiction becomes blurred or dissolved. Indeed, their book was entitled "*Writing Culture*".

A brief glance at many of these postmodern writings would indeed invite the conclusion that they fetishised language and obscurity. This was deliberate. Post-modernism, in rejecting science, also rejected the clarity of scientific language, epitomised in Maggie MacLure's denunciation of clarity as disguising power and exclusion (cited in Hammersley 2008: 141). As I have noted above, the anti-science, linguistic–post-modernist turn, was not a direct challenge to realism, but rather a more ambitious assault on rationality, science and post enlightenment values. Some have claimed that its epistemological and moral relativism are at least partially to blame for the rise of "post truth" politics, authoritarianism and specifically, the rise of Donald Trump (Anderson 2017: 307–309).

I do not intend presenting a refutation of these ideas, partly because others have done it very eloquently and in great depth (see, e.g., Holton 1993, Tallis 1995, Jones 1998, Boudon 2004, Hammersley 2008), but rather I will simply observe that the epistemological relativism of post-modernism and its manifestations in social "science" are very obviously contradictory, but more importantly would render any attempts at a felicitous explanation or understanding of the social world pointless or impossible. However, through the smoke of battle of the culture wars that ensued in the 1970s to the 1990s, one can discern some genuine problems and insights that have survived into more temperate and considered versions of methodology. I will briefly mention two of these, because they have important implications for what follows in subsequent chapters.

The problem of language. Winch, Derrida, Clifford and Marcus and many others, reify language. According to them, one might say that there is nothing other than language. Language can define who we are and is the means of the feedback mechanism in the social world. One can even (to an extent) agree with MacLure's view that absence can exclude. I myself, am a member of an ethnic minority that has (up until recently) been excluded from history and from contemporary recognition, less by sanction, than by deliberate absence of linguistic description or acknowledgement. Language is important and any realist account of the social world cannot ignore its enabling and constraining social properties (Sayer 2000: 35–41). Indeed, one can go as far as to say that the social is language and Winch was at least partially right. But he and those that followed were wrong in three ways. Firstly, that language does not always predate action. We do not need a word for something in order to create it. Where I live rural stone walls are called "hedges". In the Cornish language that preceded English, they were called *keow*. Some are over a thousand years old and after they were built, they were named, but those ancient farmers did not sit around a fire contemplating a name before they built them to keep their animals enclosed!

Secondly if, Winch was right, then members of society S would be unable to communicate rules or meaning with members of society S1 and vice versa. To know those rules, according to Winch, you need to be within the society in which they are created and know the language of that society. But this produces an empirically and historically unsatisfactory dichotomy. Because there are extra linguistic referents and many things S and S1 have in common, initial and at least partial understanding is possible. All societies will have some notion of hunger, food, defecation, reproduction and so on. S and S1 may have differing views on the presence or absence of phenomena, but they will agree on the existence of a notion of presence and absence.

Thirdly, language is real, because it is real in its effects, yet it does not exhaust reality. As Bhaskar and others (1998, 2008) have argued, reality is deeper than what we can observe. In 2016, the UK, in a referendum, voted to leave the European Union. Politicians and journalists have each utilised (to use the late Alan Bryman's phrase (Bryman 1998: 142) "rhetorics of persuasion" to advance their favourite theory to explain a vote for an action that will primarily economically damage the very people who voted for it. But, this vote was complex, and it will need much more than linguistic dexterity to provide an explanation for it. It will require explanations that can identify overlapping and intermeshing historical and contemporary mechanisms. Some of these mechanisms (as with many others) will need both linguistic and statistical description. Statistical description, though in its presentation, is indeed a language, it is based on many non-arbitrary mathematical rules and the law of large numbers and these transcend language.

A realist theory of language, must acknowledge its centrality, but also that linguistic description and narratives more generally, do not exhaust the causal efficacy of social reality.

In one respect, the linguistic turn is more directly anti-realist in that it maintains that what we know of the world, both social and physical, is constructed in the social realm through discourse. It is well summed up by Kenneth Gergen as follows:

> ... all claims to "the real" are traced to the processes of relationship, and there is no extra-cultural means of ultimately privileging one construction of reality over another.
>
> Gergen 2001: 8

Social constructivism does not (usually) deny that there is, or there may be, a reality beyond construction but, at least for contemporary constructivists, such as Gergen, there is no point talking about it because what we perceive is a world that is a product of culture and cultures are ever changing in time and space. Constructivists are then saying that the world can only be known under a description, but this is actually something realists can agree with! The "founder" of critical realism, Roy Bhaskar (2008: 250) puts it very well, "things exist and act independently of our descriptions, but we can only know them under particular descriptions". There are, however, two key differences between the social constructivist position and that of realism. Firstly, social constructivism ignores ontology, whereas realists, prioritise ontology. For social constructivism, there are no "things", just social constructions of "things". Secondly, social constructivism maintains there is an epistemological equivalence between discourses, whereas realism aims to match description and reality and consequently implies that some descriptions will be "better" or more "realistic" than others. That is, there will be statements about the world which have a greater truth content than other statements. There is a midway position between social constructivism and realism. For the former, there are only descriptions and for most realists, there are descriptions and things. Yet whilst we can agree with the latter that there are descriptions and things the separation between them is not discrete. The descriptions themselves can become "things". This was recognised a long while ago by W.I. Thomas and Dorothy Thomas (1928: 571–572) when they said "when people define situations as real they become real in their consequences". Thus, we can have objects and descriptions of objects and the latter may themselves become objects to be described. But they are both real. I'll come back to this when I discuss "social objects" in Chapter 4.

Although the post-modernists reached conclusions about language that are not sustainable in any methodological approach that aims to describe, explain or understand the social world, they are not wrong to emphasise the importance of language, but how that mechanism is ideologically infused and created. The feedback mechanism is not just a neutral reflection and appraisal of the state of the world, but is mostly ideological in content, reflecting, creating and sustaining power relationships. Given that researchers must intervene in the social manifestation of this, their choices, methods and actions are not neutral either. In Chapter 6, I will return to this question when I consider the issue of reflexivity.

Reality, realism and investigation

I began this chapter by saying that the biggest problem for realism, is reality. Advances in physics have led to a questioning of materialism in descriptions of physical reality and social reality is no easier. Is it that which we experience directly, those things we believe are real, or is it the myriad of interlocking actions and beliefs of others that enable and constrain the individual? I think it is all of these things. Critical realists talk of "layers" of reality or a "layered ontology", often called the "real", the "actual" and the "empirical" (see, e.g., the descriptions in Bhaskar 2008: 56–58 and in Outhwaite 1987: 44–60), but I think this metaphor is misleading, because it implies that the layers are themselves discrete. I prefer the metaphor of a dynamic matrix of interlocking beliefs and actions that are sometimes partially visible. Their properties are not always manifest, but may be dispositional. Sometimes they coalesce into, what I will call later "social objects", themselves sometimes fleeting, sometimes enduring and in turn we can sometimes identify their further arrangement into mechanisms. This is the complex nature of social reality.

But this is theoretical supposition and whilst metaphysical realists are right to say that in principle there is a reality we can surmise (on the grounds that past suppositions often become manifest in due course) scientists and social scientists must produce evidence for the nature of that underlying reality.

They must do this through the empirical tools of measurement and observation, but if you cannot access underlying reality, how can you measure and observe it? This is the conundrum. Empiricists would have us believe that all we can speak of is that which we measure and observe, but the response to that must be how did you decide what to measure or observe?

There must be some notion, however implicit that what is measured or observed stands in for what is real? Realism faces up to this and accepts that our tools of reasoning, measurement and observation are scientific constructions, but they can nevertheless help us to describe and explain reality. Constructivism shares one characteristic of empiricism: a belief that we cannot know reality. In constructivism, the researcher is simply interested in how people construct their social world, usually through the medium of language. Language and the concept of social construction, are not an anathema to realists, but it does not imply the epistemological relativism of the former position.

This said, the question for realists is *how* can we know reality? And this is a methodological question. Put it another way how can we use our methods and techniques to close in on reality? As realist social scientists, that is our destination, but to get there, there is a fair bit of philosophical and methodological work to do.

Throughout this chapter, three things have been implicit: the complex nature of social reality, the issue of causality and the inevitability of accessing reality through theoretical and methodological representation. These matters will be the subject of the next three chapters.

Notes

1 Many physicists now maintain that, at the most basic physical level, reality might be explained by, what is described as, "vibrating strings", a simple metaphor for, yes, another theory, which has yet to be confirmed! See https://www.newscientist.com/article/dn16950-string-theory-a-beginners-guide/ for a description (accessed 1/09/2020).
2 The concept of the "Meso" is valuable for two reasons. Firstly it is a description of those levels of society between micro level interaction and macro level structures, particularly for example in community studies, but is also a valuable methodological device for show the connections between the micro and macro, or even between micro level "social objects" (see Chapter 4) and mechanisms (see Chapter 8). For a good description of and argument for the "meso" in sociology (see Smelser 1997: 28–48).
3 See, for example, Haig and Evers 2016, Maxwell 2012, Harré 1986. A useful "map" of the relation of realism to other philosophies of science can be found at http://positivists.org/blog/archives/4233.
4 Critical realists often use the terms "causal powers", or "tendencies", which are equivalent to dispositions, the term mostly used in the philosophy of science. Because I refer to the latter literature in Chapter 4, I have used the term "dispositions" throughout.
5 Indeed, his PhD supervisor/doctoral advisor was Bertrand Russell, who subscribed to a version of empiricism, he described as "logical atomism".
6 In the correspondence theory of truth something is true if there is agreement with the facts. Thus, it requires an agreement between premises and conclusion, but it does present a logical problem of sentences such as: "this statement is false". If the sentence is true then what it says must be true – that it is false, but if it is false then what it says must be false, so it must be true! The logician Alfred Tarski attempted to solve this problem, by saying that the truth of a sentence can only be established in a further sentence(s) (Popper 1989 [1963]: 116). This does present the problem of a linguistic regress, rather similar to the logical positivist separation of an observation language and a theoretical language. Empirically, however, a more satisfying answer that the facts are those things for which we have currently unfalsifiable evidence. Except where I speak of other versions of truth, through my use of the term is that of correspondence.
7 Causality and Causation refer to the same thing. Roughly, philosophers call it causation and methodologists, causality, but there are exceptions. I have used causality throughout.
8 See Puri (2001: 155–157) for a description of quantum damping.
9 What he meant by this was the use of operationalised variables in sample surveys. Though the spirit of his criticism was probably right, if this is taken as a dismissal of quantitative sociology, then – in my view, he went too far.
10 Bunge has had a long history of advocating "mechanistic" and arguably realist positions. The paper Blalock cites is Bunge 1961. But see also Bunge 2004.
11 In this view, a precision about language is essential for good philosophy and science. Linguistically carefully specified theories can be tested through observations, which themselves should be specified linguistically. This begs the question of how was the observation language derived. This becomes a particularly important question, when observations must be made through complex instruments, rather than through direct sense data.

3

Complexity, probability and necessity in the social world

Complexity has become fashionable in recent decades, but it can trace its origins back to the work of Warren Weaver, in the late 1940s (Weaver 1948). He coined the terms "organised" and "disorganised" complexity. Somewhat counter intuitively, the latter is somewhat easier to describe statistically. Things such as Brownian motion, or gasses may have millions of "parts" and are stochastic, but they can be described and predicted statistically. Organised complexity may have many fewer parts that interrelate and may produce stability, or new states may emerge. Complexity is defined in many different ways and there is some debate as to how it differs from "chaos theory".[1] There are indeed similarities, but whilst the former mostly studies complex emergence as a result of relatively simple interactions amongst units (often large numbers of units) chaos is concerned with change, often sudden change in relatively simple systems (Gleick 1987). This is a conceptual distinction, but in systems the difference can be subtle. However, for the most part social systems, to use Weaver's description, exhibit organised complexity.

In the natural sciences, complexity has become an empirically fruitful interdisciplinary way of researching systems, particularly in the work conducted at, or influenced by that at the Santa Fe Institute.[2] However with the exception of economics and management science to some degree, it is less developed in the social sciences, where it is often long on theory and short on empirical engagement.[3] Similarly, the literature in popular science, though often very engaging, mostly focusses on physical systems, and when social systems are considered this is mostly through abstract examples, or rudimentary simulations.

For many, the concepts in popular science are a useful taxonomy, if not applied too literally to social science, but for others their methods and theories treat the world as "complex" without any reference to the vocabulary of complexity at all. For example, most social science versions of realism, notably critical realism, will emphasise the "open systems" nature of social organisation, but never or rarely discuss or refer to "complexity". There is no entry for it, for example, in the *Dictionary of Critical Realism* (Hartwig 2007), the critical realism *Essential Readings* volume (Archer et al 1998), or in a quite different approach to realism, in Haig and Evers *Realist Inquiry in Social Science* (Haig and Evers 2016)

My approach is somewhere between the two. I'm not too concerned, in this book, with how the complexity approach to science came about, or its theoretical positioning and terms (though I will use some of its terms where they are descriptively useful). This is for two reasons. The first is that others have already done an admirable job in this respect and I would refer you to their writings (for example Gleick 1987, Holland 2014, Ruelle 1991 and in the social sciences Byrne 1998, Cilliers 1998, Reed and Harvey 1992). The second reason is that such abstraction, often provided as a "framework" can have a methodological disconnect from empirical work. Occasionally one sees a splendid piece of analysis of large and complex data (see examples in Chapter 9), which demonstrate an intuitive feel for complexity, without ever mentioning the word, whilst other less empirical work will show a theoretical awareness of complexity, that does not translate into a complexity-informed methodology.

I came to complexity in a very different way to most people and that was through the writings of Karl Popper on realism and on probability (Popper 1957, 1959b, 1983, 1995). I think it is perfectly possible that Popper, who died in 1994, never heard the word complexity used in the way it is now, yet his later writings on his version of the propensity theory of probability embodied, in my view, a complexity approach. In this chapter I want to do three things. The first is to outline what it means to say the world is ontologically probabilistic – and thus "complex". This description largely comes from Popper's metaphysical basis to his theory of probability. The second is to introduce the idea of contingency, which I think follows from ontological probability. In this section, I will show how complexity concepts, such as phase space, strange attractors and emergence are useful descriptors. Thirdly, I want to contrast the concept of contingency, from that of necessity, arguing that whilst social life is relatively ordered, there are no things that must be, or must not be, only things that are likely, or unlikely.

Probability, epistemology and ontology

Probability can be about the character of things or estimations. Estimations can be made subjectively or objectively. The former is usually associated with Bayesian approaches, where probability resides in subjective initial estimations, called "priors", which are then revised as new data become available.

Objective theories treat probabilities as real properties, not estimations. There are many objective theories of probability (see Gillies 2000), but only two will concern us here. The first of these, the frequency theory, is the most common-place in social science and underpins the statistical reasoning employed in survey research and the analysis of quantitative data and the second is the propensity theory, which is mostly (though not universally) associated with single case probabilities (OP Cit: Chapter 6). Both the frequency and propensity theories of probability are referred to as "objective" probability, because each refers to an objective situation that exists independently of the observer's appraisal of it, whereas the prior odds in subjective probability are derived from observer estimation.

Whilst subjective, or Bayesian probability is methodologically valuable, it is not a concern in this book. However, the frequency theory and propensity theory are. The first, because of its ubiquity as a basis for survey research and the analysis of survey data and the second because, in my view, can be a valuable statistical basis for complexity. Both have methodological value for complex realism and I will explore this in the Chapter 9. Both have statistical or methodological shortcomings. Although, here, I want to advance the idea of the propensity theory as a philosophical and methodological basis for complex realism, we need firstly to contrast this with frequency theory.

The frequency theory of probability measures the relative frequency of an event A defined by conditions B. Thus, the objective probability of an event A occurring is conditional upon B and can be symbolised as p (A/B). Consider the case of a standard six-sided dice. In this case the event A might be the frequency of the dice coming up as a six. The odds of the dice coming up are 1:6 and statistically these odds are determined by the fact that there are five other equal possibilities of other numbers coming up. Though those other numbers may come up in lengthy sequences, in the long run the relative frequency of a six being thrown will be 1:6. In this case conditions B would be the characteristics of the dice itself, the way it was thrown and the surface it landed on, etc. However, whilst statisticians acknowledge these conditions, they nevertheless maintain that probability is a limiting frequency and an operational definition of the axioms of probability.

Karl Popper disagreed with this view. He said that the frequency is actually generated by the properties of the case (e.g. the dice, the way it is thrown. etc.). Popper maintained that a singular event has a probability that arises from the same generating conditions that produced the sequence. It follows, that any event, even if it occurs just once has a probability, for its probability is a property of the generating conditions, themselves outcomes of earlier probabilities.

Now, contrast this with a case in a sample survey. Although in a probability sample, every case will have an equal chance of selection, the cases selected nevertheless stand in for all of the cases in a population, with the assumption that these are relative to the population mean. But each case will, according to Popper, have its own individual dispositions that produce a probability that may be particular to that case. Or as Watts and Gilbert put it (Watts and Gilbert 2014: 10) "systems [are] composed of multiple interdependent parts, and the behaviour of the system could not be equated to a linear sum of the behaviours of the parts". We know, from the example of outliers, that the characteristics of individual cases may vary enormously from the mean and indeed, in the social world a perfect normal distribution is rare. Thus, we could say that "cases" in sample surveys are virtual, not actual (Williams 1999). This, it might be said, blurs the relationship between the non-linear generating conditions and the assumption of linearity in a model of aggregate data. Sample survey aggregate data, however useful, "smooths out" the complexity of the generating conditions of case characteristics that make up the aggregate.

The ontology of single case probabilities is simple and even trivially true, but because most quantitative analysis, in social research, depends on the frequency theory of probability, this is ignored. So, please indulge me in further stating the trivially true for the moment.

In the world some things are certain and some things are more probable than others. We can think of it as those things that cannot happen as zero and those things that must happen as one. Most events in the world and (it is my belief) all events in the *social* world have probabilities greater than zero, but less than one. Let me begin by suggesting some examples of "ones" and "zeros", those things that must or cannot happen, and the things between.

It is certain that you will die (1), that water must consist of hydrogen and oxygen atoms (1), that no human can fly unaided to the moon (0), energy in a system cannot be conserved indefinitely (0). Each of these things has a final grounding in a fundamental physical law that will always operate in any conditions we can think of. Some things are very, very unlikely. There is the very faintest possibility that I could become the Prime Minister of the UK, but it is an infinitesimal possibility. It is much more likely that I will contract a cold in the next year, or go on holiday. One of the fascinating things about non-zero probabilities (that is between zero and one) is that they change over time. Think about your own life trajectory. Some things in it were fairly probable, that you would go to school, you would have friends, you would get a job. Other things are much less probable (and therefore less predictable). In fact, our lives are so complex and so subject to change, that the probabilities (sometimes this is expressed as "odds") of any particular event/characteristic would be very difficult to estimate when we were (say) ten years old. But being ten years old in one set of circumstances can generate very different probabilities of outcomes than in others.

At an aggregate, or population level, in a given society, we can predict the likely outcomes for ten-year-olds, as a group, possibly mediated by class, education and so on, but these are based on a population mean, whereas we can say that any given ten-year-old has their own odds of a particular outcome, which may or may not deviate from the mean (or indeed the mode), but ontologically is a product of their own biographies and will be shaped by interactions with the physical and social world in the future.

Michael Blastland and David Spiegelhalter (2013: 43–45) provide an entertaining example of this. They report that the *Daily Express* informed its readers, in 2012, that a daily fry up increases your risk of developing pancreatic cancer by 20%. What does this mean? Does it mean that if you eat a daily fry up, you are 20% more likely to get cancer? As they illustrate, if we take a population of 400, where four people would normally contract pancreatic cancer, a 0.25% increase across that population is one more person! Which means, one's own risk increases by only 0.25 – which is reassuring, but possibly wrong in an important respect! The risk is almost certainly not evenly distributed across the population, that is some people regardless of their eating fry ups, will have other characteristics that increase or decrease the chances of contracting pancreatic cancer. Denzil eats a fry up every day, but he doesn't smoke, drinks only moderately, exercises and has his five portions of fruit and veg every day! He is also 29. Garfield eats a fry up every day, eats no fruit or veg, apart from potatoes and the tomato sauce on his pizza, he doesn't exercise and is obese. He is also 57!

The probabilistic character of the world is real and is not an artefact of our lack of knowledge of it. To illustrate what I mean, consider the view of the 18th century physicist and mathematician, Pierre Laplace. He believed the entire universe was composed of "different arrangements of atoms moving in accordance with Newton's laws of motion"(Tallis 1995: 12). It then followed that if all such arrangements that exist now can be known with certainty, then we can also know all possible future arrangements. Even if we could know the first, and we can't, we cannot know the second, because all of the "elements" that compose "now" are in different, possibly only slightly different states, but their interactions with other states will produce very different trajectories and outcomes. I'll say more about this later.

The Oxford Dictionary definition of propensity is an inclination or tendency, which would suggest that something has particular properties that have a potential to become a certain way, or bring about circumstances that can change other things. Philosophers call these dispositions and I will return to these in the next chapter.

Contingency and complexity

The word contingency can be used in quite subtlety different ways. For example, something that happens by chance or is unpredictable, something which may or may not happen, or something that is dependent upon something else happening as a sufficient, but not necessary condition. The way I use it is the latter, to indicate a particular form of dependency, in so far as event B (in time) is dependent upon event A, which has a degree of ontological probability. We should not think of this as a linear dependency, whereby A's probability is itself determined by a singular prior event, but rather as a nesting of prior probabilities. There may be a path dependency of A -> B, that may have a very high probability and indeed the prior paths that led to this may have equally high probabilities. In a relatively stable system, this will be the case and these paths can be modelled, using retrospective longitudinal data, as I will illustrate in Chapter 9. Equally in other systems, the paths may have quite low probabilities of happening and B can look like chance, or coincidence. Actually, what has then happened, is that the prior low probability paths have converged with a much higher probability path(s).

Take two historical assassinations as examples of this. In June, 1914, Archduke Franz Ferdinand, heir to the Austro-Hungarian throne, was assassinated. The time, place and immediate circumstances of his assassination could, of course, have been different. It was not determined, how or even if, he would be assassinated. But at the time, there was a quite powerful movement that wished to incorporate southern provinces of the Austro-Hungarian Empire into a new country – Yugoslavia. There was even a secret society, the Black Hand gang, dedicated to this through violent means. Something like his assassination could certainly have been anticipated.

Now, contrast this with the assassination of President John F Kennedy, in November 1963. There was no dedicated political movement, of any consequence, that presented a violent challenge to Kennedy. The Cold War and the Cuban missile crisis, of the previous year had brought the United States and the Soviet Union close to war, but there was no appetite, in the Soviet Union, to kill or overthrow Kennedy, whose presence arguably helped to keep the United States – Soviet relations in equilibrium. Kennedy was assassinated by Lee Harvey Oswald, who acted alone and the assassination was unanticipated. If we consider, in each case, the A -> B relationship as that of the assassin to the victim, the prior paths would have had different probabilities, though the A -> B relationship ended up the same. The prior actuarial odds of the Kennedy assassination would have been set considerably lower than the Ferdinand one[4].

I use these examples for effect, but even in our own lives we can reconstruct similar outcomes with quite different antecedent probabilities. In these examples we are working back from outcomes to envisage the different probabilistic pathways to similar outcomes. Many illustrations, in the complexity literature do things the other way around. One of the first and now iconic examples – actually from Chaos Theory, was that of weather systems. James Gleick, in his book *Chaos, the Making of a New Science* (Gleick 1987), tells the story of Edward Lorentz's "toy weather", simple computer modelling of changes in the weather that demonstrated that the smallest changes of initial variables led to huge deviations in weather patterns later on. This was termed the Butterfly Effect: a butterfly flaps its wing in one location, causing tiny perturbations that lead to large weather effects many thousands of kilometres away. This was, of course, metaphorical, but nevertheless demonstrated that very small changes in initial conditions can produce massive changes later. This showed that weather forecasts beyond a few days, were prone to huge variation.

As Byrne and Callaghan note (Byrne and Callaghan 2013: 176), "It is conventional to describe the complex as occupying a realm between simple linear determination and chaos". However, as they go on to say, there are limits to the number of states a given system can be in. Stochastic states might be thought of as those ontological systems that we have yet to produce epistemological models of, though we may produce statistical descriptions. They are the mathematical version of Dick Cheney's famous "unknown, unknowns". Actually, the chaos literature itself does distinguish between "deterministic chaos", that indicates non stochastic outcomes and stochastic states. As Byrne and Callaghan go on to say,

> In reality itself it is difficult to envisage chaos other than in terms of the heat death of the Universe. Weather systems, so often considered to represent chaos, are not ontologically chaotic. The weather systems can take any from a set of forms but that set is not limitless.
>
> Byrne and Callaghan 2013: 176

Karl Popper, in an essay entitled "Clouds and Clocks" (Popper 1979: 206–255) also uses a weather analogy. He contrasted the behaviour of clouds with that of clocks. The former has measurable properties, but these can only be approximately known and measured through time, whereas clocks (and he meant old fashioned clockwork clocks) have relatively precise mechanisms that behave in a reliable and predictable way. Some systems, he goes on to say, are more like clouds and some more like clocks.

This is an excellent illustration of the distinction between systems, such as clocks, which by definition must be in equilibrium to tell the correct time and those, such as clouds, which whilst recognisable as systems are further from equilibrium.

The complexity literature employs a vocabulary of "strange attractors" and "phase space" to describe systems that are relatively stable and the possibilities of that system. I prefer to use the term "possibility space", rather than "phase space", for the reason which will become apparent below. Strange Attractors, refer to time-ordered patterns towards which other trajectories converge (Cohen and Stewart, 1994: 200). Mathematically an attractor can be described as a set of numerical values towards which a system tends to evolve, but may begin from a wide range of initial conditions.

Strange attractors can be understood to exist within "possibility space", the space of the possible where anything can happen but not everything will happen given the structured, rule-driven nature of the social:

Equally, Strange Attractors are themselves dynamic, which if one considers it, can only be the case, otherwise they would remain in the same state in perpetuity.

Let us consider these things in respect of social systems. To go back to Popper's analogy, social systems are somewhere between clocks and clouds. The possibility space in which they can operate is less than that of clouds, but much more than clocks. Likewise, the "strange attractors" in the social world will have varying stability and robustness through time, but they are more identifiable and thus predictable, than any semi-stable cloud patterns. They also may emerge as the result of a slight change, or perturbation, in a particular environment (I'll say more of this later). But, here's the rub. Social systems may be more stable than clouds, but they are also much more complex. Cloud systems are little more than aerosols of water droplets, that coalesce as a result of temperature, air pressure, wind, dew point, etc., whereas social systems are multi-faceted, historic ensembles of self-aware agents co-operating and competing. It does not follow that the more complex a system is, the more likely it is to become stochastic. Social systems are very much more stable than clouds, but also very much more complex. This is an enormous challenge for social research. David Ruelle (1991: 59–64) discusses the methodological challenges of providing a mathematical description of strange attractors in turbulence flows, something he eventually achieved, but that had challenged mathematicians for a considerable period. It is tempting to say that turbulence flows are relatively simple things in comparison to dynamic social systems. Nevertheless, do not read this as a doctrine of despair, in social research! Whilst the social world and attractors in it are considerably more complex than turbulence flow, the former has characteristics that assist us to more readily provide descriptions.

Indeed, whilst terms like "strange attractors" and "possibility space" are handy metaphors, they can however be misleading in their use in describing the social world. Strange attractors,[5] in the physical world, usually have a "fractal structure", so called because they exhibit similar patterns at increasingly small scales, what is called self-similarity (Mandelbrot 1982: 44–46) and can certainly be observed in turbulence flows. This rarely is the case in the social world, where stability is much more to do with the convergence of a number of path dependencies. Patterns at a macro level often do *not* look like those at a meso, or micro level. Crucially stable patterns which ensue, are maintained, changed or dissipated by conscious reflexive agents. Nevertheless, one very useful concept we can take from the idea of strange attractors is that of bifurcation. Divergent behaviour, perhaps towards "chaos" is the result of bifurcations which gradually, then often spectacularly diverge to produce widely different outcomes. Whereas "strange attractors", in the social world at least, can be seen as the opposite behaviour, where bifurcations can eventually lead to convergence.

Many years ago I was involved in the evaluation of a group of Sure Start[6] projects, in Britain. Sure Starts were a Labour government initiative, in the late 1990s and 2000s, aimed at improving the health and educational opportunities of under-fives in economically and socially deprived communities in the UK. Of the Sure Starts we evaluated, one began as a "bottom up" community initiative, whilst the others were top down initiatives, their establishment decided on the basis of the socio-economic characteristics of the localities. The "bottom up" Sure Start, was started, governed and shaped by the community, using "planning for real" methods,[7] whereas the "top down" Sure Starts mostly employed "off the shelf" standardised procedures. Over a five year period both convergence and divergence occurred, creating a number of over-lapping, but sometimes antagonistic "strange attractors". Put simply the way the "bottom up" Sure Start developed became increasingly like the others, but at the same time, the other Sure Starts began to diverge from each other in the nature of their governance, services provided, local legitimacy and finally ability to survive. Sure Starts were an excellent example of the complexity of policy intervention.

In the physical world, mathematicians can calculate an attractor as a set of numerical values towards which a system tends to evolve. Though not impossible, in the social world, this is very much more difficult, so the term must serve as an analogy, not a qualitative description of mathematical specifications.

Similarly, possibility space may be a useful analogy in the social world, but cannot be as precise as that used in the physics or mathematics, for the simple metaphysical reason that except where bounded by the physical world, or the transcendental reality of time, no social system is bounded by particular possibility spaces. All possible states of the system, are all possible states of the social world – the whole lot! Nevertheless, the term can be useful to describe a relatively bounded system in which we can describe *probable*, rather than possible states.

One final term, that is of value to us is that of emergence. This term has been widely deployed in both the complexity literature and realism. See for example Lawson 2019: (197–222)

In Chapter 1, I described Paul Cilliers' distinction between "complicated" and "complex" – the first a jumbo jet, the second mayonnaise. The jumbo jet is the sum of its parts, the mayonnaise is emergent. Paradoxically, mayonnaise is both simple and yet its emergence is complex.

Emergence arises out of the properties and relations, characterising its simpler constituents. It is not predictable from or reducible too those constituents. If we had never seen mayonnaise, and we were not chemists, it would be very hard to predict that oil and egg yolk could produce mayonnaise. Equally, once produced, it is impossible to separate it into its constituent ingredients. Mayonnaise is a good illustration of what emergence is, but what is happening and more importantly and less trivially, what is emergence in the social world?

In the social world it is hard not to see emergence everywhere. New complex forms of social organisation can arise from relatively simple antecedents – the social version of the Butterfly Effect. In 2010, in the town of Sidi Bouzid in Tunisia, a fruit seller, called Mohamed Bouazizi set himself on fire, in front of a government building, as a protest against his maltreatment by the police. What became known as the Arab spring ensued, culminating in one of the most destructive and dangerous wars, since the Cold War, in Syria, and one which, at the time of writing has lasted over eight years. A spark that lit a conflagration, a stone that moved in the river enough to bring about a deluge, further downstream. At the time of writing, ten years after these events, stability has emerged from considerable bloodshed. In Tunisia this has taken the form of a fragile democracy, but elsewhere it has only been achieved through new forms of repression and authoritarianism.

Analysis of what happened and what caused the Arab spring tempts us towards a reductive strategy. Andrew Sayer warns us against this:

> It is often assumed that a useful way of understanding a complex object is to break it down into its constituent parts, either by abstraction or literally taking it to bits. For example, to understand something like employment

> change, it seems sensible to break down, or "disaggregate" the aggregate statistics in the hope that complexity and irregularity might be reduced to the effects of a combination of simple and regular components.
>
> Sayer 1992: 88

He goes on to say that we would not try to explain the power of people to think by reference to the cells in their bodies. Sayer is absolutely correct, but equally this is a bit too pessimistic and possibly a category mistake, if taken too literally.

In the case of the Arab spring and other large-scale social changes, he is absolutely correct. Things, such as the Arab Spring, are examples of "strong emergence", that is would not be possible to produce a computer simulation, because there is a multitude of other earlier systemic components that led to the emergence. A weak emergence, on the other hand (say, simple economic exchange networks) can be simulated from a small number of initial components and conditions. I'll say a bit more about this in Chapter 9.

Mohamed Bouazizi did not begin his process *tabula rasa*, rather it was itself an emergent property from earlier complex social formations in Tunisia, perhaps combined with his particular economic circumstances and psychological dispositions. In other words, to attempt a reductionist explanation that began with what was happening in Tunisia, in 2011, is an almost arbitrary intervention into a nested array of complex mechanisms.

But in order to explain, we do not need to reduce, though in relatively simple systems, taking a "slice in time" can produce relatively accurate descriptions, which can become a basis for explanation. My own work on measuring homelessness, I would suggest, can produce locally accurate descriptions, that inference to the best explanation (more of that later) are also accurate (Williams and Cheal 2002). Local, relatively determinate systems, are a bit closer to "clocks". However, non-reductive explanations, that use strategies such as narratives, case based analysis of trajectories, or even causal modelling of frequency-based data. In the latter case, some level of disaggregation (contra Sayer) can aid us in complex realist explanation. But this too is for Chapter 9.

Necessity

This chapter, so far, has been about the domain of the possible. Complexity, I have suggested, is about nested probabilities and outcomes that are the result of particular path dependencies. However, probability exists in the space of the possible, between 0 and 1. In order to envisage probabilities, we must consider their absolute limits of 0 or 1. I have claimed above that there are no zeros or ones in the social world, but let me qualify this with saying two things. Firstly, there are plenty of zeros and ones in the physical world and the physical world so very often places limits on, or makes possible aspects of social life. Secondly, there are outcomes in the social world, that are zeros and ones. These are actualised states. Before Emmanuel Macron was elected as President of France, there existed a probability that he could be elected. Initially, this probability was quite low, but maybe greater than the person who services his car, or sold him a pizza. But, from when he became a contender in the election, the probability increased and increased much further when he got to the second round of voting. Then he was elected and a 1 was realised. Further probabilities of his presidency rested on this, but he had to become President for these probabilities to exist. So, probabilities are not "free floating", they are always grounded in actual events that happened.

This brings us to the matter of necessity. There is necessity in the social world, but what it is and the way it operates, is different to that operating in the physical world.

This how Rom Harré describes necessity:

> To attribute necessity to items as various as a condition, an outcome, or effect, the truth of a statement, a conclusion, is, we contend to indicate that within the relevant context no alternative to that condition, outcome, or effect, truth-value or conclusion is possible.
>
> Harré and Madden (1975: 19)

Harré and Madden go on to elaborate this very clear definition through a description of modes of necessity. They divide these into a priori and a posteriori modes:

The *a priori* mode consists of logical necessity, whereby conclusions must follow from premises and transcendental necessity, whereby certain conditions must obtain for a rational human to have knowledge of the world. Logical necessity, other than perhaps in mathematics, requires linguistic classification and a designation of relations between linguistic concepts. These are logical relations between statements and need not be about empirical referents in the world, but there must be agreement between the premises and conclusions. So, we might say "All able bodied pigs can fly, Porky is an able bodied pig, so Porky can fly". The value of logical necessity, to social research, lies in the validation of our statements about the world and underwrites the aim to find agreement about logical structure and empirical content. We could say that an event A is logically necessary, if and only if the precise circumstances that led to A obtain. This, of course, is only something that we can say once A has happened and in this circumstance is probably only of value to distinguish it from natural necessity (which I come to below). Whilst this form of necessity can be valuable for formalising statements about the world, it was all but fetishised by the logical positivists as the deductive nomological (DN), or covering law approach to scientific reasoning. In this the *explanandum* is deduced from a set of true statements, the *explanans*, of which at least one should be a law. Thus, the rate of cooling of an object can be deduced from the known properties of that object, but in relation to the second law of thermodynamics. This model only works in relatively simple instances where reference can be made to fundamental physical laws, but this is hard to achieve, even in natural science. In the social sciences the DN model is relatively limited, or even no value, because of the rarity of law-like statements. There are many other criticisms of the use of DN model, in social science, (See Sayer 1992: 169; Williams 2016: 56–58), and I will return to the issues that the logic of the DN approach leads to in social science in Chapter 5.

Transcendental necessity was identified by Immanuel Kant to specify what must be the case for us to know the world at all. This was in response to empiricists, such as David Hume, who maintained that we can only have empirical knowledge of the world through sense perception. However, somewhat similarly to Descartes, *Cogito,* Kant argues for the necessity of the existence of mental awareness to perceive the empirical world. It can be said to follow from this, that space and time are also prerequisites for empirical knowledge or reasoning about the world. For practical purpose, this mode of necessity is important to us as a "grounding" for the origins of our thoughts, but also the limitations of time (see Williams 2016: 225–230).

The *a posteriori* mode is divided into conceptual and natural necessity. The first of these is that which is necessitated conceptually as a property of a thing, which for that thing to be what it is must obtain. A chair cannot simultaneously be a dog, its properties of "chairness" conceptually necessitate it being a chair and not something quite different. We can extend this to descriptions of people, or institutions (which may be embodied in people). To be a plumber, you must have a particular set of skills and possibly qualifications. To be the Pope, in the Roman Catholic Church, you must be elected to that position by cardinals who qualify as electors. A vote at an election is defined by a set of rules as to what can count as a vote. All of these properties are what necessitates us agreeing that someone is a plumber, the Pope, or a particular election. What they all have in common is that they are what they are as a result of social agreement. Conceptual necessity is at the heart of realist social science, because the concepts are real, in so far as they have causal properties that are locally necessary. They are Durkheim's "social facts" (Durkheim 1970[1952]: 390–392). In order to do the things only the president of France can do, you must be the president of France. If you commit a crime and are found guilty, you will receive some form of sanction that arises from the conceptual necessity of the law and its enforcement. Sometimes the necessity is more permissive, but still exists. For example, plumbers (amongst other things) fix and install water and waste flow systems, but equally I have the potential to do such things (sadly I cannot) and not be a plumber, but if I did such things I would be engaged in plumbing.

The second a posteriori form of necessity is natural necessity. Harré and Madden define as:

> When the natures of the operative powerful particulars, the constraining or stimulating effect of conditions and so on are offered as the grounds for the judgement that a certain effect cannot but happen, or cannot but fail to happen, we have natural necessity.

In this they allow for some measure of contingency and go on to say:

> When the probability of its happening falls within a certain range we have the natural necessity of a range or function of probabilities.
>
> Harré and Madden (1975: 19)

Though it is not clear from the latter whether they are referring to the probabilities assigned within a frequency distribution, or the probability of the occurrence of an event that is the property of that event.

Harré and Madden's argument refers only to the physical world (and indeed Harré has criticised modes of explanation, in social science realism, that do not make the distinction (see for example (Harré 2002). One can well imagine the relatively direct operation of natural necessity through laws of nature such as gravity or probabilistic laws such as Boyle's Law – hence, one assumes their reference to a range of probabilities. In the latter case the range of probabilities are readily calculable given a known pressure and volume of gas.

Is there natural necessity in the social world?

At some deeper level the social world may have the character of natural necessary, but this is but metaphysical speculation. Indeed, one might argue that even the most determinate *physical* laws will cease to be necessary under particular circumstances, and this is certainly Nancy Cartwright's view (Cartwright 1989: 92–93). But the received view is that *ceteris paribus*, the laws of classical physics apply, in the last instance, and for our purposes this is enough. For the most part, in the physical world, we can trace its properties to a scientifically demonstrable physical necessity and moreover we can prove this in certain key experiments. In the social world we cannot ground any behaviours or social properties in a scientifically demonstrable natural necessity. It does not follow from this that the social world does not possess either regularity, or causal efficacy, but rather that these things arise from contingency in the social world, or in some cases might be grounded in physical events or circumstances.

On the face of it there *would* appear to be natural necessity in the social world. There is a long tradition of treating social facts as things in nature, that hold as much force as things in the physical world (e.g. Durkheim 1972: 68–74). On examination of every case we find one of two things: that there existed some degree of contingency in an outcome, that it could have been otherwise (even though the alternative might have been very unlikely), or that definable social "objects" had a conceptual necessity in a time and place, that would likely be subject to change. I'll say more about social objects in the next chapter, but for the present we can think of them as identifiable "things" in the social world.

Sayer raises the possibility, of what he describes as, "contingent necessity" (Sayer 2000: 17), wherein two previously unrelated objects interact with each other and produce an emergent necessity. He suggests the following example. A football (soccer) team can be amateur or professional, but once it becomes professional certain "necessary" conditions apply to it that are the characteristics of its being professional, e.g. the need to pay players. Sayer is suggesting that up until the team becomes professional it is contingent in what might happen, but once it becomes professional then there are certain characteristics that must necessarily apply. Nevertheless, even in this example the necessity is not entirely clear cut in its application. In some countries, non-league "amateur" teams may pay players a modest sum and some lower ranking "professional" league teams may not employ players full time. However, Sayer does go on to say judgements about whether something is contingent or necessary are fallible.

Sayer's distinction might possibly be given more force in another example. At the time of writing women cannot become Roman Catholic priests, but it is only when a particular woman attempts to become a priest that necessity operates. Prior to this time the possibility of her becoming a priest may remain miniscule, but it nevertheless remains possible, because the Papal edict could overturn the rule that women cannot be priests. Consequently, a woman at time *t1* may come to feel the necessity of the situation, but a woman at time *t2* may not. This is not hair splitting. Up until the 27th of July 1967 homosexuality was illegal in England and Wales, but on the 28th of July 1967, it was not. Social life is full of these kinds of obstructions operating at one time, that cease to operate at another. It is certainly not beyond the bounds of possibility that the Roman Catholic Church (as did the Anglican Church) will at some future time admit women to the priesthood, in which case there would be actual examples of difference between time *t1* and time *t2* that would apply to particular women. There is an important caveat here. Whilst such barriers are known to operate, this knowledge may in turn have consequences for the actions of others. Women will not currently *try* to enter the priesthood, because their belief is that they cannot.

To defend the proposition that there is natural necessity in the social world there must be a natural necessity in relations between properties, events, behaviours, etc., something like the analogue of physical laws in required. But as I have said above this does not really hold in the social world. One can cite plenty of, what Robert Brown (1973: 82) calls "accidental laws" that take the same form as nomological laws (all Xs are Ys), e.g. "All industrial societies are monogamous". These are socio-historical generalisations and are hard to distinguish from claimed social Laws, such as Duverger's Law, which asserts that a plurality rule election system tends to favour a two-party system (Riker 1982). Duverger's Law, as with other claimed social laws, has plenty of exceptions and one must always enter a number of caveats, or *ceteris paribus* clauses, for these laws to obtain. Arguably the number of these one must make renders the laws applicable in only a minority of circumstances, or their explanatory power is trivial.[8]

Those that defend social laws are in a minority. Andrew Sayer describes them as "instrumental" rather than causal laws (1992: 127), which are capable of only operating within closed systems and can yield only regularities, not causal explanation. Indeed, he explicitly rejects the utility of such laws in the social world. For predictions to be made, that are worth considering, from economic "laws" "are bound to involve a long string of conditions covering not only some of the circumstances in which the mechanisms [that the laws seek to explain]operate but about whether some of the mechanisms will actually be present" (1992: 137). In other words, there is just too much contingency in the social world for laws to have explanatory or predictive value.

If there is to be natural necessity, operating at a macro level, it should yield regular relations between the components of any system, mechanism, etc.[9] This should surely manifest itself in something like "laws" (not withstanding their causally explanatory value) or relations that will hold at a macro level. One can readily agree with those who are critical of the possibility of social laws, but if these cannot exist, wherein, therefore, lies the natural necessity (of the kind Harré and Madden propose)? I would suggest that it simply does not exist in the social world, except when there is "grounding" in physical characteristics, or systems, themselves reducible to physical laws (possibly themselves operating *ceteris paribus*.[10] We can cite the necessity of physical things, such as walls, physical decay, climate, etc. as naturally necessary conditions in enabling and constraining the social, but they themselves are physical, not social. Sometimes we create those physical systems or objects and they can possess social meaning (and therefore also conceptual necessity), but that which we define and name must always be conceptual, in terms of its social properties and conditions. The social can produce only conceptual necessity.

Robert Nozick (Nozick 2001) deployed a useful term that helps us think about change and stability in the world, that of "invariance". He defined the term as a "property or relationship which is invariant under the appropriate transformations" (Nozick 2001: 79),[11] such as in any system S subject to transformation T, there will be a set of rules that describe T. This can mean first a "mapping" or copying of a function or property or second it can by dynamic change or alteration to a system. Though he uses examples from physics, we might see the first as obtaining through, for example, customs or laws, or the second through sudden change that creates new stable behaviours, such as those created in certain countries in the 2020 Covid-19 pandemic. Invariance is not stasis, there is no such thing in the universe, but some systems exhibit relatively greater invariance than others. In describing the social world, I think invariance better captures the idea stability, for two reasons. Firstly, invariance suggests the toleration of a degree of perturbation at macro level, as well as relative stability at a micro-meso level. Secondly it captures the transformations that may preserve the relative invariance through the path dependencies I have described.

Indeed, sometimes we can trace the signatures of invariance through time. The great Brexit crisis of 2016 onwards, in the UK can arguably be traced to the "gene" of English nationalism, that has existed in the UK Conservative party for all of its history, manifesting (or "copying itself") itself in many ways from opposition to Irish home rule, opposition to Welsh and Scottish devolution more recently and in its latest form, opposition to the membership of the UK in the European Union (Calhoun 2017). Somewhat ironically, something that causes turbulence and conflict, can itself have relative invariance!

Even in the most revolutionary scenarios, much of the old order survives. The Cambodian revolution of the 1970s (as in the case of the French revolution) attempted to create a "year zero" (Ponchaud 1978), a new beginning in which the old social order is repudiated. In each case, just a few years later and despite long lasting social changes – certainly in the French case, much of the old social order was restored.

The question of why and how a society remains ordered much of the time has been an important theme in sociology, particularly in the work of Talcott (Parsons 1968, Parsons and Shils 1951). His theory of individual action crucially depended on certain prerequisites being fulfilled.[12] In particular the mediating role of pattern maintenance at a meso level (say in the family) may be more important than macro-level institutions, such as elements of the state that are casualties of revolution. Parsons' work also, through the notion of equilibrium, as dynamic, prefigured the now popular notion of "self organisation" (Parsons and Shils 1951: 10–18) in complexity theory. We should perhaps not split hairs about the difference between strange attractors and invariance. Perhaps it is invariance that strange attractors produce and invariance, that in turn produces strange attractors through varying amounts of change.

However, what is important is the emergence of stable patterns through autonomous and self-reinforcing dynamics at the micro-level. In other words, as in Parsons' work, the notion of agency is retained in the creation of relative stability or invariance. I'll say more about this, in relation to social objects, in the next chapter.

But meanwhile another "Kennedy" example perhaps illustrates the importance of micro-level interaction in establishing invariance. Around one year before Kennedy was assassinated, he had been (along with Nikita Khrushchev and Fidel Castro) one of the main actors in the Cuban missile crisis. The act of installing nuclear missiles, capable of reaching the United States, in minutes, by the Soviet Union had disturbed an existing, if fragile, balance of power between the two countries. This, as we know, almost led to nuclear war, but the intervention of representatives, of each country, through unofficial "back channels", served to diffuse the crisis and restore the status quo (Isaacs and Downing 2008: 204–230). Individual agents, acting within a context but with a degree of autonomy, restored the relative invariance. Both in the build up to the crisis and its eventual diffusion could be traced back to small actions or decisions at a micro level.

This kind of agent led change is a quite specific version of invariance, because despite its seriousness for the whole of humanity, the actual invariance restored was amongst only a very few agents, perhaps no more than a couple of dozen senior politicians and I believe can be contrasted with the kind of persistent trends in social behaviour that Durkheim (1970[1952]) noted in respect of suicide data, over a 100 years ago. Suicide levels remain remarkably similar across societies and over time and in particular sectors of society.

John Goldthorpe (2016: 40–41) provides a nice example of how aggregate change can both illustrate agent-led individual decision-making, and how this creates a transformation from one invariance to another, that of changes in regulatory social norms which sanctioned marriage, to those which later sanctioned cohabitation. The transformation began with a relatively small number of couples deviating from the social norm of marriage to cohabiting. This process speeded up from just a few mavericks, in the 1950s, to much greater numbers in the following decades as the cost-benefit advantages were realised. Changes in labour market opportunities, which led to greater uncertainty, led to cohabitation being seen as an attractive alternative to living alone remaining unattached or marriage. Individual decisions to cohabit would rest on an assessment of a number of complex circumstances. These were individual events but the aggregate effect was change and the creation of new social regularities.

What I and Nozick have called invariance, corresponds to "fixed points" in physical systems, though this is, again is more analogy, than a precise equivalent. A fixed point is outcome of some transformation that finally ends up as stable. An example often cited is that of the damped pendulum, which finally comes to rest, or the final settling of particles in a solution. It is an analogy, because fixed points depend on the operation of physical laws, such as gravity, whereas in the social world (if I am right) there is no equivalent. However, what we see as outcomes, in the social world, are the result of transformations, whereby some things remain much the same through time and in their turn, may produce invariances that take on the characteristic of a mechanism operating under particular local contexts. I'll come back to this in Chapter 8.

The real is complex and the complex is real

This chapter has been primarily about probability, but not as probability theory or that expressed through linear inferential statistics, but the relative propensity for things to happen in the social world and how we might methodologically capture this. It has primarily been an argument for treating probability as an ontological property of the social world, at the same time as denying that there is any natural necessity in the social world, other than that which is grounded in the physical world. Complexity is probability and probability is real. That reality coalesces into "strange attractors" and these produce relative invariance, in the social world, through time. So, although the social world is a dynamic nested array of varying possibilities or "propensities", this is not constant flux and consequently systematic knowledge of the social world is possible. However, when we think of the social world in this way it opens up our methods to scrutiny. The social survey mainly relies on sample data and the frequency theory of probability to infer from sample to population. This works to an extent and where there are clear relatively stable patterns, it can provide valuable descriptions and explanations of invariances. Methodologically we can begin from aggregate regularities, that large scale surveys can capture, and attempt to explain them through individual events, or we can begin the other way around and look at how individual events create aggregate regularities. In Chapter 9 I will show how each can be valuable methodological tools in a complex realist toolkit.

Notes

1. See https://necsi.edu/chaos-vs-complex-systems (Accessed 26/06/20) for a description of the difference between chaos and complexity.
2. See www.santafe.edu/about/history. Accessed 27/06/20.
3. Though, as is so often in these cases, social complexity was prefigured in the social sciences, and indeed in sociology, in the systems theory and Talcott Parsons (Parsons 1968) and in Robert Merton's writing on innovation (Merton 1973).
4. James Mahoney (2000) has argued that in historical sociology some phenomena can only be explained through path dependence.
5. There are also simple attractors, with perhaps fixed numbers of points, or limited cycles, such the swing of a pendulum.
6. Sure Start was a programme of varied interventions for under four-year-old children and their parents, in some of the more disadvantaged areas of the UK. The programme was first set up by the Labour government, in the late 1990s, but has been dramatically reduced since. Many Sure Starts have become Children's Centres.
7. Planning for Real is an engagement process centred on a 3D model of a local area. Participants use the model to comment on the strengths and weaknesses of the place, and make suggestions of how they would like to see their community develop. See https://www.involve.org.uk/resources/methods/planning-real (accessed 01/09/20).
8. Arguably one could express such laws probabilistically when there is a known probability of their effects within particular domains, but this begs the question of what then is the logical difference between these and generalisations made within a given domain? (Williams 2000a: 54–45).
9. Realists use mechanism in a quite specific way to indicate how ensembles of social relations (in the social world) form coalesce into forms which then have causal potential, itself activated by a specific contextual event (see for example Bunge 1997: 415). This is compatible with my own use of the term to indicate nested dispositional social objects (Williams 2009). However, in recent times, there has been a tendency, particularly in some branches of sociology, to refer to mechanisms in a more generic sense and not defined philosophically. See for example: Morning (2008) in respect of race and ethnicity; Mahoney (2000) historical sociology Callon (1999) sociology of science; Portes (1998) social capital. I will return to mechanisms, in Chapter 8.
10. Even if Cartwright is right and the laws the physics lie, then this only undermines the concept of natural necessity *tout court* and does not change the proposition that there is no natural necessity in the social world.
11. Lest it is said that I have misunderstood Nozick's term, I am using it in a much more informal way to describe a process of complex change and relative stability. I think Nozick's concept could be more formally developed to describe social transformation processes or rules, but that task is beyond the scope of the current work.
12. Parsons claimed there were functional imperatives that social systems must fulfil to maintain stability. This is his AGIL schema "Adaptation, Goal Attainment, Integration, Latency" (Parsons 1968).

4

Causes and complexity

Realists believe in causes. If only a belief in causes was as simple as a belief in association. In the latter case you need only show that two or more things occur together, but in the former case you must show how something created, changed, generated, produced or prevented something else. Yet in everyday life not only do we have no real problem in using "causal language" and often identifying what causes what, we use causal language constantly in our discourse. Words such as "because", "produced", "made", "prevented" …… indicate that something came after something else and would not have been the case, but for the first thing.

But causes are hard to identify and, as Nancy Cartwright observed a cause is "one word, but many things" (Cartwright 2004). In one sense this is a philosopher's problem, but it is only such because scientists (and in the century and the last) policy-makers have had difficulties in describing or explaining causes of things. This has not stopped scientists cheerfully saying what causes what, but as I observed in Chapter 2, science is a history of error. In my long career of red wine drinking I have been told, by scientists that red wine will variously bring me good health, bad health of many different kinds, longevity, desperation and death. In social policy the failure of causal pronouncements has possibly been even more dismal. However, I would be the last person to derive an anti-science conclusion from this history of error, because the long-term success of science in explaining and predicting has been phenomenal. We should not confuse weather with climate! The implication being, that causal reasoning can been successful. In social policy and public health, the successes are greater than the failure, with many of the failures the result of politics, not social research.

This chapter is in the spirit of Cartwright's motto. Do not expect to arrive at the end of it with a neat and packaged version of causality.[1] The difficulty of doing so was neatly captured by Hall and Paul,

> Causation is a deeply intuitive and familiar relation, gripped powerfully by common sense. Or, so it seems. As is typical in philosophy, however, that deep intuitive familiarity has not led to any philosophical account of causation that is at once clean, precise and widely agreed upon.
>
> Hall and Paul 2008: 100

One could devote at least one book to summarising the various philosophical and methodological approaches to causality, so inevitably my approach will be selective, but to a great extent those selections are conducive to the realist complexity approach I take, or indeed their oppositional stance serves to contrast with the approach I take.

So, what I want to do in the first part of the chapter is to examine some of the attempts to define causality and the consequent methodological strategies that arise from these. I will claim that these are too restrictive, philosophically narrow, or that probabilistic versions in social science practice, are operationalised in models that depend on statistical linearity. Consequently, they under-describe the complexity of the social world. In the second part of the chapter I want to outline an alternative view of causality that is grounded in the probabilistic approach to complexity I presented in the previous chapter. This approach is *ontological*, rather than *epistemological*, as in the case of the previous probabilistic versions I describe. I will say that there are causes, but their realisation is the result of a complex array of the realisation of prior probabilities.

However, if there are causes in the social world, they imply the relative invariance I claimed, in the previous chapter, that is a characteristic of that world. How does this invariance manifest itself? In the third section of the chapter, I will show how individual beliefs and actions create patterns of differing invariance, in social objects.

My conclusion will be that causes are complex and whilst this sets limits to what we can know of them, it also means that our causal claims and the way to them must be ecumenical.

Defining and operationalising causality

Determination

Bertrand Russell (1992: 193–210), so wise in many ways, nevertheless thought that the concept of causality in science had had its day and in quantum physics been done away with altogether. This pronouncement of Russell's has never been taken seriously, but in a way he was sort of right! The kind of causality he had in mind was much narrower than that discussed today. We might broadly describe it as "deterministic causality", where there is a universal and direct correspondence between cause and effect. And indeed, in quantum physics, it was apparent, even in the early 20th century, that there is no such thing as a determined cause. Russell's attempt to do away with causality was answered by the theoretical physicist, David Bohm, in the very important book *Causality and Chance in Modern*

Physics, in which he set out the case for an understanding of causality in quantum physics as being neither deterministic or probabilistic, but actually having a character that transcends both (Bohm 1984 [1957]).[2] But I'm getting ahead.

The problem with causality is that whichever verb we use, create, change, generate, produce or prevent, etc., like getting spaghetti out of a pot, they pull a lot of stuff after them. As I noted in the example of the Arab Spring, in the previous chapter, making sense of the death of Mohamed Bouazizi is not possible if we treat it as a discrete event. It was an event in a chain, or array, of cause-effect relationships, where effects become future causes, so attempts to find determined pathways can never be realised.

To be sure we can identify singular causality. We can say that self-immolation caused Mohamed Bouazizi death. In this case there is a clearly identified cause–effect relationship between his act and his death. It is when we attempt to generalise cause–effect relationships that we run into trouble. Let us consider a fictional less tragic example.

Denzil and Garfield are arguing. Denzil hits Garfield and Garfield falls over. A witness at the subsequent assault trial has no difficulty, and is believed, when she says Garfield fell over, because Denzil hit him. A simple cause–effect relationship, but people fall over without being hit and people get hit without falling over. OK, if we introduce the observation that they were arguing and therefore angry with each other, we might say anger can lead to hitting, but it doesn't always and hitting can be done (as in boxing) without anger. We cannot generalise from these particular events to events in general. There have been more formal attempts to produce such generalising statements, through the deployment of *sufficient* and necessary *conditions*, which to constitute a cause must both apply. This is all but impossible. Sufficient conditions, on their own, are easy. Being angry is a sufficient condition for hitting, being hit is a sufficient condition for falling over. The problem comes with the necessary bit. Very few things in the world are necessary and this is especially true if we apply the condition of natural necessity, which must be grounded in the physical world. Even here and even in respect of the laws of nature (as Cartwright has claimed) the necessity can be suspended, at least locally. In the last chapter I argued that in the social world there is no natural necessity. There is conceptual necessity, but specific manifestations of this only hold in particular times and places. We might say that to drive legally it is a necessary condition that you pass a driving test. But what does this mean? In Belgium there was no driving test at all until 1977 and even now many countries, such as Egypt, India, Honduras, Pakistan have driving tests that lack challenge to the point of being comedic! So, the conceptual necessity in the phrase "to drive legally" is quite different in other times and places. Trying to think of social causes that might be candidates for both sufficient and necessary conditions is itself hard, even when we allow some flexibility for conceptual necessity.

The philosopher J.L. Mackie recognised and attempted to circumvent this problem. Suppose, he says, we wish to determine the cause of a fire in a house. The fire was supposed to have been caused by an electrical short circuit, but this is not necessary a condition. Other things could cause a fire. It's not a sufficient one either, because a short circuit could only cause the fire if there were combustible materials nearby.

> The short circuit which is said to have caused the fire is thus an indispensable part of a complex sufficient (but not necessary) condition of the fire. In this case, then, the so-called cause is, and is known to be, an *insufficient* but *necessary* part of a condition which itself is *unnecessary* but *sufficient* for the result.
>
> Mackie 1965: 245

This he called an INUS condition (Insufficient but Necessary part of a complex of Unnecessary but Sufficient conditions). This, apart from sounding somewhat like Groucho Marx's "contract" clarification in *Night at Opera,* probably captures the logic of the possibilities, but it is little more than a lawyer's definition that does not advance our understanding of the manifestation of cause and effect in the real world (and especially the social world) very much. There are philosophical defenders of more metaphysical definitions, for example David Papineau (2001), who maintained we should not conflate methodology with metaphysics. I'm sure this is correct, and my concern is more with methodology. In the social sciences metaphysics is never completely absent in methodology, but methodology is often celebratorally absent in metaphysics!

The central problem for causality is that whilst very often A will lead to B, this is not always the case and whilst C rarely leads to D it might do so and whether A is followed by B, or D follows C is dependent on a lot more antecedent relationships. In a closed, or relatively closed system, the possibility of all trajectories can be modelled. In Chapter 9, there is an example of this, from a study conducted by Brian Castellani and his colleagues on co-morbid depression and physical health trajectories. In a model of 259 cases, 38 variables and 11 trends, all possible trajectories could be modelled. Because it was modelled on real data, it is likely a good representation of the real world, but nevertheless a toy world in which other antecedents or noise are eliminated.

Empiricism and the denial of causality

Empiricism has dominated much of the history of science, first through the influence of philosophers such as Hume and Locke and later through logical positivism This does imply that all the science that was done was empiricist, but rather it created the conditions for scientific practice by ridding it of much of the metaphysics that was present in the early Enlightenment (Phillips 1987: 39). Practices such as parsimony, testing, objectivity (Williams 2000a: Chapter 2) developed in this period and persist into modern science as *empirical* (as opposed to empiricist) practice. Possibly the most important legacy was that of inductive reasoning, which is as the heart of probability and statistics. A handful of 19th and early 20th century statisticians gave us the core and even majority of our statistical methods. Karl Pearson alone gave us the chi-squared test, Pearson's R, standard deviation, correlation and regression coefficient (Hacking 1990: 180–187).[3] There is an historical line that runs from Hume and the early empiricists, through the development of modern science and statistics, down to the causal modelling techniques of contemporary social science. Anti-causal thinking and probabilistic causal reasoning can be said to have the same historical antecedents.

It is all too easy to assume Hume and empiricism more generally were "against causality". This is not the case. Hume said that our experience of one event following another led us to believe that this indicated an underlying cause. This belief, he held, was due to our psychology and the assumptions of cause and effect are not upheld by observational evidence. Consequently, a whole philosophical industry developed around Hume and causality (see e.g. Beebee 2006) and it is less ironic than one would think that much of the causal reasoning, in quantitative social science has its origins in Humean scepticism.

Mid-20th century sociology produced its anti-causal militants, such as George Lundberg, Paul Lazarsfeld and Stuart Dodd. They very much emphasised statistical association over causality and in Dodd's case advocated, what he called "pan sample", a saturation sample of hundreds of observations of thousands of people to produce a giant correlation matrix (Platt 1996: 86). The pan sample research never got funded though, as Jennifer Platt observes, (op cit: 86*ff*) at times he even seemed to suggest the possibility of isolating true causes.

These sociologists were the exceptions and in fact can be more properly seen (particularly Lazarsfeld) as the progenitors of what became known as causal analysis. Indeed, in the above cited paper by David Papineau, he maintains that probabilistic causality had its origins in the logic of survey research (Papineau 2001: 16–17). And, I might add, survey research itself depends on a particular theory of probability, the frequency theory (which I described in the previous chapter.) I will return to causal analysis below, but first what is meant by probabilistic causality, at least in its empiricist lineage?

Probabilistic causality

The micro-level example of the causal relations of Denzil and Garfield's altercation above (rather like Hume's billiard balls in Chapter 2), is an "active" one, the observation of one thing "causing" another, but as D.H. Mellor (in a book confidently entitled *The Facts of Causation* (Mellor 1995: 6) notes that causes and effects seem to be of two different sorts, the singular events, of the above kind, and those with general properties. He suggests an example of the latter is "smoking causes cancer", but in the social world virtually all aggregate level statistical associations and causes are of this kind, though they are rarely as compelling. Sometimes a direct cause–effect relationship is claimed, possibly "mediated" by other factors in a mechanism, other times somewhat gnomically. For example, in the first case the relationship between father and son's occupation, whereby given moderating factors a father's occupation produces a causal pathway to a son's occupation (Blau and

Duncan 1978). But this was not a simple A -> B relationship, but was via a number of moderating factors, such as differential social capital, that constituted a mechanism. I'll come to causal pathways below and I'll discuss Blau and Duncan study in a little more detail in Chapter 9. Blau and Duncan's causal claim was based on logical inference and multiple association, but narrative can often show the same kind of relationship. This is explored qualitatively in Paul Willis' book *Learning to Labour: How Working Class Kids Get Working Class Jobs* (Willis 1977). Again, the occupational transition was moderated by complex cultural and economic factors. Willis's study was at a micro level, but the occupational transition he described could reasonably be assumed to be typical at that time.

In the second case, (for example) ethnicity is often cited as associated with differing life chances. Certain ethnicities seem to confer advantages on their bearers, whereas others confer disadvantages. Given the complexity and subjectivity of ethnicity, such a causal mechanism is inevitably complex – possibly even mysterious![4] In my own work I have noted that across several measures (e.g. employment, health, housing), repeated in a number of studies, those who self-identify as of Cornish[5] ethnicity are much more likely to have poorer life outcomes than those identifying with other ethnic groups in Cornwall (Williams and Husk 2013). Yet the category itself has only become standard in surveys and monitoring instruments, in Cornwall, recently and the identification is a subjective choice? So …. we have an association (for instance) between identifying as "Cornish" and suffering long-term health problems! The association is both probabilistic and most certainly an indirect one, yet this fact of the association is of great interest to policy-makers in Cornwall.

These "causal" examples are very different. In the first case things like education are readily identifiable mediators, but in the second case ethnicity is probably standing proxy for a complex inter-relationship of economic factors, education and cultural practices.

That the relationships I describe are probabilistic is evident, but at what point do we say (or indeed can we say) these associations, when mediated by other statistical associations become "causes"? How do they become "active", rather than just passive associations of characteristics? Every day, the tide comes a 100 metres from my house and every day I eat food, but the tide coming in is not a cause of my eating food and my eating food does not cause the tide to come in.

Probabilistic causality is the philosophical and methodological approach that aims to distinguish between mere association and causal properties.

Probabilistic causality is simply stated: A causes B if A's occurrence increases the probability of B occurring. Patrick Suppes defines this a little more precisely as follows:

> An event B is a prima facie cause of an event A if and only if (i) B occurs earlier than A, (ii) the conditional probability of A occurring when B occurs is greater than the unconditional probability of A occurring.
>
> Suppes 1984: 48

Probabilistic causality can be interpreted in two ways: that it reflects an imperfect knowledge of what is ultimately held to be a deterministic system, or that the system itself is indeterminate. The second of these is associated with the propensity theory of probability, I introduced in the previous chapter and will return to later in this one.

Empiricist versions of probabilistic causality are of the first kind, though methodologically most of its advocates in social science at least are silent on whether they believe the system is deterministic, because this is an unanswerable metaphysical question. Logically, though, the two interpretations are not mutually exclusive. In practice, most analysts who support the idea of probabilistic causality would say that it is imperfect knowledge of an indeterminate system. Imperfect knowledge needs some clarifying, for it begs the question of why would you bother if the knowledge is imperfect? Informally it means that a causal explanation can tolerate a certain amount of error and still be a good enough explanation of real phenomena. The methodological aim is to reduce error.

Probabilistic causality, in the social sciences, therefore begins from the notion of error. The concept of error can be described as a number of small and random variations, which combine to produce an overall error.[6] The amount of error in a measurement, if known, can tell us how close we might be to the "truth of the matter". Measurement of error became embodied in tests of significance on sample data. The idea being that a test of significance is able to indicate how reliable our results are, whether the finding would have occurred by chance or not. Thus, conventionally,[7] if the p value is $p = <0.01$ or even $p = <0.05$, then the finding is statistically significant. The smaller the p value, the smaller the "error".

A statistical association between two variables simply indicates that their association is likely not an accident. Quite apart from the difficulty of moving from this association to any kind of causal conclusion, is that as sample size increases, then more associations between variables will be found and this is just a function of the law of large numbers.

For the reasons I indicated above, association is not enough, so the very least one can do is to control for a third variable. So, for example, in both the "occupation" and "ethnicity" example, controlling for social class provides at least some enlightenment. In the ethnicity example, it can be shown if you identify as "Cornish" and you are from a manual class, then there is a stronger association with poor health, employment or housing outcomes compared to those who do not identify as Cornish. But the majority of people of Cornish origin, in Cornwall, are members of manual classes (Williams 2003b).[8] This is the beginning of an explanation, but it is not a causal explanation, merely an elaboration of a statistical relationship that provides more information about associations.

What is often described as "causal analysis" aims to move beyond this (Barringer et al 2013). This has become almost a methodological tradition and one which began from relatively simple statistical techniques to extremely sophisticated ones nowadays. Yet the logic of these is probabilistic and is captured in what is known as the General Linear Model (GLM). In this the relationship between variables are assumed to be proportionate. Changes in a variable, or variables, produces changes in other variables, which can be described by a linear equation (or system of equations). Information about one or more independent variables is used to predict the "variability" of a dependent variable(s).

So assuming we wish to explore the contribution of various factors to ill health (the dependent variable), social class, ethnicity, poor housing, income might each "explain" some portion of the statistical variance in the model, but although these are additive, they might each have an effect on the other, so for example low income could lead to poor housing. Many models, nowadays, will include many more variables and their interactions within the models (say income and poor housing) can be expressed.

Causal analysis is usually based on variants of path analysis.[9] The causal relations between several variables are represented by a path diagram with path coefficients providing the estimates of the strength of the relationship between two variables (cause–effect) whilst "controlling" holding constant other variables in the model. So, for example, whilst there is a path form father's occupation to son's occupation, it is perhaps "mediated" through son's education, but these things might be moderated as a result of context, such as particular times, or characteristics such as ethnicity (Jose 2013). Path analysis differs from standard multiple regression, in that direct and indirect pathways from independent variables, to be dependent variable can be calculated, along with the size of those effects.

One of the most sophisticated is Structural Equation Modelling (SEM) (Hooper et al 2008). These models contain a number of equations (models of models!) that might theorise relations between latent (that is unobserved, but theorised) variables and observed variables. The admission of latent variables into a model is a very un-Humean step, because it is an admission that there is possibly something making something, that has not been directly measured. SEMs and other models which attempt to account for unobservables are a move in the direction of realism, because they permit the introduction of theorised entities as connections, without letting go of the underlying logic of statistical relationships between variables.

More obviously, some variables particularly in a cross sectional model could not be said to "cause" other things, simply because of absence of temporal ordering. So, educational attainment may contribute to the "cause" of occupation, but occupation cannot contribute to the "cause" of educational attainment – though it may contribute to an effect in the next generation. Even with temporal ordering, cross sectional models are in themselves only associations and causal properties can only be inferred.

Wesley Salmon did not quite take this view and argued that for one event to be the cause of another, is simply for the former to affect the latter's probability (Salmon 1971: 105), thus the statistical associations are *themselves* causal, rather than evidence for a cause. David Papineau reads this as arguing that controlling for a third variable, rules out the association between a dependent and independent variable, by "screening off" the independent variable, so as to eclipse one of the original variables as the cause of another. (Papineau 1978: 72). The difference between this and an additive model (above), where adding in variables explains more and more of the variance in the model, is that this approach adds variables that will serve to eliminate or weaken other associations. So, father's occupation may be strongly correlated with son/daughter's occupation, but once we control for parental education, the former relationship is weakened. The reasoning is simple – perhaps deceptively so.

A version of this kind of reasoning ("what happens if") can be found in the concept of "counterfactual causality", which though it has venerable origins in empiricism, going right back to Hume, was developed a few decades ago by David Lewis. Counterfactual thinking proposes outcomes that would have been observed had the world evolved differently. Lewis expressed it thus:

> Where *c* and *e* are two distinct possible events, *e causally depends* on *c* if and only if, if *c* were to occur *e* would occur; and if *c* were not to occur *e* would not occur
>
> Lewis 1973: 161

This reasoning is incorporated into a number of contemporary modelling approaches, initially suggested by Judea Pearl (2000), but developed further by Don Rubin. The Rubin causal model (RCM), also known as the Neyman–Rubin causal model (Rubin 2005) depends on the logic of random assignment. However, in surveys we can only know total sample outcomes, unlike experiments where there can be random assignment to experimental and control groups. Rubin has suggested ways in which thus can be accomplished with survey data and indeed other approaches have shown how assignment can be effectively achieved with survey data Techniques such as propensity score matching will assign units in a survey to "control" or "treatment" units on the basis of similarity, expect in terms of outcomes. However, as with SEM, propensity score matching, in sample data, will only provide probabilities ultimately dependent on what is theorised and measured.

In a paper which assesses the viability of regression models in social science, David Freedman (2011) is sceptical that technical advances in modelling methods have successfully closed in on causes. Data are collected and a number of assumptions are made about the process which generated it, then

> … the model is fitted to the data and quite intricate statistical calculations may come into play: three stage least squares, penalized maximum likelihood, second order efficiency, and so on. The statistical inferences sometimes lead to rather strong empirical claims about structure and causality.
>
> Freedman 2011: 165

Freedman is perhaps using some dense statistical jargon here to emphasise his point that complex statistical procedures disguise the problems about the assumptions of the data. He provides several examples where unwarranted conclusions are drawn from such models. Their failure arose from a number of sources: multiple correlation assumptions in which $p < 0.001$ was all but universal, but was simply due to the very large sample, the ecological fallacy where one variable (class) stood proxy for one that was not measured (smoking), and the use of dummy variables, not treated as proxies, for other un-measured variables.

As he also notes:

> Indeed, causal arguments based on significance tests and regression are almost necessarily circular. To derive a regression model, we need an elaborate theory that specifies the variables in the system, their causal interconnectedness, the functional form of the relationships, and the statistical properties of the error terms ....
>
> Freedman 2011: 152

The output from this model is then seen as a test of the original theory. Freedman, though not wholly dismissing the value of causal models, nevertheless claims they cannot be said to deduce causes, but rather quantifies already hypothesised relationships.

Douglas Porpora provides a sociological critique of the understanding of causality in American sociology (Porpora 2008). He accuses analysts of reducing causality to simplistic statistical connections between concepts, themselves under theorised, but just stated as given.

> Consider the criterion that there is a causal connection – as opposed to a merely "spurious" correlation – only when other possible causes have been ruled out. In terms of sociology's favoured talk of variables, this criterion means that the association between some putative independent and dependent variable remains even after controlling for some third variable.
>
> Porpora 2008: 198

One could say the Porpora himself somewhat oversimplifies things, but the essence of this and the paper more generally, does capture well the existing empiricism, as evidenced in the practice and application of causal analysis in US research, and because their methods and techniques have been taken up more widely in countries such as the UK, Netherlands and Germany, to an extent it exists there too.

The models themselves are complicated and sophisticated and the simplification lies outside of the statistical model's reasoning. The initial research hypothesis is often expressed as a straightforward causal relationship between two variables.

Porpora is right, concepts are often under theorised, but more than this the variables which are supposed to measure them often do not validly capture social reality. An important sub-theme in the papers of Freedman and Porpora is the inevitable and necessary role of theory in causal inference. This view was advanced, some years before the Freedman and Porpora papers, in the 1980s, a time when few others were saying it, by a realist inclined researcher, Cathie Marsh (1982). Her argument for this is discussed at length by David Byrne (2002: 66–69). Essentially Marsh argues that we cannot avoid theorising our models, that no one model can uniquely provide a "fit" which can show a cause–effect relationship, that the models are therefore much simpler than the actual cause–effect relations in reality.

Byrne, though applauding the clarity in which Marsh expresses the need for theoretical inference from statistical models, nevertheless argues that the models nevertheless cannot capture the dynamic of time or unmeasured complex interactions that take place at a micro level. He illustrates this with a "causal story" that might better explain the relationship between health, income, and marital status than a statistical model could.

> [a woman] establishes a relationship with a partner in full time employment with a median level income and they decide to live together. The woman's children [by a previous relationship] are at primary school, so it becomes economically sensible for her to take a part time job. The earned household income is now well above benefit dependency levels and moreover the payments made in support of the children by their father now accrue to household income rather than being confiscated and set against benefit payments. The couple buy an ordinary middle income house in an ordinary owner occupied estate.

He goes on to say …

> All the changes in this process are non-linear and interactive. We can best understand them by considering not the variables, but the case itself. The woman's life and the life of her children have been changed in a qualitative way.
>
> Byrne 2002: 70

One can read this as an appeal to look for causality at the singular level, perhaps through qualitative methods. But this is not the direction Byrne goes in (though he does not eschew quantitative methods), but rather his methodological strategy, particularly in later work, leads him to case centred analyses, using Qualitative Comparative Analysis (QCA)[10] and a more broad brush qualitative spatial–historical analysis at the city/regional level (Byrne and Callaghan 2013).

My own view, which I will return to in Chapter 9, is to be methodologically more ecumenical. With Freedman I would agree that causal modelling can rarely reveal straightforward causal relationships, but they may be valuable as a partial test of the research hypotheses derived from our theories and as John Goldthorpe has argued (Goldthorpe 2016: 112–125), they may also help us identify causal mechanisms and much more complex phenomena.

Earlier in this section I posed the following question: *at what point do we say (or indeed can we say) these associations, when mediated by other statistical associations become "causes"*? My answer is twofold. We *cannot* say we can identify a cause from probabilistic causality, as operationalised through causal modelling, if this is to have the same ontological status as singular and active causality. Causal inference in samples of "open systems", is subject to large amounts of unexplained variance. The variance can arise from individual difference, unanticipated environmental circumstances or omitted variables (Cartwright 1989: 107), that is the things we don't measure, we measure by proxy, rather than directly. Even more problematically one cannot usually tell which of these is responsible and quite often in causal analyses the error terms are greater than that which is explained by the causal model! However, I do not think that we should not write off statistical inference of causal analysis. "Counterfactual" type techniques, in particular, can be good evidence and therefore these kind of techniques have the potential to allow us to infer the existence of complex causal mechanisms. Although it has the empiricist mark of Cain on it, its methodological sophistication can be an ally of realism and complexity and I will mount a partial defence of it in Chapter 9. My partial defence of causal modelling will be on methodological grounds, but I now want to introduce the version of probabilistic causality, which seeks to capture indeterminacy on both methodological and metaphysical grounds.

Probability causality and complexity

In the last chapter I supported the view that the probabilistic character of the world is real and is not an artefact of our lack of knowledge of it. I further suggested that cases themselves have probabilities and this can be captured through the propensity theory of probability. Here, I want to pick up this theme again, with a view to showing how probability and causality are ontologically coterminous.

In causal modelling we measure the statistical relationship between things. We observe an effect and we want to measure those things that account for that effect. But the measured relationship is a static one, whereas in the real world the relationship between things is dynamic.

In the previous chapter I considered the informal probability path that led to the assassination of John F. Kennedy, in 1963. Stephen King wrote an excellent novel called *11.22.63* in which a time traveller, Jake Epping, makes several trips back from the 2000s into the late 1950s and early 1960s. In his time travels, his interactions with people – often fairly minor ones, changed the life paths of these characters. But at the centre of the plot, is his attempt to prevent Kennedy's assassination, in which he succeeds. I have given enough of a spoiler already, but suffice to say his participation, or interference, in most of the events leading up to his success in this enterprise, each changed the world only subtly, but finally led to his prevention of the assassination. Then, with this one single change in the course of history, the world became dramatically different. Each of the actions of Epping and his companion on the day that would or would not see Kennedy being assassinated was quite small. King's narrative provides a superb description of the micro-level detail. When reading this, I was struck by what was really a fictional account of the Butterfly Effect.

King's novel is a very good example of the multitude of micro-level cause effect relationships that can be discerned in a *post hoc* examination of a much bigger cause–effect relationship. But a simple thought experiment of one's own can reveal something similar (though hopefully with a less dramatic endpoint!). Trace back a "causal path" from a current situation or event that you are in, or experienced and what you will find is a whole lot of bifurcations that led to that particular point. Some will have had only the tiniest consequence and it is quite possible other bifurcations would have produced very similar outcomes, others most definitely would not. We have all heard stories of people who avoided tragedies as a result of some prior trivial change in their actions or circumstances. I know, for example, that had not the person who came first in the interview selection at my first academic job, not pulled out, it is quite possible I would not have become an academic social scientist and I would not be writing this now. Though I'm not sure where the tragedy lies in this!

Two terms help us to describe what is going on and in doing so show what is the relationship between probability and causality.

Propensities

Popper's propensity theory of probability is advanced by him as a theory of causality. At the risk of over interpreting Popper, we might say that he conceived of causality as something which must happen. Things, such as fundamental physical laws, which have a natural necessity of realising causal outcomes. He talks in terms of push–pull forces (Popper 1995: 21–22) But, these he maintains, (somewhat prefiguring Nancy Cartwright), actually never manifest themselves in this way. Gravity, for example, is mediated by environmental conditions. So, for example, we might say that Newton's apple must fall, because of the immutable law of gravity, but a real Newtonian apple, cannot just be described as falling but will fall when the biological and environmental conditions of stem rot, wind etc. reach critical proportions. And apples fall off trees at different rates, because of this.

Every event, Popper claims, has a probability of occurrence, unless it is something that cannot happen or must happen (as in my example of unaided flying or the inevitability of dying). Deterministic causality would have it that P will cause Q if the P-> Q relationship is always the same. The problem is, that it isn't. Rather, it is the case that in every P-> Q relationship there are competing probabilities and there is no certainty in which one will be realised. Hence the recourse to the "long run" in frequency theory.

For Popper, causality is a special case of probability when a probability equals 1. Up until this point we can only talk of the propensity of something to occur.

In the previous chapter I said that Popper maintained that any event, even if it occurs just once has a probability, for its probability is a property of the generating conditions, themselves outcomes of earlier probabilities. For Popper then, each situation, has a varying propensity to cause something and some things are just more likely to happen (they have a greater propensity) than others.

This thesis is essentially a metaphysical one and a key criticism of it is that the probability of a single outcome, even though we can recognise intuitively that it has one, is difficult – even impossible to know, because there is no reference class with which we can compare it. Popper's methodological prescription was somewhat vague. Quite rightly he maintained that if, as in the frequency theory of probability, we treat each instance initially as an equal possibility, then we should treat each case as having a weighted possibility. The weight can be thought of a product of the particular circumstances, such as those inherent in throwing a dice (air pressure, surface, force of the throw). The scientific equivalent for him is the whole experimental set-up (Popper 1995: 10–11). What we then want to know, is what is the weight of the weighted possibilities? This, he maintained, can be achieved through the repeated experiment, in which the stability of P-> Q relationships might be probabilistically determined. I take this to mean that each experiment is treated as a case, but the case is the intervention as well as the other initial conditions.

In Chapter 9, I will suggest how we might do something like this (and indeed my colleague Wendy Dyer and I have attempted to do so) with case-based analyses. But, for the moment let me just reflect on what this means for a "cause".

It is subtle. Popper, unlike Russell, is not saying there are no causes, but rather (he does not actually say this) there are multi-dimensional arrays of propensities for things to occur, some of which will (1) and some of which won't ever (0), thus producing both actualised outcomes and preventions of other things. Presumably to fully explain these we would need quantum level description. For our purposes, we don't, but if we accept Popper's metaphysical description of probability – causality, and I do we have at least a metaphysical theory of causality which is compatible with complexity.

This approach to causality depends on a number of other characteristics. The first of these I noted (and illustrated through the mayonnaise example) in the last chapter, that of emergence.

Emergence

Emergence is the opposite of determinism. In determinism, the final state of a system is determined by its initial conditions.[11] One of the most famous expressions of, what we might call, methodological determinism came from the 18th century. As I noted, in the last chapter, Pierre Laplace maintained that the entire universe was composed of "different arrangements of atoms moving in accordance with Newton's laws of motion" (Tallis 1995: 12). He maintained it followed from this that if all such arrangements as exist now can be known with certainty, then all possible future arrangements can be determined. Newton himself did not go this far and few have expressed such a radical view, but it nevertheless it anticipates a view that if a model has enough information we can determine precise outcomes. Now, I would agree that a model, if based on measurements of relative invariance, in the social world, can provide enough information to infer some outcomes, this is not always the case. In macro-level analyses, because measurement is often across large numbers of cases, with relatively "stable" independent variables, predictability in models is greater than meso level models with fewer people and less stable variables. This is not just a function of the law of large numbers, I referred to above, but a property of emergence in systems. In my book *Science and Social Science* (Williams 2000a) I gave an example of a thought experiment from Alvin Sapperstein (1995), which illustrates this. I reproduce it here, because I have not seen a nicer example since.

Suppose a circular table is set for dinner with four plates set around the circumference of the table and midway between each plate there is a wine glass. The first person to sit down is in the position of being able to choose whether she will use the glass to the left, or to the right. If she chooses the right then so must her fellow diners. Meanwhile other diners are milling around waiting to be seated at other similarly laid tables. Some will prefer a left handed wine glass, others a right, yet others will be indifferent, but the first person to choose on each table will determine the side each of the others on her table will take their wine. In this way those with a left preference, those with a right preference and those with no preference become distributed through the room. Now further suppose on some arbitrary whim it is decided to serve left handed diners from one pot of food and right handed from another. The "left hand" pot contains contaminated food and those diners suffer food poisoning. Even if we had known left and right handed preference we could not have predicted deterministically which diners would be poisoned. A deterministic causal explanation would be inadequate because on following the causal chain back we would reach a point where outcomes depended wholly on a chance set of circumstances. If we represented this statistically, it would correspond to a Markov Chain. A Markov chain is a model which describes a sequence of possible events in which the probability of each event depends only on the state attained in the previous event. This is not wholly stochastic and the limits of the possibility or phase space will provide some determining boundary conditions. In the physical world these are grounded in transcendental and natural necessity and in the social world, by conceptual necessity. Though most social systems are also bounded by environmental characteristics and all are dependent upon the transcendental characteristics of time and space.

In the Sapperstein example, for instance, the number of poisoned diners could not exceed the number of poisoned portions. And, given the logic of the situation, only those on "left-handed" tables could be poisoned. Thus, an analysis of the probability space will set some conditions as "1" and some as "0". All else is emergent at different decision bifurcations. Thus, a decision to do A or B, will lead at the next step to C or D, and so on. Even in a bounded, relatively small, social situation a decision bifurcation to do A and not B (or vice versa) will produce radically diverging end states – or of course they may not! But the initial conditions may not help us discriminate.

If, however, we scale up such models, such as the thought experiment here, or the actual model exemplar from Brian Castellani, in Chapter 9, then the amount of divergence may be cancelled out by the stability of individual decisions and behaviour within a large social matrix – what I have termed "invariance". In large social systems there are outliers than can produce a "Butterfly Effect", but equally there is often a regression to a normative mean, that can produce relatively stable transformations of aspects of the social over time.

So where in all of this is the cause–effect relationship? We can certainly see it at a micro level where certain beliefs, experience and decisions lead to further actions or beliefs, for an individual. For example, Castellani et al (2018) describes how the experience of pain, or other physical symptoms causes co-morbidity at an individual level and this is similar enough across several (or many) cases to produce clusters of similar co-morbidities. But scale this up into "clusters" and we have relations of similarity of individual cause–effect relationships, not a single aggregate cause–effect relationship.

This leads us to think of causes as "nested probabilities", that an individual bifurcation that is a belief or action is an outcome state of previous bifurcations. My decision to buy, say a particular phone and not another one, was an outcome state that was bounded by certain conditions (the phone had to be available and I had to have the resources to buy it), but also my assessment of evidence of performance, cost, aesthetic characteristics and so on. These in turn emerged from hundreds, thousands, possibly millions of other decision bifurcations. But, although none of these was determined and my own and all of the previous decision bifurcations might have been different, the actuality is that my own decision to buy that particular model of phone was the same as millions of other peoples' decisions. As my partner often pessimistically remarks, "its never an original idea, somebody else will always have got there first", usually as we try to find a parking space at the supermarket!

So why is there such "invariance"? To consider this I turn now to two concepts: dispositions and beliefs – desires and show how they coalesce into, what I have termed "social objects".

Causality and social objects

What I have called "decision bifurcations" mostly do not arise from caprice, but from reason, habit and preference. As Popper notes, "propensities do not realise themselves" (1995: 26), but in the social world are often the result of choosing. These choices arise from preferences that are grounded in beliefs and desires and they and their referents have a dispositional character. The realisation of these dispositions produces the invariance that is the ontological "stuff" of the social world, what (following others) I refer to as "social objects". These are what are "real" about the social world, alongside their active relations with other social objects, creating, disturbing and eliminating others. But I'm again getting ahead myself. Firstly ......

Dispositions

Dispositions are the qualities something possesses to give it its character. They are often distinguished from "properties", in so far as they have an active, rather than passive character, though whether we can distinguish between properties and dispositions, or whether properties can take on a dispositional character, has been debated (Mumford 2007: 74). Up until fairly recently many philosophers, particularly empiricists, were sceptical about dispositions (see e.g. Goodman 1973[1955]), seeing them as having an occult character, because of some implicit internal vitality which gave them the capacity to bring things about. A good question we might pose, is what is it about something that can dispose it to be "active"? Solubility in water is a simple example.

> If a substance is soluble in water, when it is placed in water, it will dissolve. Now, this does not mean that every soluble substance will dissolve, because that substance may not be placed in water. But it has the dispositional and necessary character of solubility. It is necessary that it will dissolve in water if put in water
>
> (Mumford 2007: 74).

Andrew Sayer (using the term "causal powers") said:

> The nature or constitution of an object and its causal powers are internally or necessarily related: a plane can fly by virtue of its aerodynamic form, engines etc; gunpowder can explode by virtue of its unstable chemical structure; multinational firms can sell their products dear and buy their labour cheap by virtue of operating in several countries with different levels of development ....
>
> Sayer 1992: 105

These examples beg one question and pose another. The first is, if these are disposition, what would be properties that are not dispositional? And the second, is are social dispositions different to physical ones?

In the physical world, I for one – along with Popper 1959b, find the distinction difficult to sustain. What is crucial about a disposition, is not what it is, but what it can become or lead too. This is straightforward with something like a soluble substance. To realise its disposition, it must be "activated", but remains a disposition nonetheless, even if it is not activated. The same is true of an aeroplane or gunpowder. But what about, say, the property of redness? Being red does not make it a disposition, but redness is a property of light refraction and the chemical composition of the object. What appears red under one condition, may not under another. However, whether we can distinguish between dispositions and properties is not that important to our considerations here – that of social dispositions. Though I reiterate that what happens in the social world is often prevented or made possible by physical dispositions or properties.

Three things, I think, distinguish social dispositions from physical ones. They are the nature of necessity, duration and autonomy.

It is often said (by those at least who believe in dispositions) that they must have duration (Hampshire 1972: 37–38) – though this is questioned by others (Cartwright 2007: 196). Whether, this is necessitated, or is a characteristic, it the case that in the physical world dispositions will have the same character under the same circumstances. We cannot imagine substance S, being soluble at *t1* but not at *t2*, under the same circumstances. The reason for this, perhaps *ceteris paribus*, is that they are ultimately grounded in natural necessity. Social dispositions are not. Their necessity is conceptual. As I argued in the previous chapter the complex socio-historic context is contingent and there is no "grounding".

Compare gunpowder and multi-national firms. The unstable chemical structure of gunpowder can be explained by a relatively small number of environmental contingencies themselves grounded in physical laws. However, the dispositional chemical instability of gunpowder will always be realised under conditions C, whereas multi-national firms are time specific and evolving and their dispositions explained only in relation to other evolving structures, themselves having a dispositional character and so on.

Consider your own life. Throughout, what you were at any given time, conferred upon you particular dispositions, that did not apply before and maybe have not applied since. This may be the result of environmental factors, such ageing, or social factors, such as leaving education. Outcomes for some can be dispositions for others. For example, mental illness may provide the disposition to substance abuse, but substance abuse may provide the disposition to mental illness. In the social world dispositions have some invariance, that is they exist for a period of time, but in the physical world dispositions will exist over longer periods, or they are grounded in natural necessity and they will often be less complex.

A second distinction is autonomy. Gunpowder has the disposition to become unstable under particular circumstances, but given those circumstances, it must become unstable. It is true that in the physical world, dispositions may be activated by many sufficient conditions (though at least one necessary one must be present), but there is no behavioural autonomy. The dispositional character of the social world is grounded in behavioural autonomy. Now, by this, I do not mean, that we are free to act as we will, without the constraints of our past. The autonomy lies in choosing one thing or another, but precisely within the constraints of our past and indeed present conditions of a probability space. So, dispositions have differing propensities for their realisation.

Andrew Sayer speaks of the relationship between people and labour markets: people have the causal (dispositional) power of being able to work, but these powers must be realised (Sayer 1992: 104–105). In order to work people must sell their labour, or themselves make a product that they can sell and there has to be a demand for their labour, or product. A person may possess labour power, but the circumstances under which this may be activated or sustained can vary enormously. At no point can we specify a set of conditions *necessary* to the exercise of labour power, though of course we might specify *sufficient* conditions. It therefore requires, in David Papineau's words, "the joint presence of a number of factors which together are sufficient for the effect" (Papineau 1978: 54). However, given these conditions and (say) adding in the sanctions of not earning money, or being penalised for not taking a job, a person nevertheless has the autonomy to choose to work or not work.

Beliefs and desires

Dispositions have differing propensities to occur, that is their occurrence may or may not be realised. Their realisation will depend on additional stimulation. Salt dissolves in water, but the salt must somehow first be introduced into the water, by humans or by some other means in nature. However, in the social world dispositions can be triggered by our beliefs or our wishes and desires. I have the disposition to swim. Now, ruling out physical action of which I have no control (e.g. my boat sinks) I can choose to activate the disposition of swimming. So, what are the stimuli? Well, there has to be sufficient water and fortunately, for me, there is an excellent swimming pool nearby and there is the sea. Then, I must want, or at least feel I ought to swim (for the sake of my health). So, I have the belief there is the possibility of swimming in the pool, I believe it will be good for me, so I have the desire to swim. But, there may be counter stimuli. The pool is closed and the sea is too cold, I have too much work to do, I prefer to cycle instead. So, is there any kind of cause–effect relationship to be discerned? Can we say beliefs and desires are "causes". I think we can.

A number of philosophers have attempted to codify this. One example from David Papineau, goes like this:

> Whenever an agent believes a certain action, X, will produce some desired result Y, *and* there is no state of affairs Z, whose avoidance he prefers to Y, and which he believes will also result from X, then he will perform X.
>
> Papineau 1978: 80

As Papineau rightly goes on to say, it is easy enough to generate counter examples, nevertheless *ceteris paribus* we can say that if an agent did not have that specific belief set, s/he would not have done X. In an individual, beliefs and desires produce effects.

Papineau and others (e.g. Hollis 1977, Rosenberg 1988) spent a lot of time discussing the relationship of beliefs, actions and causes. Their opponents were often the behaviourists (who were also empiricists) who were unhappy with the inference to psychological un-observables. Some also saw the corollary of this as accepting mental events as causal, which it was claimed leads to a dualistic explanation of physical events and human behaviour. However, this argument is seldom advanced now, because a straightforward reduction of the mental to the physical, is rarely supported.[12] Even at the time of these debates, psychologists and survey researchers had become very good at measuring attitudes and beliefs and linking them to subsequent actions (see for example).

So, for a realist, mental events – beliefs, desires are real, because they can have causal consequences. John Goldthorpe, notes that number of psychologists have drawn attention to the ability of humans to be aware, not just of their own mental states, but those of others "and up to several degrees [I think that he feels that she wants ....] etc" (Goldthorpe 2016: 18). At this level, beliefs, utterances and actions lead to a very complex nesting of cause–effect relationships, that are probably not measurable, but are certainly knowable at a micro level. The question for Goldthorpe, was how can we accommodate that micro level difference in aggregate measurement?

Creating social objects

The foregoing might create the impression, if not of stochasticity, certainly of fluidity and ephemerality and indeed if we take any specific belief – action nexus in an individual, it would seem that way. But individual beliefs and actions are often social and create patterns of differing invariance, some of which may have the solidity of institutions, laws etc. and these in turn enable and constrain individual agents. Indeed, something like this conclusion is reached by John Goldthorpe. His conclusion, as is mine, is that those differences certainly exist, but there is enough aggregation of commonalities to permit probabilistic measurement. This view of action and structure is certainly not new – its most celebrated variant is Talcott Parsons theory of social action (Parsons 1968). A term used by Parsons (and others) is that of social objects (see e.g. Shils Bhaskar 1998: 409, Collier 1998: 450, Mead 1910, Parsons 1951: 64–68). Moreover, Realism requires there to be "things" in the world, if not solid material objects, then certainly things that have properties. I, like others, use the term "objects" to refer to those things in the social world that have properties and indeed dispositional properties. In order to be able to think causally, we need objects and relations between objects.

Here, I will set out what I believe constitutes social objects. I will speak of them as if they are actual entities in the world, but in Chapter 8, I will modify this description somewhat in the relationship of social objects to causal mechanisms and the means by which we might identify these.

Social objects can be defined as the coalescence of actions into identifiable invariances, such as institutions, customs, laws etc. The invariance may be stable over a considerable period, in the case of institutions, laws, or customs, or they may be quite ephemeral. They are the "strange attractors" of the social world.

Although I will say that, once created, social objects have an existence and autonomy apart from particular agents, they are nevertheless created, maintained, changed and destroyed through individual beliefs and actions. Social objects supervene on individual beliefs and actions, but the particular form they take is not determined by any particular belief or desire.

In a paper some years ago I hypothesised that social objects have five defining characteristics (Williams 2009).

#1 Social objects are socially constructed and real

Social objects are not like physical objects. You cannot touch them, they do not possess material properties, although, as I will say below, physical objects can also have social properties and are often brought into being through social processes. Social objects are socially constructed. However, this does not stop them being Real. Contrast with the opposite view, that of constructivism. Constructionists say that the world can only be known under a description. There are no "things", just social constructions of "things". Secondly social constructionism maintains there is an epistemological equivalence between discourses. One description, however derived is, as I described in Chapter 2, no privileged than any other one.

Realism, in contrast, aims to match description and reality, what Roy Bhaskar calls transitive (descriptions) and intransitive objects (reality) (Bhaskar 2008: 21–23). And even though we are constrained to know things under a description, nevertheless the implication is that some descriptions will be "better" or more "realistic" than others. But, as I argued in Chapter 2, there is a midway position between constructivism and realism, whereby descriptions themselves can become real.

When Bhaskar referred to transitive and intransitive objects he was referring to science generally and provided we keep in mind that the transitive objects may themselves take on a second order intransigence, there is no reason why we cannot think of the social world in this way. Thus, we have objects and descriptions of objects and the latter may themselves become objects to be described. But they are both real. The self-fulfilling prophecy in economics is a good example of precisely this process. The collapse of a bank or a fund is real enough, but the description of this through discourse can lead to a run on the deposits of other banks and so on.[13]

#2 Social objects are real but contingent

Social objects are real because they have causal properties. Whether something can be "real" without causal properties is a metaphysical question that I will not pursue, but if something has causal properties then it must be real, certainly consistent with my description above. Social objects are therefore real if and only if they have socially causal properties. The key causal property is, that the existence of an object increases or decreases the probability of the existence of future objects. This causal process may not be a simple one to one relationship between object X at *T1* and object Y at *T2*, but, the causal relationship will exist within a nesting of probabilities. The realisation of object Y at *T2* will have a causal and retrospectively discoverable history. By coming into existence it has a probability of 1. In the social world probabilities of zero, the impossibility of the existence of an object is probably universally the rather banal flipside of the creation of a specific social object.

The causal properties of objects make them real, but some objects will possess greater causal efficacy than others. That is, their existence has a greater likelihood of bringing about future social objects than others. For example the existence of a law banning smoking in public places will have greater causal efficacy than a voluntary code of practice. There are two caveats to enter here: first that by causal efficacy I mean comparatively higher probabilities of bringing about a given state of affairs. The "voluntary code" may have causal efficacy in bringing about quite different social objects, such as segregated smoking areas. Second some social objects, such as laws, just have more causal efficacy than (say) the brief social encounters of which we may have scores every day.

#3 Social objects are dynamic

Some social objects have greater invariance than others, some are fleeting (though not as fleeting as the isotope Hydrogen 7!) and others have relative stability, visibility or longevity (or a combination of these things). The British Monarchy is a good example of this. But although the monarchy is a quintessential social object, it is composed of other social objects, such as customs, laws, family relationships, economic activities, ceremonial occasions etc. So we talk of the monarch as a noun, yet embodied in this are actions, which we would express as verbs. For example, the Queen *opens* parliament, the Prime Minister *bows* to the Queen etc. These are obvious examples of actions that might be said to cause the monarchy, but there are thousands of other much smaller actions within the object of the monarchy and indeed any other such "large" object that cause it to exist. Indeed, when we breakdown a social object, such as monarchy, it consists of actions (such as the above) and physical things with social significance (e.g. thrones, carriages, signed Parliamentary Bills etc.).

Social objects, rather like atoms and their sub atomic make up seem to consist of the actualisation of relationships. And depending how we choose to look at them, they will look like things or relations between things, but really they are one and the same thing.

Social objects are then, the outcomes of contingent relationships that have a greater or lesser probability of bringing about other social objects. Though they may appear "thing like" they are dynamic and continuous.

#4 Social objects are continuous with thought objects and physical objects

Ontologically they occupy the mid ground between physical and thought objects. Some physical objects are not social because we have never seen them, or acted towards them socially (see Chapter 2). They exist independently of us. Inductively we can infer such things do exist, because there are plenty of hitherto unknown and unnamed physical things that are now known and named. The latter are both physical and social objects (the thrones, crowns etc. of the monarchy). We can infer about future futures from past futures. At the opposite end of this ontological spectrum are thought objects, that is thoughts individuals have that do not have social outcomes. Though it is tricky to specify which of our thoughts have no later social outcomes, because these may be indirectly socially efficacious via other thoughts. So, as with physical objects, thought objects often, perhaps usually become social. Conversely social objects may create physical or thought objects.

#5 The causal efficacy of social objects depends on their relationship to other social objects

If social objects are the outcome of contingent relationships, what is it that makes them causal, that is raises the probability of the existence of future objects (or indeed lowers the probability)? As I have suggested social objects are ontologically diverse and this diversity goes beyond socialised physical objects and individual actions. If agents perceive social objects in the world under different descriptions and act toward them differently, then surely we have an infinity of objects that only know their bounds in the collectivity of human thought? Logically this is possible, but the objects would be physical and thought objects. But the social element of objects enters through common cultural and linguistic agreement about their characteristics. A much used, but nevertheless useful, example is money. Banknotes have a physical existence to both those who know their social use and those who do not. The latter may see the notes in many ways and use them in ways not intended by their creators, but the important thing about banknotes is that they would not have come into existence without the existence of a social process that gave them their conventional role. Thus, for the vast majority of people who use banknotes there is common agreement about their functional and objective properties.

Social objects are bound together by social rules and the rules are themselves social objects. The banknote and the social rules governing its use are each social objects. We know the rules under which banking and a money economy operates. We do not know all of the rules, but we know sufficient to be able to participate in the money economy and by doing so we affirm and reproduce the social objects. We do not need to be aware of the structure in which the objects exist and we can even have false beliefs (Searle 1995: 127), though, false beliefs themselves can be causally efficacious. The money economy did not arise *ex nihilo*, but through the complex development of contract and its embodiment in the exchange of tokens, but the more such contracts are honoured and expectations met, the stronger the money economy becomes. These developments have long been known to social scientists and have formed the basis for social contract theory (see e.g. Ardrey 1970, Shapiro 1987, Soloman 1995). Indeed, apart from my emphasis on the contingent and probabilistically causal nature of objects, the foregoing description of the relationship between social action and the creation and maintenance of social structure is a relatively commonplace one in social theory. For our purposes it is the strength of these interlocking mutual expectations that produces more, or less, causal efficacy.

We must conclude that here is a dynamic world of social objects that often exist independently of us as individuals. They are variously causally efficacious and they are also "bound together" in patterns or structures that have different degrees of invariance. We may use the term social structure, social aggregation or social mechanisms. As with other realists, I will use the term "mechanism". In Chapter 8 I will pursue the argument that social objects cohere in complex mechanisms.

Causality and complexity

Causes, those simplest of common-sense notions, turns out to be a most difficult thing to define or show. Yet, in all of the sciences we seem to require causal explanations. In this chapter I have tried to give a flavour of attempts to define and operationalise causality. These are partial successes and work within specific domains, but no one definition or methodological strategy can uniquely capture causal processes.

In my view most non-probabilistic philosophical accounts of causality fail, because they set limiting conditions for what can count as a cause (e.g. INUS conditions), or their considerations are those of cause and effect in the physical world, where there might be a "grounding" in fundamental laws. I have argued that there is no such grounding in the social world and no natural necessity, the basis of laws in the physical world. At a micro level, causal accounts have enough efficacy to at least be described through sufficient and locally necessary conditions (themselves nevertheless conceptual), but at a macro level only probabilistic causality seems to do the job. But this is limited. Frequency based probabilistic causal methods are not without explanatory value (I return to this in Chapter 9), but they are dependent on the assumptions of linearity, a characteristic largely absent in the social world and they are often built on shaky theoretical constructs.

The alternative approach to probabilistic causality, that of single case propensities is an ontological theory which is very conducive to complexity approaches.

It provides us with an ontological description of things in the social world and how they might causally interact. But, it too, has its methodological limits and could not (at present) do universal duty as a strategy in quantitative research. Again, I will discuss the methodological possibilities and limits of this approach in Chapter 9.

Nancy Cartwright, at least temperamentally, reaches the same conclusion as I do. But she reaches this conclusion about causality *tout court*, whereas I do not feel qualified to pronounce on the possibility of deriving causal accounts of the physical world (though I am attracted to her arguments).

Her argument is essentially ontological – that there is a variety of different kinds of causes, which can operate in different ways (Cartwright 2004).[14] If this is true of the physical world, it is true in spades of the social world! Our causal language, when we talk about the social world is diverse: institutions (banks, parliaments, universities) are treated as causal agents, individuals cause things, ensembles of individuals take on characteristics, such as poverty, which will have highly complex causal antecedents. We treat things such as ethnicity and gender as proxies for causes .... and so on. Trying to capture this plethora of so many different things, through one thing – social causality, is to chase a rainbow.

Cartwright's book *The Dappled World,* (Cartwright 1999) refers to a poem by Gerald Manley Hopkins. The world is not regular and ordered, but "dappled", there are some regularities, but also too much diversity to be described by simple and elegant laws. Because causes are highly unspecific, a single methodology will not capture all we wish to capture. Though she does not ground this in complexity explicitly, this surely is the message? Causes are complex, they are not one thing. I think it follows, that the best we can do as social researchers is to be ecumenical about what we say a cause (or causes) is and how we might investigate them. It also depends on our purpose. We might take a broad macro-historical approach to describing the causes of change over long periods, as do Byrne and Callaghan (2013), or we might want to provide a societal level explanation of why a defined social group has poorer life chances. Here we might use few relatively simple measures of a sample, which might provide a statistically robust and theoretically intuitive answer. For example, in developing countries, access to fresh drinking water will dramatically change the health and life chances of those hitherto deprived of it (see e.g. Nguendo Yongsi 2010). Or, we might wish to research the life trajectories of a particular group, looking for key differentiating moments that provide different outcomes, such as the accommodation outcomes for young people leaving care.

Finally, because realists seek macro-level explanations, they search for mechanisms and mechanisms are ensembles of causes and effects. Mechanisms are also complex, because causes are complex. This will be the subject of Chapter 8.

Different methods will be deployed to look for different kinds of causes. Ultimately, although causes are real, but complex, as social scientists we aim to tell plausible causal stories!

Notes

1 Causality is the relation between cause and effect, and causation either the causing of something or the relation between cause and effect. However, in the literature, causality and causation are often used interchangeably. I have used the former, because I am primarily concerned with cause–effect relationships, but others whose work is quoted sometimes use the latter, in specific circumstances.

2 That the world was fundamentally probabilistic, rather than deterministic, entered physics (from social actuarial science) in the 19th century with Robert Brown's discovery of, what became known as "Brownian motion", the random motion of particles suspended in a fluid (Feynman et al 1963). Ian Hacking notes that Francis Galton, the statistician, abandoned causality for correlation, because once we abandon the idea that A caused B and introduce, C, D etc., as mediating variables, then eventually we would need to "involve all the factors of the universe" (Hacking 1990: 188*ff*).

3 Karl Pearson, was an enthusiastic eugenicist. Ian Hacking (1990: 22) notes that he believed, with Malthus, that the poor should have fewer children "not in order to help the poor, but to save the rich". Nevertheless many of the techniques he invented chi square, Pearson's R., etc. are universally used and are not tainted by the context of their invention.

4 This is more than a rhetorical device on my part. Biologists and clinicians, whilst often acknowledge a complex mechanism, have made little progress in understanding how those mechanisms work. See for example: Sleigh et al 2014.

5 The Cornish are the indigenous inhabitants of the extreme south west peninsula of Britain.The UK Government officially recognised the Cornish as a national minority under European rules for the protection of national minorities on the 24 April 2014.

6 The term error, in statistics, does not denote a mistake, but rather inaccuracy as a result of the constraints of sample size, measurement etc.

7 Significance levels are conventions and could be otherwise. Moreover, their value in hypothesis testing has come under considerable scrutiny in recent years. See, the discussion in Chapter 6 and Gigerenzer 2008, Anderson 2019, van Witteloostuijn 2020.

8 And indeed, as I will say in Chapter 5, "social class" as measured by occupation is a far from satisfactory operationalisation of what we can mean, nowadays, by class.

9 Most techniques now seem to be forms of path analysis, but this was not always so and causal analysis may follow constant conjunction, regularity, or correlation, and as I note below counterfactual frameworks (Barringer et al 2013).

10 See Chapter 9 for a description of QCA.

11 It is important to note that the concept of supervenience, I mentioned in Chapter 2, does not imply determinism (though some of its stronger forms might). One fact grounds (or supervenes on another) when the second obtains, by virtue of the former. Therefore, the second is an emergent property of the former.

12 See my discussion of supervenience in Chapter 2.

13 See Merton 1968: 128–129 for a discussion of examples from history.

14 Cartwright (2004: 3) lists six approaches as aiming to provide universal accounts of causal laws. I simply list them here, but she provided an account of why each one fails beyond particular domains:

    1. Probabilistic accounts of causality and Bayes – net causal inference
    2. Modularity accounts
    3. The invariance account
    4. Natural experiments
    5. Causal process theories
    6. The efficacy account

5

Representation and reality

The greatest empirical problem facing realism is that of "closure". Put simply, how does the researcher "capture", through measurement or interpretation, what is real in the social world? At a non-quantum level, no such problem troubles the physicist or chemist. A volume of gas, its temperature, its rate of expansion, can be reliably measured. It is absolutely true that at the quantum level, or in those domains described by relativity theory, the physicist faces problems of closure, if not like those of the social world, certainly as challenging. But at least the day-to-day bread and butter physics and chemistry can rely on a set of procedures, that for the most part, there will be agreement that a given measurement validly and reliably measures what it is supposed to measure.[1]

Many social researchers fantasise that they too share this measurement certainty, of at least basic concepts. Although validity and reliability are achievable, they come hedged with qualifications and limitations. In realist closure, measurement is a necessary, but not sufficient condition.

In this chapter I want to explore how we can "represent" the real and the relationship of representation to theory. But firstly, I want to return to the issue of complexity and to show why it is that even our quotidian science is so difficult to specify.

Representing the complex real

In quantitative social research much of our methodological thinking was inherited from early 20th century natural science and in particular the logic of experiment and control. This was described by Carl Hempel (1965) as the deductive nomological (DN) or "covering law" model that I discussed in Chapter 3. As I noted there, the model only really works in the relatively simple instances where reference can be made to fundamental physical laws and its scope and veracity has been called into question, even in the natural sciences (Salmon 1989, van Bouwel and Erik Weber 2011) (see also Nancy Cartwright's objections to "fundamental laws" in the Chapter 2), but nevertheless the logic of it persisted into social science and specifically survey research. Though laws were rarely invoked, the definition of the things measured were treated in the same way as known physical properties, even though the former were derived measurements (say social class) as opposed to (say) the invariant properties (such as those of stable elements), or properties whose variance was limited within a given domain (such as gases). The second characteristic, was that of control, whereby the effect of A upon B can be separated from other exogenous variables by holding them constant.

Survey research, unlike much laboratory work, is dependent upon statistical measurement and control and assumes a linear relationship between variables. The assumed predictive ability is therefore of the same logical kind as that which might be achieved through the covering law model. As David Byrne put it:

> If we can establish the relationships so that our formalised linear mathematical models are indeed isomorphic with the real world … then we can predict what will happen in a given set of circumstances.
>
> Byrne 1998: 19

But as Byrne goes on to say, much of the world does not work in this way. And especially the social world.

Social categories, such as behaviours, states, attitudes and so on are multi-dimensional, fluid and may be known under different descriptions, or the same description can apply to different phenomena.

Let us take the concept and measurement of homelessness as an example.

Homelessness is a major social problem in most countries around the world. But it is not a simple or singular phenomenon (Tipple and Speak 2005). The form it takes is very different across countries. Indeed, in extreme examples, where shelter is precarious for large segments of the population – say, where a large proportion of a population live on the streets, then it is hardly a meaningful word at all. Even in advanced western societies it can take multiple forms. Glen Bramley (Bramley 1988) writing only about the UK at a particular time, identified seven different homeless states.

In the research on homelessness, in which I participated, (Williams 2005b, Williams and Cheal 2001, 2002) it was found that not only are there multiple types of homelessness, some situations are recognised as homelessness in official definitions, but those experiencing them do not regard themselves as homeless. An example of this was encountered with elderly men living long term in Salvation Army hostels who did not see themselves as homeless, because they had no anticipation of leaving the hostel (Williams et al 1995). Conversely, UK law does not recognise a person under notice to leave accommodation as homeless, until they have left, despite their often very precarious housing situations. So, subjective definitions of homelessness frequently diverge from policy or research definitions.

Even when definitions can be settled, the "trajectory" of homelessness is far from straightforward, with many of those experiencing it not remaining in the same situation for very long. In the UK (and it is very different in other countries) only a very small proportion of the homeless live "on the street" for extended periods. Most people move through a number of different shelter situations over a relatively short time, say between hostels, short-term accommodation in some form of housing, staying with friends, sleeping rough on the streets, etc.

Finally, and perhaps controversially, homelessness may be a symptom. Brian Cheal and I (Williams and Cheal 2002) argued that we might say there is no such thing as homelessness, just many sub-optimal housing situations. Rather what we have are things like migration (for many reasons), substance abuse, leaving care or the family home, leaving an institution (such as the armed forces or prison) as primary social problems and housing need, in its many forms as secondary. But then, of course, being in one of these situations, itself becomes something that impacts upon other things, especially employment. However, from a research perspective we could treat homelessness as the dependent variable, with things like substance abuse, leaving an institution and so on, as the independent variables. Conversely, we could treat substance abuse as the dependent variable and homelessness as one of the independent variables. The results from each, would almost certainly point to different causal patterns, hence my claim at the end of the last chapter that we aim to tell plausible causal stories.

Homelessness is a major social problem and one, as citizens, that we feel we have a hand waving grasp on what it is. Yet, it is a quintessential complex system, where we can indeed discern path dependencies through individual housing histories (the "strange attractors" or invariances). Because the possibility space will be limited by laws, accommodation availability, employment opportunities, rehabilitation programmes, etc., in any particular location and time, these pathways will be often be patterned very similarly, they may converge or diverge over time. Bifurcations at various points in an individual's life, such as acquiring a tenancy or not, can lead to major changes in life chances. The process of bifurcation, as I indicated earlier, implies neither simple linear determination (where if A happens then B happens), or random process where anything can happen. Instead what is implied is complex change, so that starting with A, in the first bifurcation if B or D happens, then C or E happens depending upon initial variations in the form of A (as in a Markov chain). If we then multiply this up, across thousands of individuals, through time, we do not see a stochastic process, but we do see an indeterminate one.

This does not mean we cannot research homelessness (or housing need), but what we are researching is subject to variation between locations and through time, multiple definitions, subjective understandings and association with many other individual characteristics.

Representing in the social survey

In the homelessness example, I mentioned only briefly the definitional issue, sufficient to make the point that it is heterogeneous and contested. Yet, the definition one arrives at, that subsequently becomes a measurement makes an enormous difference to the results obtained. This is not to suggest the results are a fictitious construction. Taking a selfie, from a different angle, when you are in a different mood or place are each representations of you, none of them are false. But to extend the analogy, you might say that a particular photo better represents what you are "like", more than another. But they are not fictions. In homelessness, there is "something going on". People live in precarious housing or shelter situations, they have no work, they are often ill or malnourished and may have substance abuse problems. This is real. But how do we represent that reality? Well, clearly one single word, or uniform concept – homelessness will not do. Yet somehow, we have to represent the real, so that it is amenable to description, measurement and explanation.

The description, measurement and explanation of homelessness is but one example of the realist problem of representation and empirical closure.

In this section I want to look in a little more detail at measurement and representation in the social survey. I use the term social survey very broadly, meaning everything from opinion surveys to major government surveys and censuses.

In survey research the process of operationalisation describes the move from abstract concepts described by a theory, for example as alienation, to concrete and specific measures. How well these measures represent the concept is described in the literature as construct validity. de Vaus (1996: 57) illustrates this with the example of alienation and class. Suppose we have developed a new measure of alienation and we want to evaluate it. Our theory may postulate a relationship between class and alienation, whereby the "lower" the class the higher the amount of alienation. If subsequently the research shows this to be the case then we might say that the new measure has construct validity. But, as de Vaus points out, there are two dangers here:

Firstly, if when using the new measure, the theoretical proposition is not supported, how do we know whether it is our new measure that is invalid, the theory that is wrong or that the measure of the other concept (class) is invalid.

Second, we must avoid developing a test so that it supports the theory. If we use a theory to validate our measure and then use the (valid!) measure to test the theory then we have established nothing (de Vaus 1996: 57) other than a logical relationship between variables. De Vaus's example of alienation, is itself, like homelessness, a concept that may be theorised very differently and may in fact be standing in for a heterogeneous individual behaviours and emotions. But more of that later.

The problem is then, how do we represent the "real"? This is not always such a deep philosophical or methodological issue. It may be no more than a technical one. For example, age, biological sex and many behaviours can, with the caveat of respondent truthfulness and good survey technique, be readily measured.[2] The UK censuses ask respondents to say how many rooms there are in their dwelling (https://census.ukdataservice.ac.uk/use-data/censuses/forms.aspx). This question is answered badly, because although rooms are defined, respondents misunderstand or count rooms wrongly. But this is a technical issue that can be checked in a post-enumeration study (ONS 2014) and these things directly represent the construct through the measurement. The validity and reliability of the question can be improved.

Measures of attitude or belief, or what we might term "sociological" variables are more difficult. By the latter, I mean such things as social class, ethnicity, gender, religion and, of course, the aforementioned homelessness. The things that these constructs represent are socially constructed by the researcher, but they are meant to be adequate representations of the real.

What I am arguing is rather similar to Bateson's "fact value" continuum (Bateson 1984: 25–30), well summarised by Byrne (2002: 65) a "fact holds constant amongst different observers and for the same observer at different times, but an opinion does not".[3] The sociological concepts (such as social class, ethnicity, etc.) I describe are in that continuum, but can take on a "factness" for different observers at the same time. Though Bateson and Byrne are talking about surveys, this continuum is logically equivalent to the value continuum I will discuss in Chapter 7.

We can go about measurement in two ways. Firstly, we can define a theoretical concept and then attempt to operationalise this through measures. Or, we can begin from what *can* be measured. The first of these is the empiricist approach and the second is that of realism. However, both of these present methodological difficulties.

Operationalism

Quite often the term operationalisation and operationalism are conflated, or used interchangeably. The latter is a very specific form of operationalisation, with its roots in logical positivism and a widespread influence across the natural and social sciences for much of the last century.

The operationalist programme in the natural sciences had its origins in the work of Percy Bridgeman, who had been impressed with Einstein's concept of simultaneity (Bridgeman 1927). Einstein's concept described signals from events occurring in physical systems which are moving with respect to one another. Judgements by the observer about the signals will depend on the relative motions of the systems and the observer. Thus, observer One on system 1 may judge that event x on system 1 and event y on system 2 are simultaneous, whereas observer Two on system 2 may judge otherwise. From this Einstein concluded that simultaneity is the relationship between two or more events and is not a fixed relation between events, but a relative one.

The methodological problem of a number of entities which have different and changing relationships to each other, is not so dissimilar to the one I described above, in homelessness. But, additionally, in homelessness and other sociological concepts, the subjective and intersubjective definitions of the bearers, or other "stakeholders" adds a further dimension of representational difficulty.

This problem impressed Bridgeman and what he saw as a solution, he regarded less as a philosophical statement than simply saying what good science should do (Bridgeman 1954 [1927]: 75). That is, it is the operations by which values are assigned that give us the empirical significance of a scientific concept. An operational definition is that which measures, for example, quantity, extension, duration, length, mass, etc. The sociologist Hubert Blalock expressed it very clearly.

> Although a concept such as "mass" may be conceived theoretically or metaphysically as a property, it is only pious opinion .... "mass" is equivalent to "mass" as inferred from pointer readings.
>
> Blalock 1961: 6

The clarity in Blalock's definition implies (a possibly unintended) sleight of hand from an operational definition, that few would deny, is necessary for measurement, to one where that which is measured becomes the thing itself. So, for Blalock, once we have an operational definition of alienation, then that is what alienation is. The epistemological becomes the ontological.

To tease out the distinction I want to make let us take the well-used concept of a "proxy" variable. In secondary analysis, in particular, one must confront the problem that one would have liked X to be measured, but it was not. But infer what difference X might have made, the analyst might use a "proxy" variable. For example, a national survey may not have measured quality of life, but instead something about quality of life might be inferred from a measurement of per capita GDP. But crucially, the latter is not an actual *representation* of the former.

So, (for example) if alienation is, that which is measured as alienation, what is the problem?

These are the problems:

Firstly, if we can only measure and therefore know a phenomenon through a given measurement rubric, then it follows that the only new discoverable phenomena are those that might be found within that rubric. So, for example, in biological taxonomy, if a particular genus of insect is defined by having characteristics A, B, C, then the search for insects with these characteristics, will only find by accident examples where A, B or C are not present, or another characteristic is. Fortunately, in the natural sciences, this does not come to pass, because operationalism is not taken at its word. We are often not so fortunate in the social sciences. Take the illusive concept of happiness, often taken as the most important measure of a society's subjective well-being. A quick Google Scholar search will uncover a massive psychology and social science literature on its measurement. At the time of writing, the first item that appears is a paper that claims to successfully measure the concept with a single item scale (Abdel-Khalek 2006). On further inspection, the validation of this scale is calibrated by reference to a number of other scales and measurements. But what if happiness is actually a latent variable and what is actually being measured is attitudes to an abstract concept? Furthermore, maybe we are measuring the wrong thing and it is security (for example) that people crave, not happiness?

There are two specific issues for the social and psychological sciences.

In natural science, the problem of relativity aside, measurement is often of constants. That is, as I have noted in previously there is a grounding in the natural necessity of laws. Temperature is a simple example. Temperature is measured in different ways: Fahrenheit, Celsius, and Kelvin. But these measure the same phenomenon, the same class of thing, but they are translatable one to the other (ICWM 2011). The measurement of ethnicity serves as a social science example that illustrates a key problem of measurement in the social world. There are a number of measures of ethnicity, but these are not always directly translatable (as in the sense of Celsius to Kelvin), because the ethnicities present will differ from place to place, whereas temperature is a universal characteristic – it's just higher or lower from place to place. Moreover, there is no "meaning" for that which is measured by a measure of temperature, but ethnicity has a (often fluid) meaning to its bearer and the definition may or may not correspond with that meaning.

Unlike the concept of temperature, in the physical world, in the social world there is mostly no readily available translation language between different measurements of phenomena and between the measurements and the phenomena themselves.

A second problem, for social science, is that changes, or different operationalisations, cannot give comparability across time or place. In the Thatcher years, the definition of unemployment was changed a number of times, perhaps deliberately, so that "increases" could be hidden, as in for example changing unemployment benefit, to sick benefit, thus removing large numbers of people from the unemployment claimant count (Webster 2002).

Operationalism, in sociology and its analogous disciplines, was less popular than in psychology. In the former it was championed principally by George Lundberg (1947). He argued that sociologists are wrong in believing measurement can only be carried out after things have been appropriately defined. Lundberg maintained, as in the Blalock quote above, that the definition of a concept is the result of measuring it. Therefore, social values can be measured (and therefore defined) by an examination of the extent to which particular things are valued. Do people value X? If so, how much do they value X? But is this what we continue to do in survey research and call it operationalisation?

The answer is complex and turns on the sleight of hand captured in the Blalock quote, as to whether an operationalisation becomes the thing itself. It is not necessarily the act of measurement, or the measure, that is always at fault, but the assumptions behind it and the social – historical context in which it is used.

A good example can be found in how concepts are operationalised in the UK Censuses.[4] The derivation of Census questions is underwritten by the assumption that there is a one to one correspondence between the question and the object it is supposed to measure. Any mismatch between concepts as measured and the measurements themselves is treated as a technical problem and the suggestion that the Census does anything other than measure "real" things in the world would probably be greeted with incredulity by the UK Office for National Statistics (ONS). Yet one can ask, perhaps, which is the "real" measure of social class: that used in Censuses up until 1991, or the newer Socio-Economic Classification (SEC).[5] In fact, the concept of class, as defined by occupation has been widely challenged (e.g. Savage et al 2013). It had its roots in divisions of labour that characterised industrial societies, that were already "de-industrialising" by the 1970s. Class now is quintessentially complex and whilst thee is a stratification through access to material and social resources, it cannot be captured in any valid way through one quantitative measure (Byrne 2020). Therefore, certainly not the way it is measured in the UK censuses.

However even if we accept that the Census is measuring "real" things, the things that it measures are there because they are items seen to be important to constituencies, such as policy makers. Before each Census, a consultation is organised to investigate what should be changed, added or taken out.[6] Like so many other "consultations", the outcomes reflect the contemporary power relations amongst policy makers, politicians and campaigners, etc.

However, once the Census variables are derived, the Census conducted and the data are analysed, those variables get treated as both constituting both important things that should be measured and their ontological character as reflecting social reality. This is a kind of naive methodological realism which manages to be object measured as real and operationalist in the pragmatic justification for so doing. If the problem, as specified by Blalock, was alternatively resolved it was done so, as Bunge (1996: 327) maintains, by just taking the reality of the social world for granted.

But lets us look at the converse, what Blalock would have called "pious opinion". I mentioned earlier Glen Bramley's definition of homelessness. It is worth reproducing in full:

Glen Bramley's definition of homelessness

1. People literally without a roof over their head, including those regularly sleeping rough, newly arrived migrants, victims of fire, flood, sever harassment or violence and others;
2. People in accommodation specifically provided on a temporary basis to the homeless (hostels, bed and breakfast and so forth.);
3. People with insecure or impermanent housing: this includes other ("self referred") hotel and bed and breakfast residents, licensees and those in holiday lets, those in tied accommodation who change jobs, tenants under

notice to quit, squatters and licensed occupiers of short-life housing and owner occupiers experiencing mortgage foreclosure;

4. People shortly to be released from institutional accommodation, including prisons, detention centres, psychiatric hospitals, community or foster homes and other hostels, who have no existing alternative accommodation or existing household to join;
5. Households sharing accommodation involuntarily;
6. Individuals or groups living within existing households where either: (i) relationships with the rest of the household or (ii) living conditions are unsatisfactory and intolerable for any extended period;
7. Individuals or groups living within existing households whose relationships and conditions are tolerable but where the individual/groups have a clear preference to live separately, including cases where the "potential" household is currently split but would like to live together. (Bramley 1988: 26).

It is possibly one of the most comprehensive definitions of homelessness and some of the specific definitions 1 to 4 are, technical issues aside, possibly operationalisable (though with the caveats I entered above) whereas 5 to 7, though laudable as theoretical constructs, seem to me, to be difficult to operationalise into measures, which capture the theoretical essence of the definition. And this is exactly what, I think Blalock was getting at.

Realist operationalisation?

We are on the horns of a dilemma. Operationalism, which I think still lives on through a naïve methodological realist version of operationalisation, is not capable of capturing the real complexity of social life. On the other hand, a deeper form of realism (and I think that is what Bramley was trying to get at) risks staying as just theorisations, that might possibly be captured at a qualitative micro-level or ends up as an under theorised construct that does not represent the complexity adequately.

I think there are three ways forward on this and with the exception of the first, requires us to come at the issue of closure with different terms of reference.

1. Some things actually measure what they are supposed to measure

Although the decision to measure these things is always in a social context, their measurement is restricted only by technical issues. These items are usually grounded (though not always) in some physical characteristic. The obvious candidates are biological sex, age, but also, we might include income, occupation, distance travelled to work, dwelling type.

The social context, such as the circumstances in which Census questions are decided (or indeed other omnibus surveys), or a specific research question will focus on a particular aspect of social reality and ignore others, but the questions do seem to measure something real – social facts. These are examples of the second ontological kind (that I suggested in Chapter 2), physical properties, that become social as a result of our interaction with them.

But what about things like occupation? Surely a question cannot capture all occupations? Is this not the same as homelessness? No, whilst it is difficult to produce a list of all possible occupations within a survey question. Filter questions, probing and an open ended question, in which the respondent is asked to describe their occupation, should adequately provide construct validity.[7] Similarly, a "sex" question could provide a third or subsequent category, should this be desired. Or indeed a follow-on gender question. Furthermore "occupation" will only be a meaningful measurement in a society that actually has "occupations", so even "social facts" such as this have a local dimension.

2. Some measurements must be developed within specific contexts – a form of "local realism"

Realism, in the natural sciences, is predicated upon universal properties (see for example Psillos 1999). So, whilst complexity is present, generalising rules describing it are themselves universal. So, whilst turbulence flow is quintessentially complex, the nature of that complexity is the same in Canada as Cameroon. Moreover, as I have suggested, much of physical reality is "grounded" in laws, in the final instance. A realism of the physical world is viably universal, but if in the social world we have only local invariance, then a universal realism may not be possible.

This is amplified when we consider the complexity of the social world. Possibly there are individual behaviours that can be universalised, but these behaviours are in social contexts that cannot be universalised. As Haig and Evers (2016: 7), citing John Searle, say "mental and social objects, such as beliefs or money are mind-dependent, in the sense that they are partly constituted by our representations of them". This does not make them "unreal", in that they have real consequences for people. It also does not mean that there is no stability in behaviours, customs or institutions. There is, in fact, a great deal of local invariance.

Moreover, this is not a reiteration of methodological individualism, at least not in its previously understood form. What it does mean is that whilst there is no social without individuals, they are nevertheless socially constituted agents. So, what is "real" extends only as far as the social context of particular behaviours, customs or institutions.

This is what might be termed "local realism" and has been advocated by Usakali Maki (2005) and Daniel Little (2009), the latter describing it as methodological localism. An immediate objection to this approach, might be phrased as "what counts as local", and a reduction ad absurdum reduces this to relativity of the immediate local. Does this then lead to the linguistic and epistemological relativism, that I discussed in Chapter 2?

I do not think so and the objection can be answered in two ways. Firstly, what might be termed an ontological thesis, that there will be general characteristics such as the similarities and dependencies of human biology, along with some environmental universalities. These, in turn, lead to second order characteristics, such as language (and the possibility of mutual comprehension in the matter of such general characteristics), sociability, social norms, deviance, etc. As most anthropologists would claim, these things are *contra* Winch, at least partially knowable (Hollis and Lukes 1982). It perhaps follows from this that some realities, will be less local through time and space than others and some particularities will persist over long periods of time and across wide geographic areas. Variously, we could cite incest taboo (Parsons 1954), the gift relationship (Titmuss 1971) and the longevity and universality of languages, such as French, Spanish and English. Others had longevity and geographical scope, but become challenged and die out, or become atrophied. Variously we could cite divine right of monarchs, revenge killing and the homosexuality taboo.

Local realities are not bounded in time or space, but actually might be seen as strange attractors, that change differentially and moreover can overlap at their boundaries with others.

The second way this might be answered might be termed the epistemological thesis and it is in this that Maki grounds his local realism and minimal characterisation that can have global application, in so far as amenability to scientific investigation and truthfulness (Haig and Evers 2016: 18). We might venture further and say that the development of investigative social science, is itself a socially constructed reality, with transcendental characteristics (Williams 2000a, 20). In other words, whilst social reality exists, whether or not there is social science, the concept and the possibility of the measurement of social reality is created by social science. In other words, measurement and its interpretation are social constructs that become real.

I'll illustrate this with a personal story, again in the area of homelessness. The paper Brian Cheal and I wrote (Williams and Cheal 2001), had the provocative title "Is there any such thing as homelessness?" and in it we advanced much the same argument, as I have above, based on data from two studies, that it is so heterogeneous, that the term can be unhelpfully misleading in a policy context, leading policy makers towards seeing it as homogeneous and consequently proposing simple and singular solutions (which they do). Some while after publishing this paper I was invited to come to City University, New York (CUNY) to talk specifically about how we "measured" homelessness. I gave my talk the same title as the paper. Which I came to learn was a mistake! Whilst, in Europe, I could easily defend my argument, there was an additional element in the concept of homelessness that was present in New York City, and I believe more widely in the United States. Being homeless has become itself an identity for many people (McCarthy 2013). This identity is important because it can be mobilised socially and politically, to help fight the problem. This is possibly an outcome of the virtual absence of social provision, means that many remain homeless for a longer period and in visible states of homelessness. The subjectivity and intersubjectivity of identity played a greater role in the United States, than in Europe. Whilst, indeed, some will adopt such an identity in Europe, this is very much less the case. My New York colleagues challenged and berated me for the title of my talk, and I came to realise they were right to do so!

This anecdote has fairly obvious ontological and methodological conclusions. Homelessness can be broadly interpreted from place to place as a concept with wide understanding, but its specific composition or characteristics differ. The methodological conclusion is that initial definitions and operationalisation will be different.

However, for me, there is a final methodological twist. Though what we can mean by "homelessness" will differ through time and place, the method of measurement I was talking about a method of enumeration called "capture-recapture".[8] This method almost certainly applicable in US cities as it is in European ones and subject only to the same methodological constraints (see for example (Neugebauer and Wittes 1994; D'Onise et al 2007)

3. Measurements are interpreted within a social or historical narrative

Operationalism evolved from logical empiricism (see Chapter 2) and retained the separation of a theoretical and operational language. This was always a problem for the empiricists, because it required translation sentences between the two languages, which apart from anything else leads to an infinite regress of statements. The empiricists were denying or ignoring the obvious, that the desire to measure X and not Y and how to measure X or Y, are themselves the outcome of informal processes and reasoning. One might say how we measure is a matter of scientific judgement as to which measure works best. But this is not wholly true. Statistical analyses go in and out of fashion. Discriminant Function Analysis was widely popular a couple of decades ago and now Structural Equation Modelling is in favour, for example, sociology, management studies and is being taken up even in areas, such as nursing research (Sharif et al 2018). It is true that some techniques supplant others, because they are more accurate, or require different assumptions, and so on, but the reasons can also be social and the result of training regimes, PhD supervisor influence or the availability of software or applications. For many, once a technique is learned and perfected, they stick with it.

I shall say more about values and methodological choice in Chapter 7, but for the moment my point is a relatively simple one, that all measurements are interpreted with some kind of narrative and only make sense, or make better sense through interpretation.

Jane Elliott, in an excellent book on narrative in social research, considers a number of quantitative approaches, such as event history analysis, optimal matching analysis and person-centred approaches, where narrative is inevitable to make sense of the data. In each of these techniques, the interpretation of context becomes important. As Elliot says of the last approach, "The emphasis is therefore on providing holistic description and retaining a focus on individual lives or careers through time, rather than adopting a more variable centred approach" (Elliott 2005: 94).

In my own research on "living alone" the longitudinal census data, collected at 10 year intervals, of individual trajectories into and out of living alone can only be explained through narratives that inevitably connect with the contemporary social trends at each point. For example, the increase in numbers of people living alone, alongside the steady or increasing numbers of marriages may be explained by the contemporary phenomenon of serial monogamy (Ware et al 2007).

Realist representation – local to global

How do these things translate into "realist closure" and how do we improve on operationalism?

At the beginning of the chapter I fingered the operationalists for defining a characteristic as that which could be measured. But the subsequent discussion indicates a deeper problem with the variable itself. David Byrne (Byrne 2002) focusses on this. Somewhat provocatively he declares "Death to the Variable" (op cit: 29), advancing similar arguments (and indeed also citing Jane Elliott) to those I have made above. His conclusion is to abolish variables in favour of identifying variate traces within specific possibility spaces. Variate traces, unlike variables, are not seen as literal features of what exists and therefore can be measured, but rather indicators of features or processes.

> So what is it then that we measure when we measure what we used to call variables? .... My argument is that we measure traces of the systems that make up reality.
>
> Byrne 2002: 32

This is classically realist and, as I argued in Chapter 2, a key feature of realism is that what is "real" is often hidden, underlying and cannot be directly known. One methodological solution to this is to go back to the individual, as Elliot had earlier remarked (and is cited by Byrne), it is individuals who have the capacity for action and reflection (Elliot 1999: 102). In analysis terms, this leads Byrne towards case-based approaches, rather than variable based and indeed this is a methodological approach that I too have advocated, however I think it is only one tool in the complex realist toolkit, and one I will discuss further in Chapter 9.

However, and whilst not disagreeing with Byrne at all, we do need to measure, even if our measures are "proxies", to use the more conventional term I introduced earlier. There are two things to say: first few of our variables are "universal" and most will be relatively "local". Second, they require interpretation both at the stage of operationalisation and at the stage of analysis.

Some concepts though very few are universal – that is they exist and are capable of operationalisation anywhere in the world *ceteris paribus*, technical issues aside. Those things I mentioned that are grounded not in the social, but in the biological and can become variables that can be measures of reality through time and space. Others are environmental and though subject to social construction, within contexts, are also possible candidates. These might be earnings, hours worked, even educational qualification. However, they can only be valid measures of "reality" within those societies that have money, the concept of paid work or qualifications.

But so many other things cannot be operationalised universally and many of these are meaningful in one place, but not another. Moreover, what they mean in localities can also change through time. Candidates for these might be (as I noted above) ethnicity, homelessness, religion, nationalism, gender roles, human rights.

Then there are concepts like health and illness, which because of their biological basis, exist universally, but are understood culturally and subjectively. Even what counts as illness, or a "disease", changes over time, psychiatric disorders in particular have been reclassified and the numbers of disorders recognised has grown considerably over time (WHO 2018). It is perhaps an irony that classifications aim to be more accurate, comprehensive and universal, at the same time as the contexts in which they are suffered become more complex. Diagnosing mental illness must itself be done in the context of the patient and the diagnosis depends to a great extent on the nature of that context. The more economically "advanced" a society and the more complex it is, the more diagnoses of mental illness there are. Now, does that mean there is less mental illness in lesser "developed" societies, or just that it is not diagnosed/measured? It would seem to follow that the measurement of illness, particularly mental illness, must be within a "local" context, at least within a society that has the same health care regimes and similar socio economic circumstances.

Limiting Long Term Illness (LLTI) has long been a standard measure of morbidity in England Wales. Some areas experience much higher levels of LLTI, for example Wales, this is significantly higher for men than women. There have been a number of attempts to explain and compare this through variable analysis. Martyn Senior (1998) for example (using Census data) controlled for a number of factors: "current and former employment in the coal industry; unskilled and semi-skilled manual occupations as a proxy for life style; a range of deprivation measures designed to reflect lack of wealth and relatively poor housing quality; and a measure of ethnicity" (Senior 1998: 266). In a comparative study, across the UK, these variable still underpredicted LLTI in Wales, but these under predictions were substantially reduced when Welsh nationality[9] was controlled for. The straightforward addition of the "Welsh" nationality variable, produced some level of explanation. Now this does not mean that Welsh nationality itself increases one's probability of LLTI, but the Welsh nationality context matters in a model with the other variables. These are variate traces and can even be discerned from standardised measurements in variable analysis, but the "local" measure of Welsh made the difference.

Senior's analyses suggested a complex interaction between a number of characteristics and it is likely that only some of these were measured and those that were, were proxies for more complex attributes or behaviours.

Let us look a little further at one of these, ethnicity, a concept I mentioned above and in the previous chapter. Although ethnicity is socially constructed by its bearers, social scientists, or both, as with homelessness there is "something going on", and despite the often crudeness of measurement, as I noted earlier, being a member of an ethnic group (as measured) can be a predictor of social, or health advantage, or disadvantage. There is, then, in Roy Bhaskar's terms some kind of "intransitive object" (Bhaskar 2008: 23–24) and we need to find a suitably representative "transitive" object that will adequately (if not perfectly) produce a realist "closure" on the former.

Some ethnic categories are very broad, others are researchers' fictions. The category "White", for example, has in the UK come to stand in for an absence of ethnicity. White is not an ethnic group. There is no "white food", "white dance", "white language". Compare this with, say, "Greek". Greek can be seen to be a social category that it real and meaningful to those who describe themselves as such and therefore the variable Greek is a better representation than "white". There is a closer fit between the instransitive object of Greekness and the transitive object of Greek as a measurement than there is in the case of "white".

A necessary, though not sufficient, condition of a realist approach to operationalisation is that the transitive objects are realistic, that is they are derived from those categories that are real for the agents that the survey researcher will produce predictions and explanations about. This is not much more than construct validity. Nevertheless, an objection to this is that why should we prioritise an individual meaning (say of being Greek) over the researcher's (or anybody else's) definition? Empirically the veracity of an agent's understanding or knowledge may vary, but perhaps there is a principle that in the social world whilst all of the features which comprise social reality cannot be known to each agent, they are each known to one or other agent at some time. When enough of these features are held in common by many agents at the same time, then this seems like evidence for "real" characteristics. Thus, being Greek may be a matter of holding meanings/characteristics individual to one agent, but also a range of meanings/attributes in common with other agents who are also Greek. Greek, as a realistic category, can be identified.

In the specific case of the measurement of ethnicity, the categories must be meaningful to those to whom they apply, even though their understanding of the meaning of being (say Greek) might differ from agent to agent. This means that in any given location prior work must be done to establish what the meaningful ethnic categories might be and in this there will be an inevitable "localism", whereby in one locality one utilises different categories.

But surely, one might say, that this precludes comparison because validity becomes completely localised? This need not be the case in practice because "local categories" can be sub-categories, allowing the possibility of both local analysis and macro-level comparison. Indeed, this is somewhat similar to the categorisation used in the New Zealand Census (Williams and Husk 2013: 9).

This in itself is not exclusively a "realist operationalisation", but it is an operationalisation that better facilitates realist analysis. Realist operationalisation is grounded in the theorisation of objects, but this theorisation must be based on empirical evidence. It is not a once and for all task. The variables measured may be evidence for underlying regularities, but the latter are not fixed, but themselves complex and emergent.

Theories

The inevitability of theory has been an underlying theme throughout the book so far. Perhaps it is this that most divides realism from empiricism. Empiricists do not ignore theory, but they see it as a separate matter to observation and testing. Realists, on the other hand, see theory as both central and a dynamic interrelationship between it and observation and testing. The relationship is both more holistic and less formal. In the above I have tried to show how measurement is cannot be separated from context. But also, measures and concepts are the product of theory and theory is shaped through measurement. This is not a restatement of the DN, or covering law model, it is much richer than that.

Sometimes it feels that the social sciences have had too much theory. My own discipline (though I should say I'm on the edge of it) of sociology, has often wallowed in theory that is little more than punditry with long words. Empirical appraisal of a social situation is conducted from an armchair and societal level conclusions follow. As John Goldthorpe, is reputed to have remarked, theory is too important to be left to the theorists. So, when I speak of theory, I do not speak of grand theory, that is the abstract and ambitious theories of functionalism, Marxism,[10] critical theory and so on. The problem with these theories is twofold: firstly they are far from "local", in the sense I meant above and usually have ambitions to provide explanations valid in all or many societies. For the same reasons I set out above, in respect of the operationalisation of concepts, I do not think this is feasible. Secondly and possibly more importantly, it is difficult to derive testable propositions from them. One of the easier concepts in Marxism to operationalise is alienation and, as de Vaus suggested, above, this is extremely difficult and open to multiple definitions and interpretations.

What I mean by theory is much closer to what natural scientists mean by theory. Though unlike natural science theory, I think that virtually any testable theory will only be capable of explaining specific concepts limited by time and space. I do not rule out that some elements of such theory can have explanatory power that extend widely through time and space. What I have in mind is, as you might suppose, Merton's "middle range theory".

Robert Merton described middle range theories as those

> That lie between the minor but necessary working hypotheses that evolve in abundance during day-to-day research and the all inclusive systematic efforts to develop a unified theory that will explain all the observed uniformities of social behaviour, social organization and social change
>
> Merton 1967: 39

Middle range theory allows the testing of "minor theories" that in themselves may have only relatively limited explanatory scope, but can cumulate to provide wider and deeper explanations. Middle range should generate testable generalisations from one context to another. As Ray Pawson notes "abstraction" is the key here. We need to be able to say that if P holds under circumstances S, then it can also explain Q. However, as Pawson goes on to say this does not solve a major problem of theory in empiricism. He describes it as a "flat ontology", that is "concepts may be said to be 'flattened' in the sense that they do not discriminate between the different layers of social reality" (Pawson 2000: 290). To return to the example of ethnicity above, ethnicity as measured, even when a "local" dimension is incorporated into its definition, does not capture the underlying processes that it seeks to represent as a variable. Ethnicity, as a variable, stands in for a complex mesh of meanings embedded in historically dynamic cultural forms. We may, for example, regard "Pakistani" as a valid ethnic description of people who identify as members of this ethnic group. But what this means to a 70 year old first generation migrant, from Pakistan, to the UK and what it means to an 18 year old "third generation" Pakistani, in the UK, who may never have visited the country of his or her grandparents, is very different.

Theories are inevitably developed from a perspective. This may arise as a result of the observation of a phenomenon, possibly because it is considered a social problem. For example, a falling birth rate may be seen as a social problem, because of the socio-demographic impacts at a future time, such as skills shortages, rural depopulation and so on. So, explanations of this are only sought because it's a problem and its theorisation begins from that perspective. Consequently, the descriptions and explanations that are the outcomes of the research depend on the theoretical position adopted.

But, turn this on its head. If we observe particular phenomena, perhaps through descriptions. Say, for example, demographic data over time indicated a falling birth rate, more than one theory could explain the data. Rarely, in social science, is there a simple uncontested fit between theory and data. Theory is under-determined by the data.

Counterurbanisation an example

Before I suggest some ways that we might approach this problem, let me illustrate this with an example. The example, that of Counterurbanisation, comes from population geography.

For much of the 20th century, in much of Europe and North America, the movement of population was from rural areas to cities and towns, as these settlements became major centres of manufacturing and commerce. But in the 1960s, first in the United States, population geographers began to notice an opposite trend developing and finally becoming the dominant form of population movement. This was termed "counterurbanisation" (Berry 1976)

Berry's discovery, that this had become the dominant migratory pattern, was serendipitous, but as further work progressed, became a good example of testable middle range theory, that could begin with the "local", but could be testable more globally over time. Indeed, much of the subsequent work focussed on Western Europe and furthermore the flow and rate of population movement varied from country to country (Rowe et al 2019). Whilst the UK, for example, was dominated by counterurbanisation flows, in France, even in the 1980s, urbanisation and rural depopulation was dominant.

Counterurbanisation theory might be summarised as "a process of population deconcentration … a movement from a state of more concentration to a state of less concentration" (Berry 1976: 17). It is the opposite of urbanisation and will become the dominant form of movement in advanced industrialised and post-industrial societies.

Although counterurbanisation theory generated testable hypotheses, the data have often been confusing and contradictory.

Initially researchers in the UK and United States claimed to have identified clear evidence of population movement from urban to rural areas (Robert and Randolph 1983), but questions arose on how this was defined and measured (Vining and Kontuly 1978). Is moving 20 kilometres from a city, counterurbanisation or must it be 100 kilometres? What population density is "rural" and what is "urban"? Two definitions are now routinely applied and give rather similar results, those of "clean break", where a migrant is moving beyond a defined near metropolitan area (Coombes et al 1989) and population deconcentration, where movements in the whole of a country (initially the UK) was measured according functional zones and areas of metropolitan influence. However, as with any spatial measurement, "lines" must be drawn, such as regional or city boundaries, whereby person A is classed as a "migrant", because they are beyond such a boundary and person B, not a migrant, because they did not move across that boundary. An example of this is the regional boundary between Wiltshire (in the UK South West region) and Berkshire (in the UK South East region). A move of just 100 metres could constitute "counterurbanisation"! Furthermore, the kind of settlement may actually be more "urban" in the destination (say a medium-sized town in the UK South West region) as compared to the location of origin, a small village in the UK South East region.

A second issue arose, again about measurement and definition, that of motivation to migrate. Migration could either be for economic reasons, such as the relocation of enterprises, or "environmental", whereby migrants chose to move for reasons of lifestyle, or to rejoin friends or family (Perry et al 1986). Again, such decision making is not readily discernible from attitudinal or behavioural research. A respondent may move for a mixture of reasons, that intertwine economic and environmental concerns and their post move attitudes and behaviour recall may be subject to rational reconstruction.

The story of counterurbanisation theory is perhaps typical of middle range theories. They may arise from accidental observation or informal hunches, then they develop into theories that purport of explain phenomena in one location, or in one social group and enjoy some empirical success, then their testing in further locations or times, throws up anomalies, requiring further amendments. Over time they may then be superseded by successor theories. One of the most important UK researchers or counterurbanisation, Tony Champion, suggested the description population deconcentration better captures what is going on (Champion 2001), that generally there is a movement from more urban locations to less urban – not necessarily rural ones. But this suggestion retains only the broadest feature of counterurbanisation. Most would nevertheless agree that counterurbanisation takes on different forms in different societies.

One might conclude that counterurbanisation is a quintessentially complex process. Widespread macro-level patterns, like turbulence flows, are readily discernible, but composition of migration flows, in the case of counterurbanisation, encapsulates differing lengths of migratory moves, structural factors in the economy, house price differentials, destination location imagery (as more prosperous or environmentally attractive) with a multitude of individual subjective (or indeed intersubjective) reasonings. Local "strange attractors" can be discerned, such as an almost uninterrupted migration flow from South East England into Cornwall (in the far South West) for over 50 years. Here data indicates an extremely complex mix of environmental and economic factors, combined with fluctuating "push" and "pull" motivations from origins to destinations that demonstrate different layers of "reality", from individual motivations and understanding, meso-level economic drivers and the broader economy at different times. Often, in counterurbanisation, data runs ahead of theories and in turn challenges earlier theoretical assumptions. But more of this in Chapter 8.

There is one last twist to counterurbanisation as a middle range theory. Although it is classically complex, in its broad features of migratory motivation it fits well with another higher level and broader, yet testable, theory of the migratory elite.

This proposes that those persons who migrate are those in the originating society that will have the economic or social capital to permit migration. In other words, the migrants will not be the "poorest" in the originating society (Musgrove 1963). Though, as with counterurbanisation, this theory requires specification for different local contexts. An "elite" in the originating location will be subject to different definitions because the societies themselves will differ greatly. Compare, for example, skilled migrants from newer European Union countries to Western Europe with migrants from sub Saharan Africa, who pay for illegal transportation, into European countries. Both are "elites", in

Musgrove's sense, because they had forms of capital to permit migration. But the resemblance stops there.

Moreover, not all members of a potential migratory elite, will migrate and there will likely be more non-migrants in this category, in the originating country, than migrants. Lastly, not everyone who migrates will have the specified "elite" characteristics and may actually have fewer resources than those who remain. In other words the higher level theory is also probabilistic.

Nevertheless, the theory is testable and in very many locations is confirmed, at least at a macro-level. I will return to the example of counterurbanisation in respect of mechanisms in Chapter 8.

Closing in on closure

In this chapter I have considered how we can represent social reality. Survey researchers have, for the most part, claimed to do this through operationalisation. But operationalisation is still much influenced by *operationalism*, the doctrine that a concept is that which we can measure. It is inevitable that we must represent reality, through theories and measurement and our theories and measurements will never achieve a one to one correspondence between what is and our conceptions of it. Yet *operationalism* defines the world as what we can measure and is deeply inadequate approach, because measurement is predicated on a single description and the possibilities of measurement change over time. More sophisticated operationalisations, do accept that singular measurements cannot capture deeper realities, but these too are subject to an informal naïve realism, which simply "reads off reality" from measurements. I demonstrated this in respect of ethnicity. One single measure of ethnicity cannot capture its dynamic complexity.

Measurement and theory are bound up together. Both are social constructions, but the intention is to close in on reality through theoretically informed "realist operationalisation". In this "local" and amendable measurements are derived from middle range theories, which offer explanations of phenomena within limited social, geographical and historical parameters, but can be tested under other parameters to establish whether the explanations have a wider currency. What I have, therefore, proposed is a version of "local realism" that may have trans-local features and is a version of Merton's "middle range theory".

This, I believe, goes some way towards realist closure, but it does leave us with two major difficulties. The first of these is the problem of the "underdetermination" of theory, which can be discerned in the counterurbanisation example, but at the same time data anomalies arise that cannot be explained by the existing theory, even in its several variants. The second, the criticism of middle range theory, made by Ray Pawson, that it is a "flat ontology", that fails to grasp deeper realties. In other words, the terms of the theory under explain what is going on, because what is going on must be explained in relation to other aspects of reality beyond the theory.

To achieve a methodology that will provide realist closure, these problems must be addressed.

In the next chapter I will focus on the first of these problems, that of the verification or falsification of theories. In Chapter 8 I will address the second problem, by considering theories and measurement in relation to underlying mechanisms.

Notes

1 Though this is very much more the case in the natural than social sciences, precise measurements and procedures are often differentially interpreted or applied. Anthropological studies of scientists have shown the importance of things like translation and inscription of concepts/ procedures within interacting networks of "things" ideas and people, which have formed the basis of Actor Network Theory (Latour 1986, 2005).
2 At the time of writing there was a vigorous debate on the measurement of biological sex versus gender. See https://www.tandfonline.com/doi/full/10.1080/13645579.2020.1768343 (Accessed 16/06/20) and https://www.tandfonline.com/doi/10.1080/13645579.2020.1768346. Accessed 16/06/20.
3 Though a note of caution here. That a number of people hold that something is a fact must, nevertheless, be subject to empirical testing. Coherence of opinion is not necessarily the truth of the matter (see Chapter Two).
4 There are separate censuses for England and Wales, Scotland and Northern Ireland.
5 See: https://www.ons.gov.uk/methodology/classificationsandstandards/otherclassifications/thenationalstatisticssocioeconomicclassificationnssecrebasedonsoc2010. Accessed 15/06/2020.
6 See: https://www.ons.gov.uk/census/censustransformationprogramme/consultations/the2021censusinitialviewoncontentforenglandandwales Accessed. 15/06/2020.
7 But what about those without occupations? An earlier filter question is used to screen out these respondents.
8 The technique rests on the principle of two or more independent observations of the same population. These observations can be simultaneously of two sources that represent approximately the same population, or they can be of the same source at two time points. In the latter case the observations should be at approximately the same time. In order to estimate the size of the population (Nt) the researcher needs to know the number of persons observed at the first count (N1) the number of persons observed at the second (N2) [or subsequent counts] and the number observed at both (M) [or each of subsequent] counts. Thus the estimate of the population (Nt) is: N t = (N1 X N2)/M (Williams 2010)
9 'Welsh Nationality, in the Senior paper refers to Question 10 in the 1991 Census "Country of Birth".
10 I have included Marxism here, not so much to indicate Marx's own works, but the massive edifice of occult and often antagonistic theory that followed. Actually, I think that Marx's concept of historical materialism is empirically useful, because it allows for different historical and developmental modulations.

6

Theory choice – verification, falsification and inference

Theories are social constructions, but they are not fantasies, at least middle range theories are not, because they propose testable consequences, which should show whether they are right, wrong, or partially right. However, it's not as simple as that. The overall problem is that a number of different theories can be consistent with the data we have (the problem of under-determination I mentioned in the previous chapter) and even at the same time, we can have data for which there is no available theoretical explanation. The focus of this chapter is on how we might discriminate between theories and how we might develop a theoretical framework from individual theories, that might then provide viable and testable inferences about deeper realities. The chapter will not finish this task, because this strategy is dependent upon identifying social mechanisms (the topic of Chapter 9) and a realist approach to objectivity (the topic of Chapter 7).

The social and psychological basis of theory choice

In the previous chapter I described how the DN (deductive nomological) or covering law model claimed that an explanation can be deduced from a set of true statements, one of which should be a law. This is difficult enough in the natural sciences and all but impossible in the social sciences, where laws are rare, if existent at all and even generalisations of invariances will be far from universal. The DN model was, at best, an ideal type and became largely discredited in the 1960s, with the demise of logical positivism. The logical positivists had wanted to all but hermetically seal scientific reasoning from social and psychological externalities, but this became unravelled through the work of several philosophers of science, who in quite different ways, demonstrated that scientific knowledge does not progress in an orderly way through history and that social and psychological factors play an important role. Two of these philosophers are directly important to the case I set out in this book – Karl Popper and Imre Lakatos. However,

I will first briefly describe the ideas of two others, Norwood Russell Hanson and Thomas Kuhn, because their work indirectly influenced much subsequent thinking, especially in social science, about observation, theories and the progress of science in a social context and, as we will see, the latter's argument about reasoning has a direct relevance to a realist approach to theory choice.

Norwood Russell Hanson

Hanson's ideas were the first major challenge to logical positivism, at least in the English speaking world[1] (Hanson 1981[1958]). Nowadays Hanson's ideas are mainstream when we consider the relationship between observation and theory. The gist of his claim was simple, that what we observe is filtered through the lens of our prior knowledge and experience. He used the concept of the optical illusion to illustrate his point. For example, the famous duck-rabbit illusion can look like a duck or rabbit, and which it is due to the perspective of the observer. It follows that our prior expectations will influence what we observe and how we observe it. Take for example the reading of an X-ray. A lay person, or even a medical student, will see much less or not see what is important, compared to an experienced doctor. Because the X-ray will be of a particular part of the body, a doctor will bring prior experience and medical training to bear on the observation. Michael Polanyi (1973: 101) describes how a medical student begins observations with puzzlement, but listening to the commentary of doctors experienced in the field will gradually see the picture differently, in light of understanding their descriptions. I mentioned this in relation to the interpretation of simple regression, in statistics, in Chapter 2.

Hanson, (unlike Popper), to whom I will turn below, did not believe we begin from a theory, but rather that the scientist begins from observation (Hanson 1981: 70–71) and later develops, or fits the observation to the theory (or in his words the hypothesis). But, the observations are not *tabula rasa*, but originate in prior experience and practice, and there is a reasoning process between observation and theory. Berry's "discovery" of the counterurbanisation process (discussed in the last chapter) was serendipitous, but whilst he was not looking for a pattern of population turnaround, he was still looking at migration patterns with his geographer's training and experience.

Theories do not usually simply emerge from the scientist or social scientist's fertile imagination. What comes first, theory or observation, is not answerable, because as I suggested in the previous chapter, theory and observation are intertwined. Hanson was not saying we cannot, or should not believe our senses, but rather when we speak of "seeing" this must involve our prior beliefs and knowledge.

Thomas Kuhn

Kuhn's focus was much less on the specifics of science, such as observation, and more on its history. Prior to Kuhn the zeitgeist of science was that it was both rational and progressive. That observation and theorisation produce a pattern of discovery and confirmation that drew scientists ever closer to the truth. His book *The Structure of Scientific Revolutions* (Kuhn 1970) had an enormous impact in challenging these assumptions. Karl Popper was an intellectual contemporary of Kuhn and in his essay "The Aim of Science" (Popper 1979: 191–205) he describes physics as a progression of scope, detail and successful prediction. His example of this is Galilean physics, but as George Couvalis observes (Couvalis 1997: 87) the actuality of this was that Galilean predictions were only successful within a narrow domain and were widely off the mark beyond that domain. For example, he asserted that that the rate of acceleration of an object in free fall is constant, but as Isaac Newton correctly found, as objects come closer to the earth their acceleration increases. Whilst the description of the falling of objects was correct, other than matter of acceleration, other aspects of Galilean physics were completely wrong, that (for example) a missile launched over a long distance will describe a parabola in its trajectory, when in fact it describes an ellipse. Yet, it is the case that Galileo's physics was more successful in its explanations and predictions than Aristotelian physics, much of it was wrong in respect of later Newtonian physics, and this too was in import respects supplanted by Einsteinian physics.

Popper's version of this is that there is a meta-rationality that guides scientific progress of criticism and refutation that allows scientific progress to build and develop through time. Although, as we shall see Popper's ideas were themselves revolutionary, there was something of an orthodoxy in his general view of scientific progress he shared with the logical positivists.

Kuhn challenged these kinds of claims of scientific progress. As the title of his book suggests, Kuhn believed that there were "revolutions in science", in which whole orthodoxies of thinking, reasoning and researching were overturned.

Pre-scientific thinking (in particular disciplines and in science more generally) produced a "normal science", in which theoretical assumptions, investigative tools and procedures were developed and agreed. What Kuhn called a "paradigm" developed, in which these things were unchallenged, because they were productive in producing new discoveries and explanations. Normal science is good at "puzzle solving", but eventually errors, anomalies and un-solvable puzzles will lead to a crisis in the "normal science" and someone (or several scientists) will propose radical new ideas, that ignore the normative assumptions of the paradigm and there is revolution. Then, post-revolution, a new normal science is established and the pattern repeats itself.

As, in the case of Popper, Kuhn's emphasis is the history of physics and what we might call the "heroic" physics of the great discoverers, such as Newton or Maxwell and the subsequent "paradigms" that were established on Newton or Maxwell's laws.

Accounts of "heroic" physics often paint a picture of scientific work that depends on clear rules, procedures and structures. But Kuhn, following Wittgenstein (Wittgenstein 1953), maintained that paradigms were more like a game, recognisable in its broad characteristics, but one where necessary and sufficient conditions of what counts as that game cannot be articulated, that in fact much of science was based on "tacit knowledge". That scientists, like people in informal everyday situations, use "tacit knowledge", is now widely accepted and indeed how this is done has been explored in detail by sociologists – particularly effectively by Harry Collin (Collins 2010). But what do we mean by tacit knowledge?

Tacit knowledge is not just psychological, but it is also social because though (by definition) not codified, it is passed on. I remember my mentor, the excellent social statistician, Angela Dale, suggesting I "eyeball" the data. I did not initially get what she meant, because there are no precise rules for this procedure, but rather the seeking of patterns, anomalies and interesting things. It's something you get better at the more you do it, but the better you get, the harder it is to articulate your own procedure for doing it. Moreover, I can attest that if you don't do it often enough, you get out of practice, but you don't forget. Like riding a bike. How do you keep balance? If you don't ride for a while you are a bit more wobbly, but you don't forget.

I have talked of tacit knowledge for two reasons. Firstly, it demonstrates very clearly how science is not just a social construction as an enterprise in itself, that was born of particular historic and material developments (Williams 2000a: Chapter 2), but that within itself science socially constructs and much of its procedures and thus, discoveries, involve a large component of social-psychological interplay. Secondly, and I will come to this below, it can and should play an important role in inference.

Despite the sophistication and subtlety of Kuhn's account of scientific "progress" it was heavily criticised, particularly for the relativist implications of his account (Doppelt 1978). How can there be "progress" in science, if all of the work and procedures on one paradigm can be completely overturned by revolution? A new paradigm is really not better than the one it overturns? Is there no progress in science? Sociologists of science later embraced this apparent consequence of Kuhn's reasoning, some concluding that there could be no demarcation between what we called "science" and (say) astrology (Barnes and Bloor 2002). Indeed, Kuhn himself, in a postscript to the second edition of his book, maintain that later scientific theories are better than earlier ones for solving puzzles, because they are applied in different environments (Kuhn 1970: 206).

Whether we should take Kuhn as a relativist or not is less important here than a more central idea of whether, given the undoubted social content of science, our theory – observation procedures can build knowledge over time? Both Hanson and Kuhn did a great service by establishing the importance of social and psychological factors in this process.

Falsification

Falsification resurrects a problem identified by David Hume, that is the problem of induction, I considered in Chapter 2. Logically, no amount of observations of a phenomenon can conclusively confirm the characteristics of that phenomenon. Famously, this principle was upheld by the first sightings of black swans in Australia. Hitherto, it was believed, that all swans were white. One sighting of a swan that was not white was sufficient to falsify the statement – "all swans are white". As I explained, though Hume identified the logical problem of induction, he saw inductive reasoning as an inevitable psychological trait in humans.

It was Karl Popper who identified this as a problem for science and developed it into a methodology (Popper 1959a). Popper's initial views on falsification were shaped by logical positivism of the Vienna circle and the theoretical claims of psychoanalysis and Marxism. Indeed, Popper claimed it was his concept of falsification that killed off logical positivism. Popper wanted to find a demarcation criteria between science and non-science. During his youth, in Vienna, Marxism and psychoanalysis were very influential and both claimed to be scientific. But, Popper pointed out (Popper 1976: 31–37) that in each completely opposing evidence was marshalled to support theoretical claims, rendering Marxism and psychoanalysis, unfalsifiable. Their theories were specified in such a way that they could not be wrong.

Popper, restating Hume's problem, said that whilst no amount of evidence could finally show a theory to be true, just one empirical counter instance could show a theory to be false. The black swan, for example. On this simple logical point, Popper built his philosophy of science, that of conjectures and refutations. Science, he maintained, proceeds through criticism. Bold conjectures about how the world is are tested in the most rigorous way, by the scientist, and if they fail these tests, then they are falsified and the theory is shown to be wrong. What Popper was proposing was an almost Darwinian selection process amongst theories and indeed later in his career, he built this into an evolutionary theory of knowledge (Popper 1979).

If, having been exposed to the most rigorous of tests, a theory is not falsified, then it is corroborated for the time being, but certainly never confirmed. Popper's pivotal example was Einstein's theory of general relativity and a "crucial" experiment, carried out by Arthur Eddington in 1919. The implication of Einstein's theory was that light should bend when it passes near to massive gravitational objects, such as the sun. It followed from this that a star, situated behind the sun, would be appear displaced from where it was normally be observed by this bending. Eddington set up an experiment to test this conjecture, by observing an eclipse in Africa. The light was duly bent and Einstein's predictions were shown to be correct. Popper, used this fairly straightforward example, to claim that if the light had not been bent, then the theory of relativity would have been falsified.

This, for Popper, was a bold conjecture, a theory that claimed a lot and made risky predictions. But things are far from that simple and Popper's early views of falsification, were seen as naïve. Even a simple appeal to the kind of "heroic" science Popper, Kuhn (and their contemporaries) cited as evidence, would show that theories are often multi-faceted and whilst some parts of a theory may be refuted, other parts survived. We see this in the case of Galileo and Newton. The gist of the former's theory of gravitation was right in many respects, but wrong in respect of acceleration. Newtonian laws of gravity, which supplanted Galileo work perfectly well on earth, but become a limiting case within a broader framework of Einsteinian relativity.

Whilst it is reasonable to aim for a theory to have as much falsifiable content as possible and a simple, yet ambitious theory which explains more than its predecessor, is to be preferred, in practice theory development is much more messy than this and only some parts of the theory will be immediately falsifiable, but these once tested may provide greater clarity and precision to other parts of the theory, making these more open to testing as they are developed. The counterurbanisation theory, I described in the previous chapter, began with a relatively falsifiable premise, that developed societies population movement would shift from rural to urban, to urban to rural. Within the limits of particular societies, North America and the UK, in particular, this theory was confirmed. But, when applied to other societies, it was falsified (see Chapter 5). The theory could be saved by better specifying "developed". Later other conjectures about what counted as migration, or urban/rural, reasons for migration, were all tested and either falsified or corroborated, but certainly the theories were amended.

Often theories are amended with "ad hoc" modifications, that is modifications that are proposed to simply "save" the theory, but have no basis in the theory itself, or observations. Popper's hero, Einstein, was guilty of just this when he added in the cosmological constant,[2] to his General Theory of Relativity, to allow for the existence of a static universe. This was an ad hoc number, but decades later, it would seem it helps to account for the presence of "dark matter" in the universe.

If physics cannot be relied upon to provide a tenable model for falsification, then the social sciences (and indeed biology and organic chemistry) certainly could not aspire to this and if Popper stuck to his original criterion of falsification, then the social sciences and several natural sciences could not be deemed scientific.

Several sciences and most of all, social science, also rely on inference through statistics, which means that simple falsifiable statement of the kind P or nor P cannot be made and moreover, as I have shown, the ontology of the social world is subject to complex change through time and space, so rarely can such simple bold conjectures be made that will hold to falsify a theory completely, or corroborate it other than locally. Even a simple regression line (and as I have suggested these are often too simple to adequately explain a phenomenon) will rarely produce a large positive, or negative correlation and there will nearly always be outliers. Plot the regression line, with the same variables, at a different time and place and quite likely there will be a better fit, or many more outliers. Even if we accept that a theory has been falsified (say because there was no positive correlation), what about if it is tested again and a positive correlation results? Does this mean that the falsification is now falsified? Probability is the enemy of falsification, at least in the latter's simpler formulation.

Naïve falsificationism is an easy target and the meat and drink of Philosophy of Science 101, but the baby should not be thrown out with the bathwater! Popper, himself, in his later writings develops a much more sophisticated approach to falsification, which at least tacitly accepts temporary confirmation and that theories may be partially falsified, and as we have seen the issue of probability became a central focus (Popper 1959b, 1983). Moreover, it might be said that real advances are made when bold conjectures are confirmed and cautious ones are falsified and the converse is true, the refutation of a bold conjecture and the confirmation of a cautious one, do not constitute real advances and both are readily achieved. At the heart of falsification, there seems to be a fact about science (and one that can be applied in other spheres) that we learn from our mistakes. And when I say "we", I mean a broader investigative community, through time. I may set out to find as much confirmatory evidence as I can to support my theory, but assuming that theory is taken seriously, it becomes a public statement of how I believe the world is and there is nothing I can do to prevent someone else producing data to show I am wrong. I'll come back to this in Chapter 7. So, even if Popper was wrong in his specific assertions about how a theory is tested and falsified in its entirety, as a result of a crucial experiment, perhaps over time more successful theories survive and less successful ones, first struggle and then are finally eliminated. But it is rarely a simple linear process. One last example from astronomy demonstrates this.

Most astronomers and physicists in the early 20th century (including Einstein), believed that the universe was in a "steady state", but doubt was cast upon this view, with the discovery of "red shift", that the wavelength of light is shifted towards the red end of the spectrum, suggesting that as light reaches us from other galaxies, they are moving apart from us (rather like a police siren stretches and diminishes as it moves away from us). The unit of measurement to show this was proposed by Edwin Hubble (Hubble 1929) – the Hubble Constant. The idea became known as the "Big Bang", suggesting the universe began at a finite point and expanded. Initially, this idea was widely challenged, but over time the evidence for the "Big Bang" piled up, leaving very few supporters of "steady state" theory. Amongst them was Fred Hoyle, an English astronomer. Gradually Hoyle's position became lonelier. He proposed a modification, suggesting expansion might be "local", but this too was challenged. "Steady state" theory, Fred Hoyle's version of it and Hoyle himself are now dead![3]

Research programmes

Imre Lakatos was very much influenced by Popper and developed a version of falsificationism, that like the example above depended upon the *long durée*. In my view, his position avoids the simplifications of naïve falsification, but also the potential relativism of Kuhn's approach.

Lakatos introduced the concept of the research programme (Lakatos 1978). This is perhaps not as grand and epoch defining as Kuhn's paradigms, but as with Kuhn it embodies a core of principles which are the defining characteristics of the programme. A perhaps somewhat contentious, but nevertheless illustrative example from social science, would be that of Marxism. Whilst there are many versions of Marxism and indeed at least two in Marx's own work, there are a few core principles that are defining, for example the importance of the economic base determining social relations, the centrality of class struggle and the concept of the historical dialectic.

Whilst other aspects of Marxism might be contested and possibly refuted, through empirical example, the core of the research programme remains untouched.[4] In any research programme elements of, what Lakatos referred to as the "protective belt", may be falsified, without damaging the core. But, if the core is successfully challenged, then the research programme is, like Kuhn's paradigms, finished and a new research programme, or programmes will replace it.

Lakatos uses the term "heuristic" to describe the rules of an investigative programme. A "positive" heuristic are the things that should be done, such as particular methods and methodologies, and a negative heuristic, the things that should be avoided. In social science, for example, there are rules about particular statistic procedures around the general linear model. This provides the researcher with a range of tools to test theories empirically. But what about if the general linear model is challenged, as is the case by some realists (see Chapter 4)? Does this constitute an attack on the "core" of the methodological research programme?

Finally, Lakatos proposes that once a research programme is established, it should produce fruitful results. It is then "progressive". Although falsification is legitimate, Lakatos, equally emphasises the importance of confirmation within research programmes, though of course these may later become falsified. When a research programme ceases to produce fruitful results and its protective hypotheses become challenged, then this is a degenerating research programme and in due course, its core may be challenged.

Lakatos's work might help us to see falsification in two different ways, that are of value to understanding and developing a realist social science. The first is closer to Popper's original idea of falsification and it is specific theories, within a "research programme" being subjected to rigorous testing, which they may fail. This may occur very locally and involve just one, or a very few researchers, working on a problem. The second refers to a whole body of research, that over a long period may turn out to be wrong in respect of its central claims. This falsification would not (I can't think of a counter example) be the result of a crucial test, or experiment, but through the gradual erosion of the empirical–theoretical credibility of the programme. This is not to say there will be none of John Worrall's "elderly holdouts" – such as Fred Hoyle in physics, or that elements of the programme might not be resurrected later. Furthermore, single tests and their subsequent falsifications or confirmations are examples of Pawson's "flat ontology", they can only access one, or at best a few, elements of social reality. A better picture of the depth and breadth of social reality, above all, takes time.

When trying to think of non-trivial examples in social science, of a Lakatosian, research programme one is not struck by an abundance of examples. Two things seem to get in the way. Firstly, that quite viable research programmes go out of fashion. Functionalism in anthropology might be one. But these are not like the examples from natural science, where once they are dead, they stay dead. In social science, they often come back later, and become fashionable again. Secondly, social science programmes are hampered by the almost complete lack of replication of studies (there are honourable exceptions) (Freese and Peterson 2017), so again programmes are not fully articulated, or subjected to enough empirical scrutiny, before the social science community gets bored with them. But in social research methods, particularly quantitative methods, with the advent of big data, we may be witnessing the end of one "research programme" and the beginning of a new one.

I suspect that if I were writing this book twenty years from now, I would say that our ways of statistically modelling the social world that dominate now, will be seen as not up to the job of capturing the complexity we know now is the hallmark of social reality. Well … to some extent I'm saying this now, but there is too much "noise", to be able to say definitively we are at the end of one methodological era and the beginning of another. Brian Castellani persuasively argues just this in an article provocatively entitled *Complexity and the Failure of Quantitative Social Science* (Castellani 2014). In this paper, Castellani, as I have done in this book, begins from the premise that the ontological character of the social world is that it is complex and the quantitative approaches we have used in the past are not up to the job of modelling complex data. Yet, we still hang on to our traditional methods and teach them to new generations of students. Castellani, is not necessarily talking about "big data", but his argument most certainly applies to this. In a provocative paper in the journal Sociology, in 2007, Mike Savage and Roger Burrows questioned whether the advent of big data and transactional data (data gathered from customer transactions, etc.) present a methodological crisis for sociology (and of course by implication allied disciplines) (Savage and Burrows 2007). I'll say more about this in Chapter 9.

Since Savage and Burrows published their paper, both the number of data sources, the size of these datasets and the technologies to analyse them has dramatically escalated. One of the areas that has developed rapidly is the analysis of new social media data. Over the last two decades technological innovation in digital communications has shifted from information to participation, and social networking, blogging and micro blogging, provide both a rich source of data for social research, but also methodological challenges. Some have suggested that these data and their methods of analysis can be treated as a surrogate for more traditional research designs and analyses. Whilst others believe these may be tools that can augment the latter (Edwards et al 2013).

Finally, and quite separately (and mainly in psychology) the concept of significance testing has been under sustained assault for the last few years. The case against significance testing goes back to the 1970s. Back then Ronald Carver advocated abandoning all statistical significance testing and returning to the examination of data and the replication of research, rather than relying on statistical significance testing to validate results (Carver 1978). In more recent years, the target of criticism has been hypothesis testing, primarily used in experiments, but also less often in the analysis of survey data.

Statistical hypotheses allow the researcher to accept or reject a hypothesis, thus emulating the laboratory procedure of the natural sciences, whereby a hypothesis is either confirmed or falsified. A statistical hypothesis is initially posed negatively and is called the null hypothesis (its opposite is usually called the alternative hypothesis). If something is found to be statistically significant then the researcher *rejects* the null hypothesis and *accepts* the alternative one.

Gerd Gigerenzer et al (2004) has questioned the rigour and efficacy of hypothesis testing and suggest the following parody of the procedure that is followed:

1. Set up a statistical null hypothesis of "no mean difference" or "zero correlation". Don't specify the predictions of your research hypothesis or of any alternative substantive hypotheses.
2. Use 5% as a convention for rejecting the null. If significant, accept your research hypothesis.
3. Always perform this procedure.

op cit: 392

There are two objections contained in his criticism: (a) the arbitrariness of the significance level (which wrongly often then becomes associated with substantive significance; (b) the tendency to accept the alternative hypothesis on the grounds that the null one was falsified! In other words, the test says nothing about the confirmatory level of the alternative or research hypothesis.

I don't want to get too carried away with this notion of the end of one "research programme" and the beginning of another in quantitative social science and indeed I will argue in Chapter 9 for the continued value, at least for the present, of some of our more traditional methods, but my general point remains, that the theory-research process, the confirmation and refutation of theories is a social act, that exists within a particular scientific and historical context. An understanding and explanation of social reality requires the attention span of the social scientific community over a long period. In this respect, I find the analogy of research programmes, or something like that, a useful framework for thinking about a pluralist approach to the theory–testing relationship, that can combine more informal and even tacit knowledge, with more formal methodological procedures.

A realist methodological framework

In the second part of this chapter I will propose a methodological framework that is grounded in research programmes over time and space. It retains the idea of Popper's conjectures and refutations, perhaps more in spirit, than the letter, it reintroduces middle range theory and it introduces two other methodological concepts, reflexivity and inference. I will begin with these two latter concepts.

Reflexivity

Positivist approaches to methodology stressed a formal to science and social science (things like the DN model, or the importance of statistical techniques, such as significance testing). I don't want to dismiss this formalism entirely, because good science still depends on rigour and some standardisation of method. But through this chapter, and to an extent the previous one, was the need to move beyond formalism. Realism's weakness and strength is its need to rely on unobservables. In other words, formal methods will partially describe the world, but they will under describe it. As I suggested, in the previous chapter (and following others such as David Byrne and Jane Elliot), interpretation is central to methods and methodology. In realism, that interpretation is what binds together theory and measurement. There can be no measurement without some theory and theory without measurement is indulgence. The social science equivalent of fantasy football!

Moreover, we do our social science within a social context, because science itself is a social construct, albeit one that can transcend that context. I will say much more about this in Chapter 7. How do we interpret our theories, our methodology, our measurements? How do we achieve the critical stance that can produce falsifiable statements and the most rigorous tests? Furthermore, how do we as researchers, locate ourselves in both the milieu of social science research and within the context of those we research? It is often said that this is achieved through reflexivity.

Reflexivity, at least as applied in social research, is an act of self-reference, a psychological and social accounting procedure that is said to lead to more authentic research. Usually it is framed as an individual act, but one deeply embedded in a social milieu (see e.g. Archer 2007, 2012, May 1999).

Reflexivity is deployed in several different ways as a methodological tool, substantive property of social systems, or source of individual enlightenment (Lynch 2000). Here, I will consider only its methodological use and as with falsification, I will not rehearse, in any great depth, its development or deployment.

Although reflexivity, either in name or at least as a concept, has been around a long time, the 1980s marked, what has become known as the "reflexive turn". One can see its antecedents in twentieth century sociology in the "bracketing" strategy of phenomenology, or the agnosticism of ethnomethodology. Indeed, the tradition of interpretive sociology has always had, at its heart, a questioning of, or a search for a deeper or more authentic understanding. As Schleiermacher stressed in his version of hermeneutics, the aim of interpretation is to avoid misunderstanding (Schleiermacher 1998). Reflexivity is not old wine in new bottles, however, because it emphasises the importance not just of seeking a deeper more "authentic" interpretation of the social milieu researched, but turns a critical gaze on the researcher, her background and the context of the research.

Reflexivity began as critical reflection in textual criticism, but was then applied to fieldwork in anthropology and sociology. Michael Lynch (2000) discovered twenty uses of the concept. Within these he identifies four versions of specifically methodological reflexivity: philosophical self-reflection methodological self-consciousness, methodological self-criticism and methodological self-congratulation. The last of these refers primarily to the relationship of sociology of science to natural science, but the second and third (though frequently underpinned by the first) are what most social researchers mean by reflexivity. He describes methodological self-consciousness as an awareness of assumptions, prejudices and biases in their research that may arise from the position they occupy in relation to the researched. The third one, which is also found in ethnography, can also be found in natural science and he attributes its identification to Karl Popper and Lewis Wolpert. Methodological self-criticism goes beyond awareness to rejecting any idea (or theory) that does not survive rigorous criticism. This might be seen as an individual virtue or (as he maintains Wolpert says) a communal virtue which distinguishes scientists from lay-persons. What does Lynch mean by "methodological self consciousness".

Considerations of political, or ideological context, power relations of gender, class, ethnicity, institutional contexts and researchers' biographies are the kinds of things seen as shaping knowledge production in ethnography. Thus, who you are and where you are situated socially and historically will shape the assumptions you have, the questions you ask and the way/context of asking them. Such epistemological fluidity, which dissolves any objects of research focus into manifestations of subjectivity, leads – perhaps inevitably to epistemological relativism, whereby no one research account can be privileged over another. As I described before postmodernist inclined writers, particularly Clifford and Marcus (Clifford and Marcus 1986), suggested that fieldwork accounts were little different from fictions and indeed some proposed that there should be a blurring between fiction and empirical accounts.

However, not all ethnographers embraced such a radical conclusion and for most reflexivity (rather like falsification) was a mode of engagement with the empirical world. Methodological reflexivity (or in Lynch's description, methodological self-consciousness) can be summarised as a critical examination of one's own biography and the social context in which the research is conducted. It can take a number of forms, awareness of one's perceptions, behaviour or judgments. It might relate to one's theories or concepts. As Charlotte Aull Davies (Aull Davies 1999) notes, one can place it on a spectrum from private and introspective at one extreme to a very public social reflexivity at the other. It may be partial, or total. But, of course, how one assesses each particular manifestation of reflexive practice, is itself a matter of subjective or intersubjective practice, which unlike the specification of a crucial experiment to falsify a theory, does not make any claim to specificity.

This lack of specificity is both its strength and weakness. To be reflexive is to engage in a process of examination which cannot be specified a priori, but equally how it is done, or the extent to which it is done lies primarily with the researcher. Assuming the good faith of the researcher and a willingness to be reflexive about both her own biography and the social context, how can she know whether her interpretation and assessment of her biography or the social context is either complete or felicitous? One might argue that she should subject her own reflexivity in a particular matter to a "second order" reflexivity – that is being reflexive about reflexivity! But as Steve Woolgar (1988) points out there is an infinite regress arising from the claim that knowing is never fully reflexive until the knower reflects upon the reflexive process itself. Moreover, a methodological principle or strategy of reflexivity is hard to separate from a wider principle of reflexivity. As critical realists maintain, social sciences are part of their own field on enquiry (Bhaskar 1989: 47), so even to think of social science as investigative is to invite an all-encompassing principle of reflexitivity.

Pierre Bourdieu was aware of the kind of problems Woolgar identified and tried to frame reflexivity in a way that overcame them (Bourdieu and Wacquant 1992). Bourdieu, in the words of Samuel Knafo, points out,

> it is not sufficient to examine oneself and disclose interests and value commitments we have. For reflexivity requires a methodology to excavate what is not readily transparent to the scholar: the deeper structures that condition and shape scholarship itself .... one needs to objectify the objectifying subject in order to understand the very process by which [*for example*] world politics is constructed as an object of enquiry.
>
> Knafo 2015: 26

In practice this means using the methods of sociological analysis to examine one's own social trajectory and relation to social structures, rather than informal subjective or intersubjective reflection. It means examining our approach to and construction of the objects of research, capturing the sets of practices and norms that constitute a social field (such as sociology) (Ibid).

However, whilst this approach has its merits in respect of rigour, it is not without its limitations, many of which Knafo notes, but primarily can be seen as a regress in objectifying the object of inquiry. That is, one might use the rules and procedures of a discipline (such as sociology) but these rules themselves must be subject to objectification and so on .... One might add, of course, even if this methodological regress is not empirically a deal breaker, is there methodological agreement as to how this might be achieved, particularly in such a methodologically fractured discipline as sociology?

A further and related problem of reflexivity, is that in accounting for those things that may compromise authenticity, there is a danger of privileging the meaning systems of those investigated (Bryman 1988: 85), thus ignoring the social processes or structures that give rise to that meaning system, producing, as Paul Rock (1973: 20), maintained a form of phenomenalism.

Paul Rock's point begs a further question of what would count as an authentic account. Is it the experiences of informants, their understanding of their experiences, or a social reality that might be revealed (or partially so) through their accounts? Each of these is a perfectly valid goal and the way reflexive accounting is deployed, or at least what the researcher is accounting for, will be different in each case. An account of a respondent's experiences requires only a methodological auditing of one's own understandings and background. To move beyond the descriptive and to ask respondents to reflect upon their experiences, asks the respondents themselves to be reflexive. But seek underlying reality requires each of these plus some theoretical proposition about what that reality is. The foregoing suggests some kind of narrative approach from the researcher, but with a little imagination one can see how this might also play out in observational settings. It is also analogous with survey research which might be merely descriptive or explanatory.

Let us consider the elements present in research which aims to discover the nature of the reality underlying the experiences of those studied. Firstly, we have the motivation to undertake the research and unless this as, C Wright Mills termed "abstracted empiricism" (Mills 1959: 50–79), then there will be some theory, however informal, that seeks to account for the empirically observable. Even in those situations where one begins research, or enters the field, there are inductively held beliefs, suppositions and experiences from past research that create an either articulated or implicit set of beliefs, expectations and so on.

Secondly there will be other aspects of a researcher's background, her cultural positioning, her training and perhaps predilection towards particular methods or practices.

Thirdly there will be the immediate social context of the research as experienced by the researcher and researched.

Finally, there will be those who are researched, their biographies, attitudes and beliefs.

These things are possible to one extent or another, certainly in ethnographic research, but also to a great extent in survey research and secondary analysis. As with falsification, there is no doctrine of perfection, but this does not stop reflexivity from being a valuable methodological tool in uncovering the complexity of social reality.

Inference

The logical point made against induction "Hume's Problem" and later as the cornerstone of Popper's falsificationism, is a powerful one. No number of positive instances can confirm, but just one negative instance can falsify. This claim is enumerative, as of course is the basis of hypothesis testing, though here falsification is the significance of the alternative hypothesis versus the non-significance of the null hypothesis. These are forms of formal inference, but what about the informal inference of our everyday lives?

Here inference is more qualitative. We do not enumerate a person's failings before we decide to like or trust them. We way up the evidence more informally. Subjectivity is inevitable. Much of the time, enumeration would not be possible. Why do I vote for politician A and not B? I hope, as a reasonably informed citizen, I make this decision on the basis of many characteristics, some the politician themselves, but also the programme of their party and how, if implemented would advance or impede the interests of those parts of society I care about. I am sure, others are more considered than I in these matters, but equally I know people vote for politicians and programmes that are not even remotely in their interests.

Now, with these illustrations, I am not advocating that science abandons rationality, but I am saying two things. The first should be apparent from much of the foregoing, that social and psychological factors play a part in how science is done. I will develop this theme further in next chapter. The second is that more informal kinds of inference have a methodological part to play in general, but specifically in theory choice. It is the second I will develop a little further here.

The psychologist Gerd Gigerenzer (2008) has developed the concept of "smart heuristics". As a psychologist, he is as much interested in how we make decisions, as the decisions themselves. Unlike some other psychologists (e.g. Kahneman and Tversky 1972), he maintains that human decision making is not primarily irrational and has shown experimentally that partial knowledge can often lead to better decision making than when there is more and better knowledge. As with Lakatos, he uses the concept of "heuristics", a process of assisting discovery often by trial and error. Heuristics that are used, will differ from one environment to another. The mind is an adaptive toolbox, a modular system of heuristics and their building blocks and capacities, which can evolve (Op Cit). An important aspect of his work is the distinction between risk and uncertainty. When all relevant consequences, alternatives and probabilities are known, we should use statistical thinking. But, when these are not known and there is uncertainty, we should use heuristics.

Gigerenzer has carried out much of his work in medical decision making and medical advice to lay persons, but the idea of a psychological heuristic decision making in the context of theory choice, in science, is at least compatible with the broader notion of a "heuristic" suggested by Lakatos. Gigerenzer has tried to show the process by which this occurs and indeed can be optimised in other contexts, but social science in particular we are often confronted with data that can be interpreted in quite different ways. Fitting different statistical models can produce different results. For example, Kreft et al (1995) demonstrated that centering around a group mean, a grand mean, or using raw scores, in a multilevel model, produces quite different results, that they concluded can only be interpreted theoretically. Jane Elliott's book, that I mentioned in the previous chapter, (Elliot 2005) is a detailed argument for the importance of narrative, not just in qualitative research, but also quantitative research. Her argument about quantitative analysis might be summarised as statistical methods are a necessary, but not sufficient condition in doing good quantitative work. That the models require reasoning beyond the models to be of value, that they do not stand on their own. This is how she concludes:

> … statistical models cannot provide definitive answers about the relationship between variables and that it is important to take account of human agency and cultural influences on behaviour. This means that researchers who are conducting "extensive" research increasingly recognise the value of "intensive" research for illuminating the processes that underlie the statistical associations they have discovered.
>
> Elliot 2005: 186

If Gigerenzer is right about statistical uncertainty and Elliot about the need to interpret data, then the need for realism to rely on unobservables, a frequent criticism from empiricists, seems unavoidable in all science and its reasoned use, the hallmark of good science.

Inference to the best explanation

What I am saying is far from new and was recognised by Charles Sanders Peirce (Peirce 1931) in the 19th century. He termed this reasoning "abduction" and indeed many realists continue to use this term to describe the following (Haig and Evers 2016: 73–90, Hurrell 2014: 255–263, O'Mahoney and Vincent 2014: 17–19). However, by abduction Peirce emphasised reasoning in choosing hypotheses, but inference to the best explanation (IBE) is primarily a means to choose an explanation. It neither follows deductive inference, or enumerative induction, but rather it is a means to choose the most plausible explanation, consistent with the data available. It is also consistent with Gigerenzer's argument that heuristics are contextual.

There are many formulations of IBE and most of these are thought of in the context of natural science. A simple version is something like this. Suppose we have theories *T1*, *T2* and *T3*. Evidence (or models) is logically consistent with each, thus our choice to provisionally accept (say) *T3* will be based extra-logical and informal non-enumerative inductive reasoning.

A common version of this is expressed as:

Given evidence E and candidate explanations $H_1, \dots, H_n$ of E, infer the truth of *that* H_i which best explains E.[5]

Bas Van Fraassen, amongst several others, have criticised IBE (van Fraassen 1985). One of his criticisms is that if one theory (or explanation) is more informative than another, then it must have greater content, which itself is more open to refutation. In the social sciences, theories are usually much more informal and indeed, as I have suggested often local and sometimes subject to fashion. Van Fraassen's criticism has force, then when (as is common in social science) theories are modified ad hoc to account for empirical challenge. But this is bad science anyway and offends the spirit of Occam's Razor, by introducing extraneous content. This criticism of Van Fraassen rests on the logical problem of induction, that no amount of observations (or in this case statements about observations) can be confirmed. Nevertheless, IBE is useful and even may be a way of better specifying or building our theories, as well as testing them, if it is conjoined with the stance of reflexive fallibilism, I outline below.

However, first I will illustrate how informal use of IBE can benefit research, in a practical way, with a further story from my own research on homelessness. When we began the first project (this was in a UK city) to count the homeless population, political pressure from the city council required that before we use the virtually untried enumerative method of capture–recapture (Williams and Cheal 2002), we should first undertake a headcount. The population of the city was, at that time, around 270,00, so this was quite an undertaking, and various organisations provided volunteers to undertake a headcount on a given night. I should say we were very sceptical of this method, because of its tendency to over or undercount. The volunteers counted over 150 rough sleepers! This seemed to be an extraordinarily large amount, even in a city with an evident rough sleeper population. Our belief was that, as with the old saying "give a person a hammer and they will find nails", these volunteers were temperamentally inclined to find rough sleepers, because they cared about the problem and wanted to demonstrate its extent.

Consequently, we organised two further counts with selected enumerators, not connected with homelessness organisation. They were given training and the nights of the enumeration were kept secret, until the evening of the count itself. We found 9 and 11 rough sleepers respectively over the two counts. Now, logically there was no reason to prefer the second and third count over the first, but the latter two (for the reasons I have said) was our preferred explanation. Subsequently, much more rigorous enumerations, using capture–recapture confirmed that this was largely correct. Although this sounds like a very local form of reasoning, it can also be read as an instance of a theory which holds that most homelessness in Western countries does not take the form of rough sleeping and when it does, most rough sleepers remain on the streets for a relatively short period at any one time. Most forms of homelessness are hidden (and as I have already suggested, very heterogeneous). The data-theory match from the lower head counts was an inference to the best explanation, and in this case one that could be tested later through statistical methods.

The criticisms levelled at IBE have led to attempts in the philosophy of the natural sciences to put it on a on a more formal footing (see e.g. Psillos[6] 2000). In social science I think it can be of empirical value, even if expressed more informally, or qualitatively – which theoretical explanation is the most plausible explanation of the data? But this is but one element in the testing or the development of a theory. And this is where falsification and reflexivity return.

Reflexive fallibilism

What I have termed "reflexive fallibilism" is an informal strategy that may help us to infer the best explanation from a theory-data relationship. It exists both at the "micro" level of the researcher, or research group and at the "macro" level when we examine a body of theory or research.

Reflexivity and falsification can be viewed as trying to do the same thing, to discriminate between our rhetorical statements about the world to get to a more authentic, or more accurate description or explanation of it. Reflexivity, is as I described above, a many faceted concept. It has been primarily associated with qualitative and humanist approaches to research. It has been about making clear background assumptions, beliefs, purposes, values, perhaps unseen prejudices, both at the level of the researcher, the discipline and the levels between. It has not usually been deployed as a device to uncover deeper social realities. Not because it can't but rather that reality has often been seen as a subjective or intersubjective construct. Also, and importantly, the process of reflexivity follows the logic of *modus ponens*, rather than *modus tollens*. It uncovers characteristics that might impede authenticity, but once this is done, it is assumed the authentic is available. Hence, the criticisms of people such as Lynch or Bourdieu (above).

Falsification, in its naïve form, sets out to falsify singular statements, with the assumption that theories can be so simply expressed.

But what about if reflexivity was about subjecting both theory and data to a process of falsification? Not, what is it that is plausible in theory or data, but what is it that is implausible? Now, on the face of it, this sounds like informal IBE, but in the spirit of Popper, what I am suggesting is that we take the most plausible explanation or data and subject them to the most rigorous tests (either theoretical or empirical)? Popper himself, said that we should not attempt to falsify the weaker elements of a theory, but attack it at its strongest point.

Let me provide an example. In this example, some of the follow-on empirical work has been done, some has not. Geoff Payne, Suzanne Chamberlain and I undertook a small project of sociology journal content analysis (Payne et al 2004) as part of a broader investigation of, what has become known as, the "quantitative crisis" in British social science (MacInnes 2009, Payne 2014, Williams et al 2008). In this we analysed the content of five British general sociological journals issues over a two-year period, to enumerate the number of papers with a quantitative content and to describe their characteristics (author characteristics, levels of analysis, differences by journal, etc.). Amongst several conclusions, which prompted a response from Jennifer Platt (Platt 2012), was the claim that the paucity of quantitative papers (about one in 20 of published papers in the mainstream journals) was an indication of the nature of the discipline, at that time, in Britain.

Platt's objection was that this may not be the case, because quantitatively inclined papers may be published in specialist outlets, or in non-UK journals. Our view, was that if this was the case, and general sociology journals are not publishing much quantitative work, if this work is being done, then it is odd that he leading general sociology journals are not publishing it. Which may well be true, but a rhetorical claim, nonetheless.

Let's subject our original claim to reflexive falsification and how that claim might be empirically tested.

1. Platt's empirical conjecture, is not equivalent to our rhetorical one. The rhetorical riposte does follow from the evidence, but it depends on a number of implicit evaluative claims, such as what counts as sociology, that publishing quantitative work in these journals is appropriate for their authors, that the journals should reflect the work being done across the discipline. Although our riposte perhaps seems initially more plausible, Platt's claim is empirically testable.
2. The difficulty in what counts as sociology is the most difficult thing to establish. However, that does not preclude further journal analysis. A starting point might be that one of the journals, Work, Employment and Society (WES), had a greater quantitative content than the other journals, which gives some indication that a plausible line of enquiry might be initially in other journals that published papers in these areas, perhaps followed up from citations in WES itself. Repeat this exercise for journals that report research in (say) social aspects of health and medicine, education and gender. Then, in a sample of papers, look for citations back to the general British sociology journals. As far as I know, this work has yet to be done.
3. Ask those who count themselves as professional sociologists, what kind of research do they do and publish. This was done by Charlotte Brookfield 2017) through a census of British Sociological Association (BSA) members and academics working in British university sociology departments and units. Brookfield's findings did not support Platt's empirical claim and Brookfield found that in terms of subject content and status, the discipline was strongly skewed towards the arts and humanities (op cit: 140–144). But Brookfield's findings too might be subject to falsification.
4. Brookfield's respondents were either BSA members and possibly self-selecting to a style of sociology reflected in the BSA journals, which constituted three of the five sampled in the original research, or they were academic sociologists in sociology units or departments. If the research at 2 above were to be conducted, then the papers published would identify the affiliation of their authors. A reasonable hypothesis might be that much quantitative sociological work, in the UK, comes from either generic social science units (e.g. the Centre for Longitudinal Studies, at University College London) or from subject specialist units, such as the Centre for Labour Market Studies, at Leicester University, The Centre for Women's Studies at York University or The European Social Survey, based at City University, London.

This is an admittedly simple example that illustrates how subjecting claims to falsification can lead to better explanation. In this example, the work is incomplete and I would speculate, will lead to support for both hypotheses. In which case, further theorising should suggest an explanation that can incorporate both sets of findings into a new testable explanation. But there may be more than one explanation then available, both of which should be testable.

The overall research programme into the "quantitative crisis" in British social science has several elements that have explored academic output, student perceptions and experiences, the experience of teaches of quantitative methods and, what can be described as a massive action research programme, in the Q-Step initiative, which operates in 17 universities with both the aim of "making a step change" in the teaching of quantitative methods, but also to do this by trialling several different approaches in the various Q-Step centres, to see which works well and which works less well (Nuffield Foundation 2014).

The "quantitative" problem itself is contextual (as I described previously, a "local" one), because it is not a problem in other countries, either because quantitative research and quantitative methods are commonly used (United States), or that are not commonly used, but not deemed to be a major problem (New Zealand).

All of this is to say that the phenomena, often described in two words, "the quantitative crisis", is a complex set of partially related social processes and outcomes, that change through time and place. As such, it is typical of much of that which we research in social science. It does not lend itself (or rarely so) to simply specified theories that may be tested, corroborated or falsified. But that does not mean anything goes and one theory is as good as another, we can be wrong and good science should help us to show when we are wrong.

Representing the real: theories and testing them

In these last two chapters I have tried to how we can "close in" on reality. In the previous chapter, I argued that our theories are inevitably representations, but representations can be framed into testable theory. In this chapter, I have tried to show how theories and the process of research is susceptible to social and psychological factors – normative factors, tacit knowledge and so on. These things have been recognised as existing in the natural sciences for several decades. As I have argued elsewhere and I will say more of in Chapter 7, science is a social construct (albeit one that can transcend particular social contexts). Yet, there have been those, such as the logical positivists, or Popper, who thought procedural devices, such as the DN model, or falsification, could avoid extraneous social and psychological influences. Indeed, in rare examples (what I termed heroic science) hypotheses can be relatively simply stated and tested. In these cases, falsification is possible, or the terms of the theories can be accommodated within the DN model.

Lakatos challenged these simplistic assumptions and described science as longer term research programmes, with empirical falsification and confirmation, but with "hard cores" of theoretical assumptions. What he describes is also a persuasive account of social research programmes over time. Here, I used two illustrations of these: counterurbanisation and the "quantitative crisis" in British social science.

Research programmes, in the sense Lakatos meant, are I think, a reasonable description, but happen on a day-to-day basis, when researchers have several theories that offer plausible explanations and data that might support more than one of these? Or, even, the expression of the data through different models, might lead to different results.

It's all very messy. The messiness mostly defies formal inference and certainly goes beyond enumerative induction. There are strategies we can take from philosophies of the natural sciences, such as smart heuristics and inference to the best explanation. Combine these with what I have termed as "reflexive fallibilism" and an informal methodological strategy that can make sense of the complex theoretical-data nexus emerges. This cannot be set out in a prescriptive procedure, but it does have some normative scientific values that may guide us. Firstly, it is inferring to what seems to be the most plausible explanation, even if this is contrary to prior theory. Though we should question our data and subject these to rigorous methodological critique (being reflexive about data). We should attempt to specify theories, or simple research hypotheses, the ways in which they can be shown to be false. That is, what would it count for me to be wrong? Finally, our research problems, our theories and our methods are socially situated and should be available for reflexive scrutiny.

I do not want to leave the impression of methodological permissiveness ameliorated through an individual credo of informal inference through reflexive fallibilism. You cannot just take a theory and pick and choose the bits you like, as is so often the case in social science. What I have said in this chapter is but just one part of a complex realist methodology. There are two other important parts: the objective ontological fact of reality and the realist methodological imperative towards explanatory mechanisms. These things I will pursue in the next two chapters.

Notes

1. Karl Popper claimed, in a number of places, that his concept of falsification killed off logical positivism (see e.g. Popper 1974 cited in Phillips 1987: 37), yet The *Logic of Scientific Discovery* was not published in English until 1959 and before this, Popper's views on falsification were not well known, though this book was published in German, in 1938, as *Logic der Forschung.* Hanson's *Patterns of Discovery* was published in 1958 and is said to have influenced the work ofThomas Kuhn.
2. Einstein later referred to this as his biggest blunder, when after Edward Hubble's discovery of "redshift" indicted the universe was not static, but expanding (Hubble 1929).
3. Physics is replete with such examples. Particle-wave duality was long challenged, by what John Worrall refereed too, as "elderly holdouts" (Worrall 1990). In the 21st century, we might think also of the diminishing number of scientists who deny the phenomenon of global warming.

4. In actuality, as Popper claimed, much of Marxist theory is rendered unfalsifiable, often through the addition of ad hoc amendments, for example to explain (contra Marx) revolutions in peasant, rather than industrial societies. It does not follow that the "core" of Marxism is wrong, though I am not sure what would count as a falsification?
5. This formulation is taken from the entry in the Stanford Encyclopaedia of Philosophy, https://plato.stanford.edu/entries/abduction/ which has an excellent discussion of IBE and abduction.
6. Psillos refers to it as abduction.

7

Objective knowledge

This chapter a realist argument for an objective knowledge of the social world.

The title of this chapter was also the title of a book published by Karl Popper (Popper 1979). His thesis was that objective knowledge of the world, is in the recorded form of books, manuscripts and indeed objects created by human beings. What he called his "third world" of knowledge (more of world one and two later) consists of objects that have an ontological status, separate to our beliefs, wishes or even awareness of them (op cit: 106–115). This does not mean it is immutable, but because it is there in the form of claims, statements, productions, that are open to revision, criticism and refutation. Could Popper's ontological thesis of knowledge apply to knowledge of the social world? I believe that it can, but with an important caveat. The social world itself can be thought of as grounded in knowledge that is translated into action and discourse. When as social scientists we seek knowledge of the social world, we are seeking knowledge of knowledge. We want descriptions, explanations and understandings of social formations and interactions, but also the beliefs, desires and actions that underlie them. This is different ontological "stuff" to the physical world, because to know these things, to obtain "knowledge of knowledge" requires second order beliefs, desires and actions directed towards the object of study. This is sometimes, perhaps glibly, described as "being part of what we study".

In much of his work Popper emphasised knowledge of the physical world, but (what he termed) his "third world" of knowledge did not exclusively consist of this, but was all forms of recorded knowledge, that would encompass, for example, the arts (in the form of paintings, sculpture, etc.), musical scores and indeed the contents of libraries (Popper 1994: 24–32). Implicitly, at least, Popper's theory of knowledge is a theory of social knowledge. In proposing his "third world of knowledge", Popper was making a realist claim, that there exists a body of knowledge that has become independent of its creators. We might say that the third world of knowledge is an expression of a social reality. But it is only one outcome made possible by prior processes that comprise social reality.

The chapter is in three sections. The first corresponds to an ontological thesis of what social reality is, not particular forms of social reality, but what is in the social that can allow us to declare it real and incorporates the concept of social objects, I described in Chapter 4. My claim here is that their reality is different, but equivalent to objects in the physical world.

The second section is an epistemological theory of social knowledge. If the first thesis is correct, then there are "objects" in the social world, that can be known. If this is so, then how can we have objective knowledge of them, when our second order constructs are themselves subject to beliefs and desires? Moreover, the first and second order constructs are very much intertwined. Put it another way, if social science is a construct of society, then how can the investigative strategies of social science transcend the constructed nature of the enterprise? Or simply put, how can researchers achieve objectivity?

In the third section I will return to Popper's theory of knowledge in order to show how the ontological independence of objects of knowledge can underpin a socially situated objectivity.

The ontological thesis – social objects

Physical and social reality revisited

In Chapter 2, I described the core metaphysical claim of realism is that there is an actually existing world that is independent of our perceptions of it. Although contested, it seems easier to say this of the physical world than the social world. The physical world is complex, it has emergent properties, it has feedback loop, it changes constantly, yet despite these things it has at least some properties that exhibit natural necessity, because they are grounded properties and this characteristic, in turn, produces invariance in many systems. To recap: invariance implies that there are objects and relations between those objects and that these things remain relatively unchanging over time and space. There is also plenty of variance, but that can often be captured within higher level invariance. Biological systems, for instance, can be subject to stochastic change, but the nature of that change is captured within a higher level and simpler set of transformation rules to that higher level (Nozick 2001: 76–93). Invariance does not mean stasis, it is always relative, but the relativity can be captured by some transformation rules, as I described in Chapter 3. Though there is invariance in the social world, this is the result of either grounding in the physical world, or the conceptual necessity of the social world.

The social world is reducible to an ensemble of human mental properties, that are a subset of physical reality. Though they are not determined by particular properties of physical reality, they nevertheless supervene upon physical reality. So, the realism of the social world, is a subset realism, albeit with special properties. So, what is it that makes the social world real? As I described in Chapter 2, what the physical world is, is far from a straightforward question, it is certainly not the "solid matter" of 19th-century physics.

However, what we mean by mental states is also not straightforward. Mental processes are in the brain and only in the brain and cannot exist without the complex material existence of the brain. Even if we do not know what the mental is, we do know that it has physical origins it is incapable of operationalisation without the physical electro-chemical stimulus in the brain, Although we can say mental states are emergent properties, they nevertheless supervene on physical properties.

All this is to reiterate, in a somewhat different way, the argument of ontological naturalism, I made in Chapter 2. However, I think something else follows from this, is what we call "reality", physical or mental, is that it is dynamic, complex and often contingent upon immediate past states. There are, however, two important differences between physical and social reality. The first is, as I have argued, that physical systems are defined by much greater levels of invariance and this is grounded in natural necessity. The result is that most properties of the physical world remain stable. Local disruption or variation might impede the workings of gravity (wind, turbulence, magnets, etc.), thermodynamic entropy (energy capture or generation, chemical change, etc.), but gravitational attraction and entropy will always "win" in the end. The social world will exhibit invariance, but it is much more local, is weaker and is grounded only in conceptual necessity.

The second is that consciousness, in humans, is a reflective self-awareness that produces constant feedback loops at the level of both the mental and social. Although there are feedback loops in the physical world, these are not self-aware (although possibly in some higher mammals, there is a primitive self-awareness[1]).

The much greater invariance, in the physical world and the absence of self-aware feedback loops, does however allow us to more easily talk of "objects" in the physical world, such as books, dogs, mountains, houses, hamburgers ..., etc. Chemists and physicists know that these are not immutable, but they have changing chemical properties, that are subject to entropy, that are buzzing interactions of waves and particles. But not all objects exist for as long as these common sense ones. For example, the radioactive element francium, has a half-life of only 22 minutes, when it decays into astatine, radium, and radon. The isotope of the element hydrogen, hydrogen 7 as a half-life of only – 10^{-24} seconds! Your objection might well be, is this even an object? And my answer is, where is the cut off that counts as an object between my cat Monica and hydrogen 7? So, as with what counts as "material", what counts as an object, in the physical world is not straightforward.[2] Indeed, one may take that continuum into the social world, even though, as I have claimed, it has a different ontological status.

Which brings us back to the social objects I described in Chapter 4. My claim was that these too are real things and that whilst their reality is complex, contingent and dynamic and has different properties to the physical world, we can nevertheless name them and therefore research them.

I claimed they had five properties:

a. They are socially constructed but real
b. They are real but contingent
c. They are dynamic
d. They are continuous with thought objects and physical objects
e. The causal efficacy of social objects depends on their relationship to other social objects

Let us now briefly apply these to the concept of homelessness, I discussed in Chapter 5, in relation to Glen Bramley's definitions. There my concern was methodological, but let us examine this from an ontological perspective.

Homelessness is a social construct, what it is can vary according to definition in time and place. However, once it is named and defined, it has consequences at an individual and societal level for those who experience it directly, and those who make decisions as a result of its named existence. Yet, whilst under any description, we can name the properties that are likely associated with different states of homelessness, there is no determined pathway into those states, however, they are defined. Individuals, with the same characteristics that constitute homelessness, may or may not think of themselves as such, yet alongside the social and psychological properties, there will be real physical states of sub-optimal accommodation, such as space constraints, dampness, lack of heating, that will have causal consequences for social and thought objects. Finally the chances of being "homeless" will depend on other life events, resulting from particular biographies, local and national policies and crucially, the availability of accommodation (Williams and Cheal 2002).

Whilst we might even say that there is no one thing called homelessness, but on the other there is something going on that has an *objective* existence. That is, there are objects there. As realists, we can say that social objects have an existence and are perhaps equivalent to Bhaskar's intransitive objects of nature. Our aim, as social scientists, is to theorise and measure and then hopefully improve our theorisations and measurements through an inference process – the reflexive fallibilism, I described in the last chapter. Some of Bramley's definitions, I claimed were very difficult to operationalise, but we could theorise them in a different context. For example, his description 7, the broadest of all:

Individuals or groups living within existing households whose relationships and conditions are tolerable but where the individual/groups have a clear preference to live separately, including cases where the "potential" household is currently split but would like to live together.

This could be thought of as inadequate accommodation for desired and socially acceptable living arrangements. And though, like all manifestations of homelessness, it presents as a "housing symptom", it investigation might be through affordability of accommodation, public health and local housing markets, a quite different (though complementary task) to researching those who are street homeless. So, we might revise my "it doesn't exist" claim to one, that "homelessness" is many different kinds of social objects, that may be embedded in different kinds of causally connected mechanisms.

The ontological view of social objects is, then, that they exist and we propose they have certain characteristics, which we may name through a theory and we subsequently test for these through the best methods we have.

But in the social world, there is an important further caveat, that of a moral dimension which enters our investigations in two ways. Firstly, we are investigating moral agents within the context of an historically specific web of beliefs. This matters, because the beliefs we are investigating may constitute the very object we theorise and such an object may well be socially specific to a time and place – it may well be "normative" in character. For example, a problem for US sociologists in the 1960s were increasing numbers of babies born outside of marriage (Root 2007: 42–46). Nowadays a considerable number of such births occur, but now this is not considered a problem, but babies born to teenage parents, often is. Crucially it is the society that holds these views, not necessarily the social scientists. The "social objects" have a moral dimension.

But so too must the decisions to investigate have a moral dimension. The problems considered worthy of investigation (and importantly the provision of resources to do so) will be socially situated. Thus, a "value free" social science is impossible, firstly on the grounds that it is often values we investigate, but also in choosing (or being increasingly constrained through funding) to investigate a particular thing, the researcher makes value decisions. We could, then, add a further property to social objects, that they have a moral ontological character and that they have a moral epistemological character as worthy (or not) of investigation.

Relativism is implicit in this line of thought, that if social objects (even if we consider them "real") have a moral character and our decision to investigate is situated within the values of the society in which these objects exist. So, what saves the realist from such relativism?

Well, firstly to say that the objects have a "moral" character is not the same as saying they do not have an existence. The term "homeless" is a social construction, as was once the negative concept of babies born outside of marriage, but once people are so described, or categorised, the description or categorisation has causal consequences for them. As I said earlier, in the United States the category of "homeless" can take on an identity dimension. Realist objectivity must begin from an ontological premise of the real existence of objects and our desire and aim to know them "realistically" – that is, as completely and accurately as possible. Secondly moral descriptions or evaluations exist in the third world of knowledge, but this is something I will return to below.

The epistemological thesis – situated objectivity

A realist objectivity needs objects to be objective about! If there could be a world in which there were "objects" and those who sought to know those objects could be separate from them, then the issue of objectivity would be a simple one. As I said at the beginning of this chapter, social objects constitute second order constructs, they are "knowledge of knowledge". Furthermore, in Chapters 5 and 6, I argued that we are constrained to have representations of reality – we cannot directly access reality.

Science, both social and natural, are a social construction. It does not follow that a society will develop a scientific culture, or if it did, it does not follow that such a culture will develop into the kind of science we have now. Indeed, in China and the Middle East, the scientific culture that developed in Europe, in the Middle Ages, was hindered by social and religious beliefs and practices (Needham 1976: xxvii), despite these societies' early advances in technology and mathematics. Natural and social science are human social enterprises that arise from social values. Given this, how do we transcend those values to produce knowledge that is a true representation of the world? Knowledge that is not just a fiction, but can allow us to successfully manipulate that world through methods and technologies?

Value freedom and values

Let me come back to values. For a long while, in the natural sciences and to an extent in social science, something like the simple principle of separating the knower from the known – (the object) prevailed, in the belief that separating out what we think should be the case, from what was, facilitates such manipulation. To an extent, in the natural sciences, this was demonstrably true. Though it took a long while to demonstrate this, Phlogiston and Lysenko's genetics were fictions (I'll return to Lysenko below) and in the end were shown to be so, by nature answering back! In the philosophy of the natural sciences there have been a sophisticated articulations of value freedom. Usually these rest on the argument of the level of autonomy of cognitive values or rational practices in science from external normative social values. Those that adhere to value free positions will usually refer to mechanisms within science, in particular within theories or theory choice, which underwrite internal scientific values such as impartiality, autonomy and neutrality (Lacey 1999: Chapter 4). Such positions do not claim that social values do not enter science, but that they can be identified and controlled for to one extent or another. I (and indeed many others), do not regard this position as tenable, even in natural science (see Kitcher 2001, Longino 1990, Williams 2006).

But in the social sciences – themselves called the "moral sciences" by John Stuart Mill (1987[1872]), the separation of a value position from the process of investigation was more difficult. Actually, there are few social scientists nowadays that advocate value freedom, though its successor concept, that of "objectivity", is often confused, over simplified or ignored. Worse still, many "anti-positivists" conflate value freedom with objectivity (e.g. Guba and Lincoln 1994: 114.

The concept of value freedom, emerged in the natural sciences from the development of experimentation in the 18th and 19th centuries, a process philosophically underwritten by a Cartesian separation of the object of the experiment from the subjectivity of the experimenter. Value freedom was an early import into social science.

Some, though far from all, of the problem of values in social science resulted from a generalisation of a subject–object separation from controlled experimentation on inanimate objects, to research on people in open systems. In short, whilst it was easy to maintain emotional distance from physical objects or systems, say particles in Brownian motion, this is more difficult in conceiving, designing and conducting research on deviance. However, values also lie at the heart of natural science and the separation of human values from the objects of study has been shown to be chimeric there also. That physical objects are themselves not autonomous bearers of value makes little difference, what is important are the values we bring to their identification and investigation.

An early and quite sophisticated version of value freedom was advocated by Max Weber (Weber 1974), who tried to unite social commitment and value free investigation by accepting that in matters of policy there will be a debate about "ends", about what should be achieved and therefore what investigation should be pursued. Investigation is value driven. However, he maintained that it does not follow from this that the moral and political values of commitment should bias investigation. Weber's "value free sociology" was not a sociology without values, but rather a sociology that began with values, yet was neutral in the conduct and means of its subsequent investigation.

Weber's concept of a "value" was that of a moral or social value, but there is more to values than that.

The value continuum in science

Indeed, we can identify three important uses of the concept of value in the sciences. First it is used as a numerical measure of a quantity or number denoting magnitude on a conventional scale. This may take a concrete form such as values on a scale designed to measure a specific characteristic, or it may be used in the more abstract sense of a mathematical value. The latter can come to stand in for something concrete. A value of "32" can be 32 of anything, or it can be applied, say in the measurement of temperature – say 32 degrees Celsius. The latter is capable of numeric translation into other scales, such as Fahrenheit or Kelvin. Temperature is a good example of a conventional scale of values. Though each of the scales mentioned measures a physical characteristic, there is nothing determined about what the scales are, other than they should remain stable forms of measurement in time and place. Though in social science only a minority of our measures are of physical characteristics (e.g. age, biological sex, housing characteristics), our means of measurement denote the existences of characteristics that are taken to have enough invariance to make them measurable, or indeed we think important to measure (e.g. income, occupation, marital status, educational qualifications, but also attitudes and beliefs[3]). Our descriptive and inferential statistics are likewise numeric values that have conventional origins (see Chapter 4).

Secondly, we can identify methodological values. These play a crucial role in the success[4] of science and might include, for example: randomisation or parsimony, etc. However, these are not usually what the advocates of value freedom are talking about, indeed they would be specifically excluded because they would be seen as having no moral content. Some would dispute whether they have any social content at all, but rather they are asocial values. This is a hard line to hold because methodological values do not arise *sui generis*, but have historic and social antecedents. Methodological values may arise gradually from conventional practice, or may give rise to conventional practice. In statistics, for example, the adoption of the standard frequency interpretation of probability was by no means a foregone conclusion, but was conventional decision with social antecedents. However, its adoption changed the character of statistical methodology and assumptions (Mellor 1971).

Most methodological values are adopted gradually or piecemeal over time and are rarely universally accepted by scientists over long periods, or within disciplines or sub-disciplines. Different sciences will be characterised by particular methodological values or approaches that can trace their origins to the influence of particular scientists, or schools of thought. For example Bayesian approaches are hardly present and even controversial in some sciences (e.g. chemistry or physics), but widely used in others (e.g. epidemiology, psychology, petrology), though there are no strong reasons, other than social, as to why they should not be used in more sciences than they currently are. Some methodological values may go in and out of fashion, or be more fashionable in one country than another. Experimentation in sociology, education or criminology– in fashion in the United States up until recently, but not in fashion in Britain, yet at the time of writing (in the form of complex interventions) becoming increasingly advocated (Ariel et al 2021). Statistical tests will have a logical relationship to the distribution to which they relate, but the specific tests were devised for a practical purpose (e.g. see Hacking 1990); they are not, in his words, "natural kinds".

A third use of the concept denotes moral values. It is often argued that a decision to work on projects such as the development of the means to "weaponise" anthrax is a moral one, whereas a decision to conduct bacteriological research on anthrax has no particular or necessary moral consequences. Often the divide between the two has been presented as that between technology and science (Wolpert 1992: 25–34) in which science remains neutral of moral purpose. This distinction has been hard to sustain, and just as the divisions of labour and intent are not clear between science and technology, so there is an indeterminacy between what constitutes moral and *social* values. Many imperatives seen at a particular historic moment as timeless moral values, such as a duty to denounce witches, can be seen with hindsight to have been normative social values. Nevertheless, some moral values hold for considerable periods, as with scales expressing numeric values there is nothing determined about them and their only condition of existence is consensual or legal enforcement. The distinction between a moral and social value may be to do with its longevity and/or the strength with which it is held in a particular community.

Nevertheless, moral or social values can be seen as a third kind of value present in science. These may be aesthetic or conventional values, such as modes of dress, conduct or social practices. The distinction between moral and social values is not sharp, indeed the former could be considered as a subset of the latter. Moral values can become social values and vice versa. Moreover, there is possibly no sharp divide between social values in science and methodological values. Each can carry varying degrees of consensus or imperative. There is a very wide literature on this topic (see e.g. Cole 1992, Fuller 1997, Chapter 2, Mulkay 1991).

A difficulty in characterising the three (or possible four) types of value outlined above is that the types themselves may be differently designated, that they are not sharply divided. But this difficulty also constitutes the basis of an argument that types of values in science, however designated, *cannot* be sharply divided. There is no dichotomy between moral and social values and within social values in science there is no clear-cut division between social values and methodological values. Even within methodological values a division could be mooted, say between measurement values and procedural ones, but it is a division that does not hold for long. To show how value freedom could exist in science would entail a demonstration that each of these kinds of values are discrete and can consequently be bracketed off.

Helen Longino (1990) has recognised this. She regards science as having both constitutive values that are internal to it (things such as accuracy, reliability, etc.) and contextual values, those external things which shape what it is science is about, or what particular sciences should strive for. This position is similar to that of Weber, but she goes further and says that contextual values do and should inform constitutive values. The history of the natural and social sciences bears this out. Developments in methodology have nearly always been linked to contextual goals. For example the rapid industrialisation of the United States in the first half of the 20th century coincided with the growth of scientific sociology, both survey method and the experiment (Madge 1963, Platt 1996). Likewise, it was not just idle curiosity that led to the development of urban ethnography by the Chicago School, but the perception that the poverty that grew out of urbanisation was a serious social problem.

Objectivity as a value

If value freedom is impossible and that a value continuum exists then it would seem to follow that objectivity is itself a value, but what kind of value is it? Before we can answer this question, we need to consider what we mean by objectivity.

I realise that any answer to this question is a hostage to fortune and there have been many, many attempts to produce either a succinct or comprehensive definition before.[5] My purpose here is not to enter into a detailed discussion of the various meanings of the term, but rather to provide a minimal and possibly provisional specification[6] for a value based objectivity, what I have called *situated objectivity* (Williams 2006, 2009, 2015).

Let me start with saying what objectivity is not – it is not neutrality. This is what the advocates or opponents of a value freedom version of objectivity usually claim or imply. Objectivity presupposes purpose. Particular sciences may be completely objective, but may serve economic or political interests as their purpose. Geologists, for example, know more about oil bearing shales (because of the demand for oil) than any other sort of rock, but their knowledge is no less reliable for that (Tauber 1997: 30). Alvin Gouldner considers the role of the physician in this respect

> [the physician] is not necessarily less objective because he has made a partisan commitment to his patient and against the germ. The physician's objectivity is in some measure vouchsafed because he has committed himself to a specific value: health.
>
> Gouldner 1973: 58

Consider the converse. What would a science (or perhaps more broadly an investigative discipline) be without a purpose? At the very minimum curiosity is a purpose, but most investigation has other purposes or combines these with curiosity. However, whilst objectivity presupposes a purpose, purpose does not necessarily presuppose objectivity. An artist does not necessarily have to be objective, though s/he will probably have a purpose. Likewise, we do not have to be objective about our choice of food, clothing, music, etc., even though we may be purposeful in respect of them.

Purpose then is a necessary[7] but not sufficient characteristic. A second necessary characteristic that is also not sufficient, is that objectivity should be concerned with objects, or perhaps more correctly their properties. As I suggested above, social objects are dynamic, continuous and contingent. So, what we identify may be process or outcome. They may be states of affairs, institutions, mental states, physical manifestations of social process, etc. What they must minimally have is existential properties so that their properties, may in principle be differentiated from the properties of other objects. Let me reaffirm here, I am not suggesting we preserve the old positivist dualism between investigator and object. As I argued, in Chapter 5, we know the social world and therefore social objects, under a description.

In subjective differentiation we discriminate between objects on the basis of that which is pleasing or convenient, or just seems that way to us. The taste of chocolate is pleasing to many, but not all. I do not find rising at 5am at all convenient or pleasant and I do not like coconut in desserts. There may be much more of a consensus about some of these things than others and psychologists (or in the latter case chemists or biologists) may investigate the reasons, but we know that the bearing of these views is capricious in the population. Or, we may approach social objects as moral agents, assessing them within a particular moral framework, and acting accordingly.[8]

Whereas in objective differentiation we seek to identify the truth about the properties of objects independent of the way we feel about them. But the divide between the subjective and objective is also not that simple. The origins of all "objective" thought or statement, must begin with individual human beings, or "subjects" and they will refer to "objects" in the world. These objects may be aesthetic, art, food, literature, preferences towards other individuals, or they may be embryonic statements about how the world is. But even at that mental level, we discriminate. We can look at our perceptions of things, or states of affairs. We can question the truth of our own accounts and set aside an experience as differentiated from the flux of other experiences. Being "objective", in this sense, is not a social act, but a mental one. An example of what I mean can be found in autobiographies. An autobiographer can be her/his harshest critic or interrogator. Yet however harsh the auto biographer is in her/his judgements, the accounts lack any kind of arbitration or grounding in something beyond the self and the reflection upon the objects of consciousness.

Though, no one begins *tabula rasa*. The differentiations, the mental objectivity, will have its origins earlier encounters with the social and physical world. Again, autobiography is usually an account of earlier social encounters.

However, arbitration comes in intersubjective encounters. Again, that which is subject to scrutiny may be aesthetic, it may be political or ideological about how the world ought to be, or it may be a claim about the way the world is. A scientific claim, a political view, or a work of literature, or art may or may not survive that intersubjective scrutiny. For many non-realists these encounters suffice to establish the truth of the matter in claims about the way the world is. Though either explicitly or implicitly, what they mean by truth is that of coherence whereby the agents sharing the meanings agree on the "truth" of the matter. For example, if it is agreed that the capital of Canada is Ottawa, then that is the truth of the matter. Such arguments can be attractive and are defended on the grounds that everything we consider true is on the basis of perception and or social agreement. This is a post-Kuhnian view (see Chapter 6) and in science it is the claim that what was agreement about a scientific fact at time *T1* may not be so at Time *T2*. And if this is true in the natural sciences, then it is even more the case in social science, where there is very little agreement about particular "social facts" over time, or between places.

But this version of truth runs into trouble. In the natural sciences it conflates opinion with empirical tests. Whilst it is true that a scientific fact at time *T1* may not be a scientific fact at time *T2*, this is on the basis that a later test falsifies or modifies the earlier fact. In practice and *contra* Kuhn, there are very few instances where an important body of scientific knowledge has been wholly refuted, and more often an earlier theory becomes incorporated into a later one, just as Newton's Laws become limiting cases in later relativity (Russell 1991). One can even say that given the context dependent nature of (middle range) social theories, in practice they more often get amended than refuted.

But in social science there is a much more important objection to coherence as truth. If we go back to the early 20th century, when eugenics was respectable, characteristics and abilities were regared as biologically determined. Consequently, women and non-whites were widely regarded, as mentally and therefore intellectually inferior to white males. We no longer believe this, but most of those who would support a coherence version of truth, will both say the eugenicists were wrong and that (in various ways) life chances are mostly socially determined and shaped. But you can't have it both ways, for if one argues the eugenicists were wrong, then one must also accept that the current view may also be overturned, because both are based on intersubjective agreement! Only an appeal to extra-intersubjective assessment can rescue the situation, as indeed it did in the condemnation of Herrnstein and Murray (1994), in the 1990s, attempt to revive biological determinants as causes of inequality or ability. Though there was political critique of this position, it was their bad science that attracted the most authoritative condemnation (Williams 2000a: 118–119). Indeed, because the objects of the social world are often moral objects the ontological content of such objects is characterised by an imperative.

This digression suggests that objectivity needs more than intersubjective agreement, it needs an arbitration beyond this. The version of truth is that which is consistent with reality, Bhaskar's transitive objects of science, our theories, conventions, practices and methods, in search of the intransitive objects of nature, or in our case the social world. The aim is to truthfully describe and explain social objects.

But there are three caveats:

First, in seeking to identify the truth about properties of objects, we cannot suppose that the truth can be established, or even if it was that we would know that it was. The *search* for the truth is, however, necessary. Consider the following sentences:

a. Sexual orientation is a condition that is biologically determined
b. Sexual orientation is chosen as a result of social or psychological factors

There are only three possibilities. That: (a) is true; (b) is true or a third residual possibility; (c) that sexual orientation results from some combination of both. Now it may be the case that one may be disinclined to see an investigation of the matter as a worthwhile or proper purpose, but if one does then this requires an attempt to seek the truth of whether (a), (b) or (c) is correct.

The second caveat is that the means to seek truth is contextually different. Philosophers, theologians, scientists, judges, detectives all seek the truth, but the means by which they do this varies considerably. Consequently, the grounds for objectivity and the way it will be manifested will depend on the social situation.

The third caveat is that this version of truth – the correspondence version of truth, is itself a value, a value of science, as is parsimony, accuracy, etc. They are scientific values and science, as we know it, is a social and historical construction that could have been otherwise. But crucially, the value of truth, can and should transcend particular situations. In a pre-scientific age, Plato divided truth into philosophical and non-philosophical. The former, he saw as a universal good for the Republic, but the latter (in everyday life) is something that may not always be a beneficial value, because to withhold it may promote a greater good (Woolf 2009). If we take Plato's advice and assume science as a successor to philosophy (in this regard), though it is a social construct, it has truth and *should have* truth, as a core value and to withhold it shifts the proposition in question from science to non-science.

I do not think that a tautology, that science is truth and truth is science follows, because alongside truth as a necessary value, there must also be purpose and differentiation.

What kind of value is objectivity?

In my description of the scientific value continuum I depicted three main uses of the term value: numeric, methodological and social/moral. Where does objectivity fit into this continuum?

Objectivity is a social value, but one that has both normative and methodological characteristics. Its conventional characteristics arise from its historical importation into science from philosophy. Objectivity, in the sense I defined it above, was present in most forms of classical and medieval philosophy, though in the latter case theological doctrine often clouded the search for truth. We can find it in law, in exploration and in technological problem-solving – not always, but often. Its importation into science as a normative value was a characteristic of the historic emergence of science.

Within science (and for the purposes of broad discussion this can encompass its natural and social form), objectivity is a methodological value by virtue of the procedures that have evolved in pursuit of the truth about objects. Methodology is an operationalisation of objectivity and methodological values themselves become necessary to the pursuit of objectivity in science. These might be very general, or as I noted above, specific to particular sciences. General methodological values might be parsimony, symmetry, replicability, etc. Examples from social sciences or psychology might be the construction of attitude scales, the means of analysis appropriate to nominal, ordinal or interval level data, theoretical sampling, or the role of a moderator in a focus group. What is good methodological practice is not always agreed and will change over time, but objectivity pursued as a methodological value will use the best known means possible to seek the truth about the properties of the objects of interest. In psychology, for example, the practice of the confirmation of the null hypothesis, in experiments, was standard practice for decades, but in recent years it has been criticised by statisticians (see Chapter 6). In social science there are those who have mounted a trenchant critique of the General Linear Model (see Chapter 4). Yet methodological debate is itself an exercise in objectivity and an attempt, at least implicitly, to maximise objectivity by improving methods.

Most normative values in science have no direct pay off in terms of discovery or explanation. White coats may keep spillages off chemists' clothes and peer reviewed journal articles may assist in the quality control of scientific output, their role is at best indirect. On the other hand objectivity operationalised through methodology has the existential property of directly assisting in the pursuit of truth, or at least in the elimination of error. This characteristic endows it with a further property, as with other scientific values, the ability to transcend epistemological communities. Whilst (say) a Marxist and a Weberian may differ in, say, their theories of capital accumulation – which theory provides the best explanation, they may well agree on matters such as sample size, or significance levels. That is, though objectivity must have a purpose, it can serve more than one purpose. However, by eliminating error, or demonstrating that X is more likely to be the case than Y it can end up adjudicating between purposes.

Though objectivity is operationalised through method within science, it was imported into science as an already existing normative value. It has a life outside of science, but is manifested in quite different ways. In science the value of objectivity is situated in methodological values and outside of science it is situated within other values.

The Gouldner quote above referred to the value of health. The objectivity of the physician in opting for treatment A over B is in pursuance of that value. But that value in turn rests on a broader human value of the relief of suffering and the prolonging of life. If we subscribe to these values and presumably physicians do, then to pursue a course treatment B, when A would better serve the objective of health would be irrational. Objectivity requires rationality, both inside and outside of science. Indeed, it may well be the case that it requires a particular form of rationality, but then so does sociology, chemistry, biology, etc. for them to be recognisable as the disciplines within which we can debate objectivity in the first place. I discuss the methodological implications of this in Chapter 10.

Objectivity, is situated in contexts that may produce different purposes, but it is the search for truth about objects and their properties and the necessary conditions, I describe, transcend particular situations. The following brief example illustrates what I mean. Maria Jung and colleagues, published their research on immigrant perceptions of the police, in a leading criminology journal (Jung et al 2019).

The origins of criminology go back to the 19th century (Godfrey et al 2008: Chapter 1), but in recent years it has flourished as a popular undergraduate choice in many Western countries, often eclipsing more sociological studies of crime and deviance. Indeed, in many UK universities, criminology attracts many more students than sociology. It would not be an exaggeration to say that it is a fashionable subject, for students, and particular topics in criminology have attracted substantial funding.

The concern of this paper was to address the known characteristic (from previous research) that in Western countries (and the UK is specifically discussed) immigrant view of the police are more positive than those of the native born (op cit: 1370). But also, the longer a person resides, in a country, the more negative their views are of the police. Thus, their views change over time. In those countries of immigrant origin deemed "more corrupt" or "more oppressive", views of the police, by immigrants, in the destination countries is particularly positive initially.

Previous research had concentrated on immigrants to European countries (often using data from the European Social Survey), but Jung et al used Canadian data in order to test whether such findings could be generalised there. An analytic framework, due to Wu et al (2013) was used to test for both immigrant specific factors (length of time in the destination country and nature of political regime in the country of origin) and universal factors (e.g. race/ethnicity, experience with police and crime, neighbourhood conditions, regional context and sense of injustice).

The research used victimisation data from Statistics Canada.[9] The dependent variable used, was "overall view of the police". Independent variables, such as those above, plus control variables (e.g. age, sex, marital status, education) initially analysed using bi-variate ANOVA, then fitted to three linear regression models.

The findings largely amplified those of previous studies, suggesting a relationship between the political regime of the country of origin and the attitudes towards the destination country. The more positive the latter, the more positive were views towards the police. Conversely, immigrants from other democracies were less positive.

The "situatedness" of the objectivity was in a number of overlapping contexts. A concern, often expressed by policy makers and the police themselves, is that of negative attitudes. The origins of these are often as old as police forces themselves and develop as a result of collective and individual experience over very long periods of time. Arguably, such a concern, would not trouble authoritarian regimes, other that of a concern for keeping order. So, a worry about attitudes towards the police, is a product of the development of democratic societies, who often have a concern with policing by consent. Negative attitudes towards the police are a social problem born of a particular context. However, these attitudes, if they are shown to exist, are real – they are "social objects", because in the specific example, holding a positive attitude towards the police, has causal consequences, not just for order, but for cooperation in crime solving and crime prevention.

Indeed, one might say that the attitudes and a concern with them are social constructions, as indeed they are, but as I have argued in previous chapters they are real in their consequences.

The second form of "situatedness" is criminology itself. Like the chicken and the egg, which came first the discipline or the problems that interest the discipline? Either way, once in existence, criminology found purpose in researching the problems.

So, where lies truth? If it is accepted that different attitudes towards the police exist in different groups and prior to the research described, this was established in previous studies, then it must follow that the truth of the matter, in Canada, is that immigrants well express the same or different views, to those of immigrants to other countries. Differences are likely to be a matter of degree, rather than dichotomous. So once the initial premise is accepted, there will be a truth of the matter. The premises, themselves, can be examined, through an evaluation of the prior research. So, although the "truth" logically follows, in this case, the premises themselves could be faulty.

In the research described, effectively a replication strategy was adopted (using Wu's framework), allowing a comparison of Canada with European countries. The methods of ANOVA and linear regression were used and although no methodological justification was used, these were relatively simple methods that, again, were not vastly different to those used in prior studies and in widespread use in this form of analysis.[10]

Possibly there are methodological criticisms of the Jung et al research, but in my view it seemed to typify situated objectivity, in so far as it sought the truth about the matter, but within a particular context. Elsewhere, I have suggested examples, where either the "problem" itself was overtly "ideological", or the methods used intentionally supported the ideological stance, or were just poor methods (Williams 2005a).

Now, I realise that the last paragraph was a hostage to fortune. Poor methods and methodology, can exist as sins beyond and apart from the problem investigated, but that aside, who am I to judge what is "ideological" and what is not? The short answer is that my judgement of what is ideological is that of a citizen, but as Longino maintains, these values do and should permeate scientific enquiry. However, we are left with a problem.

Does situatedness determine what can count as true? If this is the case, then this takes us towards epistemological relativism. If, on the other hand (as I have claimed) truth is a transcendent property, is this not simply smuggling in value freedom through the back door?

The answer to this is neither simple or equivocal, and it is for this reason I want to finally turn to the idea of "objective knowledge".

Objective knowledge

Let us take stock of where we are in this chapter. So far I have advanced an ontological thesis about social objects and their reality and an epistemological thesis of situated objectivity as underpinning an investigative strategy. These two theses could stand alone. My description of social objects might stand as a realist meta-theory for the social world to count as "real". Situated objectivity, as I have said elsewhere (Williams 2015), does not require a full blown realism, merely a commitment to differentiating one thing from another (states, beliefs, actions, institutions, etc.). Such a minimum commitment could be even seen as conventionalist. However a realist methodology, because it claims to be based on a naturalistic philosophy requires to be underwritten by some form of objectivity and a realist objectivity needs a realist ontology to underpin it.

So far so good, but avoiding epistemological relativism, or the fiat of value freedom, requires a transcendency, not just for the value of truth, but for theories and methods, at least analogously to those of natural science.

Popper's "third world" or "world three" of objective knowledge may help us here. Popper's aim was, in some ways, rather similar to my own. As a realist, he also argued that there is an objective world that exists beyond our subjective imaginings, understandings, etc.

His analogy is that of three worlds. The first world is that of physical objects (in fact rather similar to my first ontological kind I described in Chapter 2). These ontological kinds exist apart from human interpretation or action: mountains, rivers, physiological states, etc. The second world is that of mental states and subjectivities. In effect these worlds are proposed as an alternative to Cartesian dualism. Though Popper supports the common sense idea of a separation between mind and body (in this sense he describes himself as a dualist) he nevertheless sees them as interactive entities (Popper 1994: 4–6), thus avoiding the Cartesian essentialism of the mental and physical.

Popper's third world is a wholly human one. It is human creation. Though he does admit that animals may possess a consciousness that might permit also a "third world" (op cit: 71). In sum, Popper's third world is that of our creations. It is a very populous world of art objects, music, buildings, books, libraries and crucially scientific theories, in fact, all of those things which create things separately to us, often by interacting with the first world via the second world. So, whilst Popper is a dualist in respect of the first and second worlds, he proposes a third kind – his third world. The important characteristic of the third world, is its autonomy. At various places he provides examples of what he means. For instance, imagine that most things in the world were destroyed, but the great libraries survived. With the knowledge from these we could rebuild our world. Or, mathematics. Though we, as humans, invented mathematics, once invented their sequences and proofs become autonomous, for example, through prime numbers, which are sequenced, but we do nor know yet what is, or if there is a greatest prime number[11] (Popper 1994: 24–34).[12] Furthermore, knowledge in the third world not just interacts with but can have unintended consequences for the second world of mental states.

Popper lived and died before the concept of artificial intelligence became a central feature of our lives. Though in his later years (he died in 1994), computing technologies were advancing rapidly and Popper discusses the idea of intelligent machines in a number of places, citing Alan Turing (e.g. Popper 1979: 224–225*ff*, 1982: 72*ff*), but as far as I am aware he did not discuss the idea of the internal autonomy of the third world, specifically through artificial intelligence and its ability to effect the kind of changes usually associated with humans interacting with the third world. I'm not sure whether he would have supported the idea of internal interaction, in the third world, but either way the existence of AI must at least increase the causal complexity of the third world.

I think it does nevertheless follow, that if one accepts the notion of a third world, then the products of the social sciences, as much as the natural sciences – theories, empirical findings, methods, etc., must be inhabitants of the third world.

So how does this help solve the problem of relativism, or the concern that I am merely substituting truth for value freedom?

Firstly, let us consider theories and methods. Both were (of course) present in the Jung et al example above, both in the research reported and in the prior research. Indeed, as I indicated, the Jung et al research, used a theoretical framework, developed and used by Wu. Thus, in publishing this framework, Wu gave it autonomy in the third world and others could later test its conjectures. Similarly, the methods used by Jung et al, were also recorded in third world documents, their strengths, weaknesses and appropriateness have been tested. Popper, of course, would claim that theories and methods may be falsified, shown to be wrong. Now, as I suggested in Chapter 6, simple falsification is naïve and hugely problematic. But, in the form of longer research programmes, as proposed by Lakatos, the court of history will hold judgement on whether they are right or wrong, or more usually partially right and incorporated into later theories. Furthermore, the value of truth itself is exported to the third world and in its correspondence form will relate directly to ontological content. Though it may well be that the ontological content changes and the truth of the matter at time T1 may not be the truth of the matter at time T2, because of this. In the social world, this is an important characteristic. Most theories, as Robert Merton recognised, are limited in their applicability. As I suggested, in the Jung et al example, the problematic itself is only relevant within certain social arrangements and the theory being tested, would be irrelevant in other social arrangements, the ontological content has changed, regardless of whether the theory is supported, falsified or modified.

Nevertheless, we can over stress the extent of variance and the relativism that might be said to follow. Max Weber (Weber 1974: 110) starting point was that in matters of policy there will be always be a debate about "ends", about social goals, about the appropriate policies and therefore which investigations should be pursued – as in my example above, the accepted "good" of trust in the police. So, whilst investigation is value driven, objectivity is preserved by social scientist's examination his/her value positions for their logical coherence and their relationship to other concepts and principles. This is the "reflexive fallibilism" I proposed in Chapter 6. Weber proposed two levels of analysis (1974: 77), the first that of the cultural significance of a phenomenon and the second an investigation of the causal factors that lead to the mass significance of such a phenomena. The existence (his example) of the money economy is a concrete historical fact, thus (he implies) existing outside of any given subjectivity, but nevertheless a product of subjectivities. So, we might say, the money economy is both a social object and has an existence in the third world.

But also the "money economy" and more specifically, capitalism, has longevity. Its key features have enough invariance to support theories that themselves have retained longevity and arguably have been tested and falsified in many respects. So, as I have suggested earlier, one may argue that social science laws may evade us, or are simply trivially true, but generalisations through time and place, can often be quite robust, simply because of the relative invariance of important aspects of the social world. I should say, this far from implies that the invariance is of beneficial social features. Oppressed groups, for example, may over time reproduce aspects of their own repression as an unintended consequence of often quotidian actions.

Within these limitations we can conclude that social science theories, findings and methods occupy a logically similar position to those of the natural sciences, in that they are testable propositions that exist autonomously in the third world. This, we might say, is the ontological "anchor" of a realist objectivity, however much that is situated within specific social contexts.

But there is a second problem, that might be described as that of morality. Popper claims that his theory of knowledge, which he describes as "evolutionary" (Popper 1979: 256–284), addresses this problem. But I am doubtful.

Values and morality in the third world

As L.M.A Francot, (Francot 2014) observes, moral choices arise out of social complexity and the complexity itself, in turn, emerges from the myriad of choices and possibilities we face. It is the self conscious feedback that I have referred too earlier. This, in turn, frames both questions social scientists ask and the legitimacy conferred upon both the questions posed and the answers provided. As I said at the beginning of this chapter, social scientists seek knowledge of knowledge.

Although Popper does not phrase the problem in the way I have, his third world and the evolutionary epistemology that follows is the corollary of his indeterminism. For him "all life is problem solving" (Popper 1999), that move towards answers that eliminate error and consequently socially evolve, in much the same way as living creatures evolve. Indeed, this is where his "third world" comes from and its contents are available to be improved upon, or in the case of scientific knowledge, falsified. There is a consequent interaction between all three worlds. For Popper, morality is the freedom to criticise in an "open society" (Popper 1999), where matters of policy arrangements, and so on, are settled through trial and error.

It seems to me that in advancing this perspective, Popper takes a philosophy of science and generalises it to a social morality. As a philosophy of science, it can be interpreted as in the long run as truth will triumph over error and particularly error that is born of ideology. The classic example is that of the Lysenko affair in the Soviet Union. Lysenkian genetics rejected Darwinism and reverted to an earlier Lamarckian principle of inherited characteristics (Medvedev 1969). Lysenko claimed that in crop plants, such as wheat, environmental influences are heritable via all cells of the organism. This approach found favour with Joseph Stalin and for a while it seemed to pay off as crop yields were increased, but this was due to other factors, such as mechanisation and the fact that it had followed a period of famine, after forced collectivisation. As time went on, it became apparent that Lysenkian genetics was ill conceived and crop yields fell.

A more recent example, from the 2000s, concerned the doubt that was cast over the MMR (Measles, Mumps, Rubella vaccine) by Andrew Wakefield. He published a paper in the Lancet (Wakefield et al 1998), which claimed a link between autism and the MMR vaccine. Unlike the Lysenko affair, there was no overt attempt to deceive, but a consensus emerged that the claimed link was based upon bad science and the Lancet itself retracted the original paper[13]. However the societal effect, in the meantime, was profound and resulted in a lowering of MMR vaccination take-up.

In the Lysenko affair the "bad science" began from ideology and was sustained for considerable period by ideology. The MMR controversy began from bad science and was sustained by a media and subsequent public reaction that became wary of the alleged consequences of the vaccine.

But in both cases, we might say that the eventual court of empirical adequacy ruled. When ideology or belief is pitted against physical reality, the latter will win out in the end.

But an evolutionary epistemology applied more generally to society is deeply problematic, for what counts as error and what counts as a solution will change over time and between places. Furthermore, societal error and success have, throughout history, been defined by those who have power – Marx's "ruling ideology". There is no equivalent of a court of empirical adequacy in matters of social arrangements. Whilst we might avoid an epistemological relativism, an acceptance of a moral relativism *as scientists* seems inevitable, though as citizens we will inevitably hold and wish to generalise moral position. The open society that Popper favoured (which was widely criticised), is itself a product of moral values, those of free speech and association, for example. But the corollary of this is an economic liberalism (of the kind proposed by Friedrich Hayek (Hayek 1944) that insists on the market as an arbiter of other values, thus often stifling the very openness Popper advocated.

But all is not entirely lost! Within the social knowledge of the third world there will exist the products of different social arrangements and ideologies. These things are real and are evidence of realities. They are available for scrutiny and comparison. That I am able to take the above view I do on Popper's social philosophy and Hayek's economics is evidence of this. At the time of writing, the UK government has made the claim that its diagnostic testing for the Covid-19 virus is on track and effective, but this claim is based on the erroneous and possibly mendacious claim that 100,000 tests per week were being conducted.[14] One cannot logically refute their claim of effectiveness, but one can refute the statistical basis of the claim, because the evidence for statistical claim is lodged in the third world and therefore open to scrutiny. Only by destroying the products of the third world, which not even the revolutions of the Khmer Rouge or the Taliban, have managed can we remove that possibility of scrutiny and comparison.

Situated objectivity

Objectivity, as with science itself and its characteristics, are values. Our world is a world of values. Yet as scientists, we need to provide descriptions and explanations that are as truthful as we can make them. This means the value of objectivity, is both a communal scientific value, but also a personal one. All scientists are citizens and we will bring, or inherit in our science, what Helen Longino termed "contextual values" (Longino 1990). As she claimed, these are both inevitable and desirable. Science does not and should not exist in a moral vacuum. But our theories, our findings and methods have an objective existence beyond us and are available for scrutiny and possibly falsification, because once created they have an existence separate to us. They, like all social knowledge, are real, they become social objects with causal properties.

As scientists and citizens we interact with the third world in complex ways, both at an individual and social level, creating a multitude of feedback mechanisms that are interactions between science (and social science) and its social context. There is no royal road to objectivity or truth, but social knowledge is real and our interactions with it as scientists, or citizens are possible and transformative. But our interactions with it as scientists, are of a special kind that are underpinned by the transcending value of objectivity.

Notes

1. See for example Bekoff 2002.
2. Dog and cat lovers should rest easy! I am not proposing that animals have no conscious awareness. In this respect, there is a continuum between mammals and humans. The most important characteristic that sets humans apart from animals is self reflection. Monica does not do much self reflecting!
3. The different ontological characteristics of these are reflected in their respective levels of measurement (nominal, ordinal, interval, ratio).
4. I realise for many that "success" is a loaded word. Here I mean it as the accretion of testable scientific knowledge, however nothing much hangs on this particular definition and one could even define it as social recognition.
5. Janack (2002: 275) identifies 17 different uses of the term.
6. I use the term specification here in the engineering sense meaning the specific performance or construction standards to be achieved to be adequate to the task. Different tasks may require different and more exacting specifications.
7. I use the term "necessary", in its logical sense here (see Chapters 3 and 4). However, the *practice* of science and social science have only conceptual necessity, though in the natural sciences, there is ontological grounding in natural necessity.
8. I have used a rather philosophical turn of phrase here, but more prosaically I mean things like political engagement, assessment of an individual's actions, particular principles and views we hold, etc.
9. Cycle 28 was the sixth cycle to collect information on a representative sample of Canadians' safety and victimization and to better understand Canadians' perceptions of crime and the criminal justice system. Data were collected from January 2014 to January 2015 from a stratified random sample of Canadians aged 15 and over, living in the provinces and territories, within households with telephone service, excluding those in institutions. Data were collected using computer-assisted telephone interviewing (CATI) and

a pilot method of E-Questionnaire (EQ), in which respondents were redirected to an online option for completing the survey (see Statistics Canada 2016 for more details around the sampling procedures)' (Jung et al 2019: 1375–1376).

10. I say this with the caveat, that the General Linear Model itself has been the subject of statistical criticism, as I have noted in several places in this book.
11. As of January 2018, the largest prime number discovered had 23,249,425 digits. https://slate.com/technology/2018/01/the-worlds-largest-prime-number-has-23249425-digits-heres-why-you-should-care.html.
12. It does occur to me that Popper's "third world" challenges Actor Network Theory (see my note in Chapter 3), if it is said that everything in the social and physical worlds exists in constantly shifting networks of relationships. Whilst, for humans to use or interpret the "third world", they must interact with it, perhaps in a "network", there exists only a contingent relationship. That is, the form of the network is not determined.
13. See https://www.sciencedirect.com/science/article/pii/S0140673697110960. Accessed 19/06/20.
14. See https://fullfact.org/health/coronavirus-100k-tests/. Accessed 19/06/20.

8

Mechanisms

In this chapter I return to the concept of mechanisms, I introduced in Chapter 3. Mechanisms are central to complex realism, yet the way the word is deployed in everyday language and indeed in a rather undefined or generic sense, in sociology, is not at all what we want the term to mean. Nor do we want to use the term, in the way it is in classical physics as "mass in motion".[1]

Popper's clouds and clocks analogy is again useful to us. The mechanism of the engineer or classical physicist is a clock and the ideal mechanism is a clock that always keeps perfect time. A clock is predictable, its mechanism can be clearly described, and it can be seen in isolation from other mechanisms. Even though, for many years, I have thought probabilistically about the social world (and very many aspects of the physical world) and at least I have a "feel" for complexity, it is nevertheless so tempting to think in terms of clocks, when I think about a mechanism.

Yet complex mechanisms are closer to clouds. They evolve in unpredictable ways and they are difficult to see in isolation. So maybe there are no complex *mechanisms* and the term is not just confusing, but downright misleading? But to concede this implies disorder, but complexity is not disorder but a particular kind of order. In the social world it is an order of discernible actions, beliefs, institutions and a very structured third world of knowledge production that I described in the previous chapter. Moreover, and crucially, mechanisms though complex have causal properties.

But consider clouds, the antithesis in Popper's analogy to clocks. Could there be a cloud mechanism? Well, if we allow that something we can call a mechanism can exist in the social, or the biological realm, then where is the cut off? When does a phenomenon cease to qualify? As I sit and write these words, I can look through the window and see some very low and dense clouds. I can see cloud formations slowly moving from east to west, they have discernible forms, which change slowly as they move. In fact, to identify the direction of cloud movement, I can fasten my eye on a particular cloud and watch it move east to west, changing but slowly in its appearance. But these clouds, in their denseness and overall character have been the feature of the sky for two days. They are part of a discernible weather pattern, a relatively weak ridge of low pressure and they are relatively low and shallow, under 4,000 metres. More precisely we can cite a number of equations that can describe weather formations.[2] I would say they are a complex mechanism *par excellence*. They have shape, form, direction, at a micro level subject to something like Brownian motion and are part of a describable, partially predictable weather pattern. But, they are much less complex than social mechanisms, because they have no capacity of self-awareness or free will.

I would readily abandon the word mechanism, but for two reasons. Firstly, I've not yet been convinced of a better term, but secondly because if there is a continuum of patterning and organisation between clouds on one hand and clocks on the other, we would be left deciding where the cut off was, perhaps somewhere between cell renewal and entropy? Mechanisms (or whatever we would perhaps call them in the future) exist from the simplest to the most complex, throughout the physical and social world.

I have two purposes in this chapter. Firstly, to show what a complex mechanism is and secondly to show how mechanistic thinking can be useful methodologically. And at the risk of providing a spoiler, we might even say that the chapter divides into mechanisms and models of mechanisms!

Making up mechanisms

This was the title of a paper I wrote, which was published in an edited collection about realist methodology and method (Williams 2019). My title was deliberately mischievous. For realists, mechanisms are … well, real. What else could they be? But my title implied an element of fiction, even deception.[3] It was, I admit, a sales pitch to get people thinking about what a real mechanism, in the social world, might be. My argument might be summarised as we need to think in terms of mechanisms which exist and what we can know of mechanisms. The first is their ontological character (Bhaskar's intransitive objects or my relative invariance), the second is what we can know of them, their epistemological character. Inevitably, if we are to talk of mechanisms, then we must describe them, but our descriptions will (as I argued in Chapter 5) will always under-describe.

Much non-realist mechanistic thinking does not dwell on their ontological status, but implicitly in analytic sociology, in the work of Elster, Hedström and Swedberg (Elster 1998, 2007, Hedström and Swedberg 1998a) they are treated as if they were real and potentially that reality is apparent to observation, for example their aim

> … could be seen as creating a kind of catalogue raisonné of mechanisms that operate in social life, ranging from the most elementary through to

> the most complex. What is then apparently envisaged is that sociologists confronted with an explanatory problem will be able to search this catalogue for mechanisms that would appear most likely to lead to a solution …
>
> Goldthorpe 2016: 114–115

John Goldthorpe, himself, seems to take a position much closer to realism when he advocates the adoption of methods that can best determine the actual operation of mechanisms, but citing Cox (1992: 297) "at an observational level that is deeper than that involved in the data under immediate analysis".

As I argued in Chapter 5, inevitably we must know things under a description, so given the inevitable gap between description and reality, pessimistically we might think of the epistemological character of a mechanism is as either an ideal type and/or, an act of faith! But it's not as bad as that, because although the act of identifying and isolating a complex mechanism is never complete, there are parts of mechanisms and even some simple mechanisms, that can come into view and can be so isolated.

Laws and regularities

To get a feel for what a mechanism is we might start from what it is not. In Chapter 3, I described the covering law model in which the *explanandum* is deduced from a set of true statements, the *explanans*, of which at least one should be a law. Now, as I have argued there either are no laws or very few and weak trivially true laws in the social world (see Chapter 3), because there no natural necessity in which to ground them. Yet, for much of its history quantitative social science has attempted to derive explanations from procedures that are grounded in a version of the covering law model.

Raymond Boudon, in discussing the work of Hans Zetterberg (Boudon 1974: 14–18), illustrates why this is a problem in the latter's advocacy of the use of axioms to more clearly specify a theory to produce testable propositions. Zetterberg suggests a theory about social mobility may be thus specified:

> Axiom 1 – if prosperity increases, the middle classes grow larger;
> Axiom 2 – if the middle classes grow larger, consensus increases;
> Axiom 3 – when mobility increases, consensus increases;
> Axiom 4 – when consensus increases mobility increases.
>
> Boudon 1974: 16

Boudon asks if this means that consensus always necessarily increases or consensus generally speaking increases? Do the middle classes always grow larger if prosperity increases, or just generally so? Zetterberg has framed this proposition as a law, but the best we can say is that it is a probabilistic one where it applies, but we have no explanation of why it is probabilistic where it applies, or why it does not always apply. Why do the middle classes grow larger as prosperity increases, why does consensus increase? And what is the causal relationship between mobility and consensus? Zetterberg's axioms may predict and consistent with middle range theory, they may be tested elsewhere, but they do not explain.

A perennial favourite to "explain" an outcome or dependent variable has been social class, say for example in educational success. In most of the western world, people from "lower" or manual social classes are less likely to attend university.

So, when we say a higher social class is a "predictor" of, or is associated with educational success, this is a somewhat coy way of saying that all of those economic and possibly cultural measures that go to make up the variable of social class are responsible for educational success! But, even then the composition of the class variable, is composed of other things, themselves, not causally efficacious – such as occupation. So, in what sense does the fact that Denzil Penberthy is a builder, make a difference to whether his daughter Talwyn goes to university?

Another variable often used in the UK to predict educational success, is that of Free School Meals. For a long time, children from economically deprived backgrounds have been eligible to receive a free midday meal, at school. So Free School Meals stands in as a measure of the economic standing of a parent(s). If their children are eligible for free school meals, then they are more likely to come from households which suffer poverty and they in turn will come to experience educational disadvantage. Sometimes it is deployed as an "area level variable", that is the proportion of children in a given area, is used as a predictor in analyses. There is some debate as to how successfully this variable does actually predict educational disadvantage (Gorard 2012, Taylor 2018), but nevertheless, in many circumstances and in models containing other variables, it may provide successful prediction, by "explaining",[4] at least some of the variance, in a model. But what does it mean? Is the act of eating lasagne and knowing its free, an inhibitor to Talwyn either deciding, or being able to, go to university? There is a mechanism and a causal one at that, but these are derived variables that are associations that, in themselves do not describe or explain the mechanism.

Contrast this with something absurdly simple. Riding a bike. Now, my sitting on my bike at place A is a predictor of my arriving at place B and if we measured lots of people sitting on bikes at a place A and then arriving at a place B, there would be a very strong, almost perfect association. A few people might just have been posing, or fell off on the way!

But this tells us nothing about what made A to B possible. But we can so easily describe a mechanism of pushing the pedals down, which turns a flywheel with the chain drive, which in turn connects to gear cogs on other smaller flywheels, which then turn the back wheel of the bike. This simple little mechanism is real enough and it in turn can be explained by other biological and physical mechanisms.

Zetterberg's proposition is one of regularities. It is not a description of a mechanism, because the causal connection between the elements of the proposition are not specified, they are a black box. The same is also true of social class or Free School Meals as predictors of educational outcomes. In contrast, my bicycle example provides a causal explanation at each stage. Zetterberg and others in the empiricist, or causal analysis traditions do, as I suggested in Chapter 3, often tell "causal stories" to say why variables are associated and this is both inevitable and desirable, but these are usually more like proto-mechanisms, that is the variables are interpreted, but statistical associations, often of derived variables, stand in for mechanisms.

So from these illustrations of what a mechanism is *not*, we can produce as summary or preliminary description of what a mechanism *is*.

Daniel Little (1991: 14) provides the following definition that might well describe a physical mechanism grounded in a deterministic or probabilistic law of nature.

C is a cause of E $=_{df}$, there is a series of events C_i leading from C to E, and the transition from C_i to C_{i+i} is governed by one or more laws L_i.

He contrasts this with, what he calls the inductive regularity thesis, in which the associative elements of the Zetterberg example would fit.

C is a cause of E $=_{df}$, there is a regular association between C type events and E type events.

Little does not defend the second statement, for the reasons I set out above. But he does offer a qualified defence of the first statement, amending laws for law-like regularities, in the social world. As with other advocates of mechanisms (e.g. Elster 1998, Hedström and Swedberg 1998). He grounds this in a moderate form of methodological individualism, whereby individuals become causal agents through exercising rational preferences (Little 1991: 18).

I think Little's definition is a good one, but though reluctantly I can live with the word mechanism, "law like regularity" is too much for me. This not aesthetic, but methodological. Whilst I fully accept that individuals can be causal agents, acting on beliefs and desires and that these can produce regularities (and indeed relative invariance), many if not most regularities are often institutional and are often emergent and they are enabling and constraining upon the individual.

What I mean by this is that individuals will create social objects, through the exercise of their beliefs and desires, but once created such social objects achieve a level of autonomy and their causal possibilities will often exist in a Markov chain. So, as in the Sapperstein example in Chapter 4, the individual decision-making at each table (whether it became a left or right handed table) was indeed a local "regularity", the final outcome of which diners were poisoned, was independent of this choice, other than the creation of the sufficient condition to avoid poisoning by being on a right handed table. But, of course, the waiters could have chosen to serve the right handed tables first, rather than the left!

So it is within a mechanism, that there may be traceability to the regularities of individual behaviour, the creation of the mechanism will involve emergent properties and the nesting of these in other mechanisms. Moreover, even if mechanisms can be said to arise from regularities, in realist language, these mechanisms may or may not "fire" and this will depend on context. Peter Hedström and Richard Swedberg (1998b: 17–19) discuss a number of examples of this kind. One in particular is almost a real world example of the Sapperstein thought experiment, that of Granovetter's threshold theory of human behaviour. In a nutshell, this theory states that an individual's decision to participate in collective behaviour often depends on how many others are participating. He identified initial threshold behaviour, whereby different individuals will have threshold limits of participation. His research indicated that very slight threshold changes, will produce quite different behaviour mechanisms. So, in this case, whilst mechanisms come into being (and they may not), the initial regularity (that there are thresholds) is only trivially true. The regularities only become established later and they are local and not just based on threshold numbers of participants, but the social and moral legitimation of the behaviour.

This is not to say that typologies of participating behaviour cannot be constructed, but the typologies of such mechanisms will be nested in other mechanisms and will operate within contexts. So, Little's definition might be amended thus,

C is a cause of E $=_{df}$, there is a series of events C_i leading from C to E, and the transition from C_i to C_{i+i} is the realisation of earlier mechanisms M … *n* operating within local context.

This is not especially elegant, nor is it satisfying, because its mechanisms all the way down![5] Indeed Goldthorpe (2016: 115) points out that seeking mechanisms that underlie regularities can lead to an infinite regress. This leads him to question where is the stopping point for identifying mechanisms? This dilemma is unsurprising when we consider that mechanisms are causal and causes are complex. But perhaps context frees us from the regress?

Contexts and mechanisms

It is this idea of mechanisms in context that has inspired the work of Ray Pawson, who suggested a simple, but elegant formula of Context (C) plus Mechanism (M) = Outcome (O). Much of Pawson's work has been concerned with programme evaluation and his (and Nick Tilley's) version of this is, unsurprisingly, termed "realist evaluation" (Pawson and Tilley 1997). Prior to Pawson and Tilley, much of evaluation research employed simplistic causal reasoning, which measured the success of an intervention programme through the measurement of a few outcome variables and moreover interventions were regarded as portable, so a crime reduction programme that had "worked" in Boston, USA, was thought likely to work in Boston UK.[6] I exaggerate, but only a bit! As Ray Pawson observes, in respect of experiments, the "why" things happen is not considered and "the findings are expected to speak for themselves" (Pawson 2013: 4–5).

Most interventions are complex in nature (e.g. Sure Start mentioned in Chapter 3) or they are interventions in complex situations and often both. A simple outcome measure of "what works" is asking the wrong question and the motto of realist evaluation is what works for whom, under what circumstances. Mechanisms do not operate independently of agents, though they can be causal upon agents, and may operate despite them. So, it is with interventions. They inevitably begin within specific contexts (C), but it is not a single C. Pawson illustrates this with the simple exemplar mechanism (M) of incentives to individuals to participate in a programme (Pawson 2013: 19–24). The incentive may be squandered by the rich and seized upon by the needy. Two different contexts. And different outcomes for these groups. Pawson suggests that the theorisation of these contexts will show a more complex mechanism of outcomes for different groups. As he notes, interventions are rarely "one trick ponies" (Pawson 2013: 23) and may include advice and mentoring support. These in turn provide further contexts and themselves increase the complexity of the intervention mechanism.

Sure Start programmes were the quintessential complex interventions, even though they had a common, but simple aim "to support young children and their families by integrating early education, childcare, healthcare and family support services in disadvantaged areas" (NESS 2008). This, in practice, meant many different kinds of intervention mechanisms in many initial contexts and unsurprisingly it was difficult to distil concrete outcome measures in common across the programmes. Initial national evaluations, across the Sure Starts, did not indicate widespread success, but longitudinal data that was more contextualised, did show benefits in child health, obesity reduction and cognitive performance (NESS 2010).

The Sure Start evaluations I was involved in, included a wide range of different programmes, of different sizes and locations.[7] Some were in largely rural areas, others in very dense urban areas. Some combined localities of great poverty with those of relative affluence. Although we were required, by National Sure Start, to make a number of standardised measurements in a formative evaluation, most of our work was "bottom up" (beginning with individual users of services) and formative in nature. That is, our evaluations were themselves formative mechanisms that changed some aspects of services. All of the Sure Starts we evaluated produced some results, that indicated unexpected emergent outcomes, but one in particular, was particularly characterised by such outcomes (Hatton and Williams 2002). For example: there was an increase in the number of women (mostly mothers) who became more active in public life through community organisations (including Sure Stat itself) and many also took up educational opportunities. Prior to the intervention fathers had a very low profile in child centred community activities, but this increased greatly. Adult literacy classes were started and were successful. Attendance at "Fun Days" exceeded all expectations. But standard health and education indicators showed only slight improvements. Yet, what had happened could be described as an increase in community solidarity, that did not exist prior to the Sure Start initiative in this location, which arguably could be said to be both worthy in its own right, but provide a more solid basis to improve early childhood outcomes. The final report on this particular Sure Start emphasised the need to respect and understand local difference in assessing the success, or otherwise, of Sure Start.

> A key problem is that as a National Initiative all Sure Starts have to follow the same guidelines and this disregards the fact that not all Sure Start initiatives are the same characteristically or geographically. In fact, they are very different in terms of community needs and experiences. One cannot treat the Sure Start initiative of an inner city in the same manner as one would, for example, Lescudjack.[8] Although all Sure Start initiatives share the common factor of significant levels of economic and social deprivation, the characteristics of each region are very different, and as such should be addressed in differing ways as a means of respecting local individuality. It is impossible to concede that all regions embracing Sure Start initiatives will become identical communities under the umbrella of a National Sure Start without considerable resistance and a loss of identity due to the ensuing dilution of the very elements which set them apart as distinct discrete communities.
>
> Hatton and Williams 2002: 38

This conclusion did not imply that every locality had mechanisms operating that were totally distinct. There were commonalities and we sought to find them. For example, neighbouring Sure Starts were within the same public housing environment, the same health and education authorities. A major characteristic, which itself produced "negative" behavioural mechanisms, was multi-generational unemployment in the same household, and this held true in all of the Sure Start localities we evaluated. Nutritional regimes were also very similar in each location. Available financial resources clustered around the same mean, with little dispersion. These characteristics alone were important contributors to complex local mechanisms that could be found in neighbouring Sure Starts, but each would operate in rather different contexts (urban–rural, public transport facilities, availability of and distance to work etc.). Mechanisms could be identified and compared, across these Sure Starts, as could the outcomes in the different contexts, allowing, what Pawson terms, "realist synthesis". This, he says, can be achieved through the synthesis of data, the theorisation of programmes, adjudication between programmes, compare theory in comparative settings, to compare official expectations with actual practice (Pawson 2006: 93–99).

CMO is elegant, but perhaps deceptively simple. It can both explain outcomes as a result of the interaction of a mechanism with its context, but the mechanisms are multi-layered, or nested, and the contexts plural and they change through time. A mechanism that works in context A may not work in context B. But this talk of contexts and mechanisms is, to an extent, question begging. When is a context the interaction with another mechanism, and when is a mechanism, just a change of context? In realist evaluation the mechanism is the resources etc. produced by the programme and the stakeholders' responses. The context is that in which it happens. This is less straightforward in non-evaluation research of mechanisms, where the researcher seeks to identify mechanisms *post-hoc* and ones which may not have been the result of the intended actions of agents or institutions, as in interventions. For example, a central bank will set interest rates, but this will happen in different socio-economic contexts, but these contexts may overlap and constitute a mechanism in their/its own right. The financial crisis of 2008 provides a ready example. It was initiated by deregulation in the financial industry, which then permitted banks to engage in hedge fund trading with derivatives (https://www.thebalance.com/what-caused-2008-global-financial-crisis-3306176, accessed 28/11/19). This was an initial mechanism, which operated on different jurisdiction contexts (e.g. sub-prime lending in the United States). When the crisis happened, there were different responses in respect of the setting of interest rates, bank bail-outs and "quantitative easing" (the printing of money). This kind of thing lends a certain duck-rabbit illusion to context – mechanism and the terms end up having only a heuristic value, despite being "real things". Whilst it is useful to talk of contexts and mechanisms and both can be "isolated" (theoretically and empirically) a context in relation to a mechanism almost certainly itself the manifestation of a further mechanism!

Nevertheless, contexts can permit, prevent or change the working of a mechanism. Some mechanisms all but stand up and shout "I'm here", they can be seen to produce tangible effects and often in quite different contexts. Similar mechanism do this, in one or other contexts, but are very shy of doing it in others. Mechanisms have a dispositional character (see Chapter 4). They can sometimes be identified, but they may be latent, that is they may be perhaps effective indirectly or not effective at all, but they retain the disposition to be effective. For example, urban to rural or peri-urban migration nearly always produces economic growth in destination locations, but this only works if the migrants bring economic and social capital with them (Williams 2003b). If their primary motivation is not economic, but environmental and they move to an area with an existing weak economy, they may serve to weaken that economy further. Even then, its more complex than that, but there are identifiable mechanisms which may or may not become "active". It is in these contexts that we can identify the causal character of mechanisms.

The dispositional character of mechanisms is perhaps what makes them identifiable, but equally their compositional character is also dispositional. Mechanisms are themselves made up of things that are dynamic, and in the character of individual agents that sustain them, actions that arise from beliefs and desires. Mechanisms must have relative invariance to be mechanisms at all and they are both social objects themselves and are made up of social objects, such as institutions, customs, laws and crucially agent interpretations and interactions etc. Some of these things have more invariance than others. Analogously we can think of Poincaré Maps (Parker and Chua 1989) where there is a relatively stable pattern of behaviour or events (in mathematical terms) a "periodic orbit" in phase space (or possibility space) that interacts within a continuous dynamic system. In urban–rural migration it is the persistent character of movement over a long period, which is both a mechanism in itself, that can be identified, but it is also the "periodic orbit" underlying and interacting with other social objects that create more complex mechanisms.

An important characteristic of many mechanisms is that they are "morphogenetic". Morphogenesis, is a concept first deployed, in the realist literature, by Margaret Archer (Archer 1995, Le Boutillier 2001, 2003) and describes a key property of the social world, the complex interlocking of agent actions and social structures (such as social norms, institutions, power relationships and language. A feature of morphogenesis that I want to emphasise, is its historic dimension (Le Boutillier 2001) in enabling and constraining future actions, or the emergence or nature of future structures. This is important in creating and sustaining mechanisms.

Research on the career differences of women and men in UK sociology, by Jennifer Platt (Platt 2004) indicated a complex intermeshing of personal, structural and historic factors that shaped outcomes. Recruitment and promotion policies several decades ago, effecting early career sociologists, had implications for later careers, for example a cap on numbers of senior academics within a department. Platt's conclusion, as she notes, were surprising and there was little difference in outcomes between women and men, but the routes to those outcomes differed considerably.

In this the causal mechanisms, though complex and interwoven, are relatively visible because they operated through time and were documented in many cases (hence the advantages of longitudinal data for showing causes). But there are other ways we can envisage complex causal mechanisms operating, where there is interaction between agent beliefs and actions and social objects, that consolidate mechanisms. Steve Vincent and Robert Wapshott (2014: 151–152) suggest a useful four way classification of "upward" and "downward" causation with "normative powers" (dispositions) and "configurational powers" (dispositions). The "upwards" and "downwards", relates to agent causation upwards and institutional causation downwards.

> Normative powers and potentials emerge from enduring patterns in the activities of agents who constitute specific institutional mechanisms. For example, employees tend to have specific levels of absenteeism and turnover, intensity in work activity, skill use and patterns of social interaction. These activities, which constitute the habitual patterns of everyday life, that continually recreate and, potentially, transform specific institutional mechanisms ....
>
> op cit: 152

The configurational dispositions are organisational characteristics, that might be higher level and have "downward" causation, or more local organisational characteristics that have "upward causation". They illustrate this with an example of a German human resources environment, where legal and regulatory systems had a downward causation (things such as appraisal and performance related pay) but came into conflict with other institutional mechanisms (trade unions) and existing local cultural norms (such as equity, autonomy and trust), which in turn led to a resistance and a modification of the higher level human resource in local practices. Consequently:

> … normative dispositions that were reproduced within a specific national regulatory regime and culture led to specific patterns in the reproduction of human resource practices at lower organisational levels.
>
> op cit: 153

We could think of each of these (the regulatory regime, trade unions, local practices) as each a mechanism, which would interrelate in different ways in different contexts, or we could think the local practices as contexts. I don't think this is important, because contexts can be thought of as just that, but they are inevitably the outcome of other causal processes and are themselves mechanisms.

Made up, but not fiction!

Mechanisms are real. Any of the mechanisms illustrated in the foregoing has causal outcomes for individuals, that enable and constrain and conversely, individuals through their beliefs and actions maintain and change the components of mechanisms and indirectly change the mechanisms themselves. That there are mechanisms that we can identify, confirms the realist ontological case, but their precise description, explanations of how they intersect with other mechanisms, what their context is and most importantly the measurement of their extent and prevalence can never match their actual character. The foregoing examples of mechanisms are under-described, because I am summarising them as illustrations. However, they cannot be anything *other* than under-described, however much detail is in the descriptions, because we cannot capture them in their entirety. Nevertheless, this is what Pawson says when he sums up seven steps to realist enquiry. Step 6 says:

> Although the social world transforms ceaselessly, this does not mean it is endlessly chaotic. Social institutions change, but not into blue cheese. There are corresponding social mechanisms that govern and limit social transformations. These too are located in the deep, underlying structures of society.
>
> Pawson 2013: 62

This is the way I understand this: the complexity of social life cannot ever be grasped, because it is too much and too fast in its change. But underlying that complexity there are ontological features which shape and limit change and give rise to the relative invariance of things that we can measure, or at least to an extent know. That means when we make up mechanisms, they are not works of fiction but will arise from phenomena that are apparent, through measurement, through reasoning or through informal observation.

Modelling mechanisms

On the shelf in my study I have a scale model of a Morris Minor 1000 pickup. It actually looks exactly the same as the real life one I had as one of my first cars – right down to rust patches! My original Morris Minor was a quintessential classic "clock like" mechanism (though it was certainly not as reliable as most clocks!). My model one is a recognisable replica, but at a scale of 1:43, the resemblance stops when one observes the very fine detail and obvious absence of an engine etc. However, for my purpose, it captures what I wanted, the visual memory of a once cherished car.

This is far from a perfect analogy, because my original car and my toy one are far too clock like, far too invariant. However, complex, more cloud like mechanisms, can be grasped to produce "epistemological mechanisms" that can sufficiently represent "ontological mechanisms". But they are not scale models.

Haig and Evers (2016: 82–83) distinguish two kinds of model, homeomorphs, where the source of the model and the subject of the model are the same (the car) and paramorphs, where the subject and source are different and the model is an analogy. Their example of the latter is computer modelling of the brain. The computer produces a model of the brain, but brains processes are of a different ontological kind to computer processing. Bradley and Schaeffer provide a nice definition of such a model. It formalises our framework for interpreting the world by abstracting from a reality that which would otherwise be too complex to understand (Bradley and Schaefer 1998: 23).

What I am saying is there are ontological mechanisms, but because of their complexity and their nesting in other mechanisms, we can know they have an existence apart from our descriptions, but our descriptions will not be the *same* as the real thing. They will be heuristics that help us describe, explain and understand. They are Bhaskar's transitive objects.

Theory and models

I said quite a lot about middle range theories in Chapter 5, and specifically Merton. As I noted there, Pawson's objection is that whilst middle range theory is a big improvement on grand theory and abstracted empiricism, it is a "flat ontology". Its predictive structure is that if *P* holds under circumstances *S*, then it can also explain Q, and that it begins from the specific and local. However, like empiricism (specifically causal analysis) variables stand in for complex arrays of social arrangements – themselves, perhaps "mechanisms". These do have the same logical structure as models, but they are too simple.

They, like the statistical models that are derived from "black boxes" (as I remarked in the Zetterberg example above), that is they may be usefully predictive but explanatorily weak and rely on inductive assumptions from regularities. It would be perfectly good middle range theorising to propose a credible theory that explains why improved IT skills, in the past twenty years, have not raised wage levels (Lauder et al 2018). If wages are not raised then the theory is confirmed, if they are, it is falsified. Either outcome is weak, if no mechanism can be identified. the mechanism is no more than a theorised black box, unless we can open that box and measure its contents.

A theoretical model, I believe, should consist of a propositional theory that is grounded in the specification of a mechanism, but also proposes how this might behave in particular circumstances. So, whilst a theory and a theoretical model might be said to have the same structure, a theoretical model is a model of a mechanism, in context, that may contain many theoretical statements and specifications of relations between these.

But how do we start to build such models? How do we avoid the generalising and abstract statements of grand theory? Somewhat counter-intuitively, we do begin from abstractions, though they should have some grounding in specific social realities, they are not just dreamed up. They are analytical in character, but they may be unobserved constructs. As Hedström and Swedberg note (1998b: 13), such concepts are routinely deployed in physics, for example protons and neutrons, and only later are they shown to refer to "real" things in the world. Some do not. The criticism, from theoretical sociologists that such analytic models are not based on "real" concepts is as Hedström and Swedberg note, to commit the fallacy of "misplaced concreteness". Where analytic models differ from "grand theorising" is that they must be operationalised into testable statements, that can provide empirical closure. The concreteness comes later.

Theoretical models are more than just speculative statements, they will have a structure, albeit one that will be developmental and may be revised as a result of empirical testing. Like the chicken and the egg, which comes first is not straightforward, it may be earlier theorising, or it may be data, in the form of "effects" that we work back from to specify a possible causal mechanism. Models may be specified in two directions, from theory and its predictions to regularities in the data and from regularities in the data, toward the predictions of a theory (Skvoretz 1998: 239), corresponding to the theory testing and theory building. Models can be specified logically, using logical operators, such as "and", "or", "if", "not if" to specify relations between terms and models that whilst common in economics, bare less used in sociology, political science etc. Nevertheless, logical operators can be specified as quantifiers. For example:

B occurs more often, if A

C occurs more often, if B

My own view is that, what might be termed, an ideal logical model, expressed through propositional terms, "and", "or", "if", "not if", is a valuable heuristic. In interpretive research (or in "fuzzy set QCA" – see Chapter 9), where variables may be less sharply defined, showing only the direction and nature of a relationship between concepts, this is still valuable, even if such a process initially over simplifies. If theoretical concepts and their relationships can be specified in an ideal logical model, this can then be compared to actual data, perhaps analysed using a qualitative data analysis package such as NVivo. Arguably this is simply a formalisation of Weber's ideal types, expressed as a theoretical model and tested against the data. In the next section I will illustrate some of the above with a story of a research programme, I undertook with others from the 1990s to middle 2000s. That this research was conducted quite some time ago, allows to fit a model of the mechanisms, that can be seen to have veracity through the continuation of the patterns observed. Moreover, whilst each individual element of the programme could identify a mechanism operating in context, the complexity of the nested and interlocking mechanisms can really only be identified through what David Byrne describes as a "macroscope" "tools which allow us to make sense of the large and complex ...." (Byrne 2002: 142). The "macroscope" is a useful heuristic and I will employ this in the next chapter.

Counterurbanisation and economic decline in Cornwall

In Chapter 5, I described, what I regarded as a quintessential middle range theory, that of counterurbanisation. Here, I will summarise how a research programme over ten years, attempted through theory testing and model building, to identify a mechanism (or mechanisms) of counterurbanisation, operating in a particular context. The programme of consisted of several empirical research projects so that there was an interplay between theorising a model, testing aspects of it and further refining the model. It had both quantitative and qualitative elements. Like so much research, this interplay was messy and whilst the CMO model of mechanisms can be retrospectively applied, the research programme was non-linear and often "reactive". In what follows, I tell the story of this.

As I noted above, counterurbanisation migration is usually associated with economic growth in destination locations of migrants, but in this example just the opposite occurred and the question was, why?

Cornwall, in the South West of Britain, is a major tourist destination, sometimes described as the "Cornish Riviera", for its benign climate and attractive scenery. Alongside this, it is characterised by a number of large areas of post-industrial decline, following the closure of metal mines and major engineering enterprises, particularly in the 1980s (Deacon 1997, Deacon et al 1988, Kennedy and Kingcome 2007). However, the decline had set in long before this decade, and Cornwall had experienced large scale out-migration for much of the 20th century, because the engineering and mining skills of its workforce were in demand elsewhere, as demand fell for them in their home region. So, there were both "push" and "pull" elements in this outward migration stream.

By the 1990s, on a number of measures, Cornwall was one of the poorest areas of Britain (Williams 2003b). Yet, since the 1960s, it had experienced "population turnaround", whereby more people were moving in, than moving out. The puzzle was, then, why were people moving from areas of relative affluence (primarily the South East of England) to a much poorer area, in particular one with very high unemployment? Around this time two "middle range" theories of counterurbanisation, in the UK, were proposed.

Theory 1: In a variant of neo-classical theories of migration, Tony Fielding (1982) distinguishes between manual workers and functionaries. Manual workers are less likely to migrate in search of new employment if made redundant, he argues, due to housing considerations, family and kinship ties, and the benefits accrued via the "social wage" (p. 26). Social and welfare benefits are unlikely to change with a change of location, nor is medical care and children's education. Moreover, to move would not necessarily involve any gain, as the work that is available in a high wage area is unlikely to be appropriate to the manual worker. Additionally, other costs such as housing are also likely to be higher in an economically buoyant area. "Functionaries", conversely, are employees in large organisations who hold technical or white collar positions. The suggestion of a move is more likely to come from the employer, and is likely to involve an "improvement in status and pay". Fielding (1982) argues that these "middle class" workers are less likely to break ties when they leave an area as they are probably already living away from the regions in which they spent their childhood. Thus, migration is seen as necessary for career advancement.

Using data from the National Health Service Central Register (NHSCR) and the ONS Longitudinal Study (LS), Fielding (1992) analysed migration flows into and out of the South East. From this he argues that the South East can be described as an "escalator region" in terms of career advancement and thus class location. Young people, moving to the South East can enhance their career prospects and maximise earning potential. Later in life, Fielding argues, they step off the escalator and migrate elsewhere.

Theory 2: Savage et al (1992) were interested in the increasing geographical mobility of the middle classes in pursuit of social mobility. Causal mechanisms surrounding social mobility may not be specifically located within the employment sphere, although they are "economically" based. They suggest that three types of assets can be called upon in the process of social mobility. Which particular asset or assets are utilised is contingent upon the specific context in which people are able to deploy them. Property assets are the most "robust" assets according to Savage et al (1992) as they are readily stored and transmitted and can be used to exploit other people's labour, through self-employment for instance. Cultural assets, such as educational qualifications, can be stored in the form of cultural capital, but need a specific set of circumstances in which to realise them. Finally, organisational assets are highly dependent upon context and can only really be deployed within the internal labour market of an organisation.

Initial work on the Cornish example of counterurbanisation, was carried out in a study, by Perry and Dean in the 1980s (Perry et al 1986). They compared stated economic reasons for migration with environmental ones, finding the latter to be a crucial motivation. Migrants saw Cornwall as offering better lifestyle opportunities and many had family or friendship connections (Perry et al 1986). But conversely, Peter Mitchell (Mitchell 1993) conducted another study around the same time, specifically of migrants in newly built housing developments and found that economic factors predominated.

The research programme, in which I participated, began with two elements: a comparative qualitative study of migrants and non-migrants attitudes to, and experiences of work and housing (Buck et al 1993) and a quantitative study that used the same ONS longitudinal data, as Fielding used, to compare three migrant/non migrant streams over ten years (Williams and Champion 1998). This latter primarily focussed on changes in employment, over ten years, between migrants to Cornwall and migrants to Wiltshire and those that were enumerated in those locations at both time points. Wiltshire was chosen because it had similar levels of in migration and out migration, as Cornwall, but it was also the richest county in the South West region.

Migrants to Wiltshire had employment levels slightly better than non-migrants, after ten years, whereas migrants to Cornwall, were much more likely to have left the labour market, ten years on, than non-migrants. The migration to Wiltshire appeared to be classic economic counterurbanisation. Wiltshire immediately adjoins the South East region and might be deemed as part of the latter "escalator" region.

So, who were these people, who moved to Cornwall, and how did their profile "fit" Fielding or Savage's theories?

> Primarily they were migrants from the South East Region.
> They were much more likely to be home owners, than non migrants.
> They were primarily from non-manual occupations (though compared to Wiltshire, professionals and associate professionals were under-represented).
> The majority of migrants were aged 35–55.

So, elements of both Fielding and Savage's theories were supported.

The qualitative research aimed to "flesh out" these findings, through testing Perry and Dean's conjecture that economic factors were equalled by environmental considerations. This was largely found to be true, but there was also an unawareness of the parlous economic position of Cornwall and a belief that work – usually self-employed and in the service industry would be forthcoming, amongst in migrants. Several respondents expressed surprise that this did come to pass and they were unemployed. These findings were confirmed by other studies, suggesting migrants were concentrated in the service industry, either self-employed, or part of family businesses (Buck et al 1993, Burley 2007), themselves subject to high levels of bankruptcy, seasonal and insecure employment.

The other major factor and confirmed in a larger survey of in migrants, by Carole Williams, was that housing considerations played a major role (Williams 1997). House prices in the South East region, were considerably higher than

Cornwall, which meant migrants could often benefit financially through selling in the South East and moving to Cornwall. This supported Savage's theory.

But what of Mitchell's "economic" migrants? They were a particular migrant stream, often moving to urban locations in Cornwall and also quite often, "key workers" re-located to Cornwall, as part of various economic initiatives, by central and local government, to attract enterprises to Cornwall.

So why did so many people become "poor" by moving and why, given their economic profile, did they not provide economic stimulus to their destination?

> Most moves were "speculative" and driven by environmental and housing considerations.
>
> Many of the migrants either did not find work and left the labour market upon moving, others left later as a result of business failure.
>
> Migrants were competing for jobs with non migrants. This, in turn, drove down wages and supressed demand.
>
> "Economic" migrants left the labour market, as the subsidised enterprises eventually relocated from Cornwall, but remained in Cornwall for environmental reasons.

The above is just a brief description, in practice, as later studies discovered, the migrant streams were more nuanced, depending on destinations in Cornwall, age of migrants and family structure, skills match and "local" connections (see Burley 2007, Kowalczuk, 2011).

So where are the mechanisms and "models" of mechanisms that would explain the unusual combination of counterurbanisation and poverty? The models were theoretical and statistical. The former tested elements of three theories: Fielding, Savage and Perry and Dean. Elements of each provided some complementary and some mutually exclusive elements. Each of the theories under-described the identifiable mechanisms. Fielding's proposition of the "South East", as an escalator region, is all but a mirror image of Perry and Dean's picture of migrants "stepping off the escalator", as Fielding suggested. The Savage model centres on social mobility, but the majority of migrants were uninterested in social mobility. The emerging theoretical model, combined elements of each, but proposed a "post social mobility" model, that nevertheless was based, not just on environmental considerations, but actual (housing) or perceived (employment) outcomes.

Statistical models (primarily logistic regression), using longitudinal census data, described the initial and outcome states and these were the basis of qualitative and further targeted survey work. From this we were able to identify several mechanisms, some of which were also the contexts in which other mechanisms operated. The mechanisms were often "nested" and were of different "strengths". Each of these mechanisms could individually be represented as a formal "model" and may were derived mostly from the statistical models, but such is the nature of their complex interactive nature, that, in their totality, they can only be made intelligible in a narrative form. Firstly, then, I will list them and then attempt a narrative to describe what was going on.

The principal mechanisms

- M1 Historical mechanism of economic decline in engineering and mining. This is the overall context in which the other mechanisms operate and has morphogenetic character
- M2 Environmental attraction arising from perceptions of Cornwall
- M3 Life course appraisal by migrants (their age, family circumstances, career/economic position)
- M4 Perceptions of economic opportunity by migrants
- M5 High house prices in the South East
- M6 Comparatively lower house prices in Cornwall
- M7 Medium term government investment
- M8 Cornwall Council policy of "population led growth"

M1 The strongest mechanism and the *context* of the other mechanisms, was the historic decline of Cornish industry. This removed skilled jobs from the job market, shifting what work opportunity there was to tourism, light industry and the public sector. This also motivated out migration. These things produced relatively lower house prices (M6). The historic morphogenetic element of prior decline constrained economic possibility, without massive investment.

M2 From the 1960s onwards tourism grew in Cornwall and this in turn created the environmental attraction. Most migrants to Cornwall had enjoyed previous holidays there (Perry et al 1986). The tourist "landscape" is a curated one, that provides the visitor with an impression of relative affluence. Few visitors were familiar with the more industrial/post-industrial areas. This provided a "pull" mechanism. This was strengthen by M4 perceptions of affluence and opportunity.

M3 Most migrants were well into their work and housing careers. But this mechanism is especially complex. Most migrants had enjoyed relative economic success and were homeowners in middle age. But there were exceptions. There were younger, less skilled migrants "taking their chances". Many of them were attracted to seaside towns, especially Newquay and these migrants were predominantly from the North West or the West Midlands (Elzey 1998). Both Perry et al (1986) and Carole Williams found substantial Cornish connections in the case of many migrants.

M5 The house price mechanism in the South East, was the outcome of that region's "escalator" character. This also provided a relatively straightforward indicator of migration. As house prices rose, in the South East, migration to Cornwall increased and vice versa.

M7 was a relatively weak mechanism. For a short while, from the mid-1970s until the early 1980s, government policies to revive economically weak areas, encouraged firms to relocate to Cornwall, which for a short while slightly ameliorated the economic decline and produced a different migrant stream. This mechanism disappeared entirely, once the investment was withdrawn. Following European Union Objective One funding, from the late 1990s, there was further economic amelioration (Willet 2011), but in this case it did not stimulate in migration, because most investment was in infrastructure, new technology and existing small and medium enterprises.

The effect of M8 was equally weak, though its absence might have produced different economic priorities for investment, rather than just (erroneously) relying on migrants to provide economic stimulation. It did reinforce messages and the narrative of M2.

Each of these mechanisms was a simplified model based on the data we had, but although key features were readily discernible, that is they had relative intransigence, they subtly changed through time, as a result of interactions with other previously invisible or non-existent mechanisms. Micro level interventions produced emergent properties that change mechanisms and created others. One example, is the restauranteur Rick Stein, whose Padstow restaurant became a magnet for food lovers and in time the growth of more exclusive leisure enterprises and a very wealthy migration stream (initially seasonal) to the North Cornwall coast. Places, such as Rock, St Endellion and Trebarwith became synonymous with a young metropolitan leisured class (King and Smith 2017). Meanwhile, the tourist landscape changed from that of people taking traditional beach holidays, to weekend breaks, surfing holidays and to a lesser extent "cultural" tourists. Migration to Cornwall, continued and the mechanisms identified above could still be discerned in their broad character, but micro and meso level changes in local migration patterns (such as those to North Cornwall) produced a more diverse picture, that does not fit the three theories above so well. The later migration has been less well researched, so its specific nature is more speculative.

One final twist, in this story, and the subject of other research, is that from the late 1990s, the character of the out-migrant stream changed from that of a predominantly Cornish, skills-rich workforce, to one of second-generation in migrants, often returning to places of family origin (Burley 2007). The Cornish workforce no longer had the skills that were in demand elsewhere, but the sons and daughters of the in-migrants did have the social capital of family networks elsewhere.

The question was a simple one. Why did counterurbanisation migration to Cornwall not produce economic growth. But the answer was not a simple one and it took ten years to get it. A middle range theory might be proposed to explain such instances:

> Counterurbanisation will not produce prosperity in the destination region if that region is economically poor and where migrants have the means to migrate to, but are primarily motivated by environmental considerations alongside a belief that such migration will not financially disadvantage them. Such migrants are likely to be homeowners, in middle age and not seeking social mobility.

Such a theory is testable in other situations, but almost certainly the mechanisms that exist in those locations, would not be precisely the same either in the originating or destination location. Moreover, it does seem that what was probably a fairly good explanatory theory to explain the migrations of the 1980s to the 2000s, would not entirely work now.

The complexity and reality of mechanisms

In this chapter I have tried to show three things:

Mechanisms are complex. Popper's analogy of "clouds" and "clocks" only partly works. Social mechanisms are certainly more complex than clocks, though their key features are more discernible through time, that that of clouds. Similar patterns of behaviour, such as those identified in the counterurbanisation example, can exist over decades and have very large numbers of people participating in similar activities. But each of them, will see their actions and beliefs through an individual lens, and sometimes, like the disruption of a strange attractor, their behaviour can produce effects that have macro-level implications for the mechanism. So, we might say that social mechanisms are actually more cloud like than clouds, mainly because the behaviour of individuals is conscious and complex at a micro level, potentially producing change at a macro level. So far, this is consistent with the methodologically individualist model of Dan Little, that I was a little sceptical of.

But, the decisions (such as those to migrate) or the later effects (leaving the labour market) are the result of earlier macro level events, that react upon the individual. For example, the likelihood of migrants to Cornwall leaving the labour market was the result of structural economic change and earlier institutional decisions (say, to close factories) over which they had no control and any actions, post migration would be constrained by these things. Whilst, in principle, one can agree with the trivially true fact that all mechanisms are traceable to individuals, downward causation is just as powerful as upward causation.

Mechanisms are real. Complexity evolves, but it produces discernible mechanisms which are at least partially visible and amenable to measurement. These mechanisms both are and consist of the social objects, I described in Chapter 4. Some are at individual level, some are fleeting and some have the solidity of Durkheim's social facts. But also they have causal and dispositional properties, that may be latent, or active, have small effects or large ones. But such effects are identifiable: for instance, the surprise expressed by migrant respondents that their skills sets were not of use in Cornwall[9] and this then led them to other employment decisions and actions.

We make up mechanisms, because they are imperfect representations of the actual mechanisms. Like my model car, they are representative enough to permit us to infer and explain. But they not analogues of the actual mechanisms, for four reasons.

Firstly, like computer models of the brain, the representations (theoretical or statistical models) and the narratives that follow, stand in for agents' beliefs and actions and the social objects that lead to these or are created by them. To say otherwise, is to commit a category mistake.

Secondly, even though representations, we cannot "capture" the mechanism in its entirety. This is because it is almost certainly "nested" in other mechanisms and it will be interconnected with other "latent" mechanisms, of which we might surmise, or be unaware of. This is a restatement of Goldthorpe's "regress", though, as I have shown, it is far more complex. Possibly the closest we could get to representing a nested or connected combination of mechanisms, is through the modelling of a neural network. Strategies, such as "self organising maps (SOMS)"[10] can model previously collected data to show complex non-linearity (Ninness et al 2013). Unfortunately, neural networks are also "black boxes", rather like those I spoke of above, that is they are essentially descriptive and predictive, rather than explanatory.

Thirdly, networks are dynamic. They may well demonstrate intransigence, indeed they must for us to know they exist, but like clouds they are constantly changing and evolving, but unlike clouds these changes originate in the conscious actions of human beings.

Finally, the dispositional character of mechanisms means that often they have potential to be active, but are not active. That is, they require some kind of stimulus, that may be available in one context, but not another. In the counter-urbanisation example, a major stimulus for migration from the South East of England, to Cornwall, was the ability to take advantage of the house price differential, between the originating and destination migration. If this was removed, many (though not all), would not migrate. So, a house price mechanism, in the South East, was then the stimulus for migration and also a context. But what of those who still moved? Such people, were usually those who had another strong motive to move to Cornwall, perhaps as key workers, or they were not owner occupiers in their place of origin.

Notes

1 There is a nice discussion of mechanisms and causality, which prefigures the contemporary more nuanced understanding of the concept in physics today in a paper by Morris Cohen, published in 1918 (Cohen 1918). "Mass" and "motion" are still useful terms in the non-quantum world, but in quantum world the physicist faces ontological dilemmas, equivalent to ~ (though not the same) as those in social science.

2 For example the Navier Stokes equations for vertical and horizontal air movement, the continuity equation for mass, the thermodynamic equation for air temperature and the continuity equation for water. (Casti 1991: 98–99)

3 I also stole the idea from an essay by Ian Hacking, called "Making up People" (Hacking 2002).

4 I use the term in its statistical sense.

5 Originally the expression was "turtles all the way down" a quote attributed to Joseph Berg (Berg and Barker 1854: 48), and indicating the problem of an infinite regress.

6 Of course it might! Ariel et al show how complex interventions in criminology can show what and how might be transferable from one location to another (Ariel 2021).

7 These were primarily located in Cornwall and the South West of England. The areas covered by some of the Sure Starts in Cornwall were contiguous.

8 Lescudjack Sure Start was centred on a council (public housing) estate in the medium sized Cornish town of Penzance.
9 A good example of this was the brick layer who believed that brick laying skills would always be in demand, wherever he moved, only to find that, in Cornwall, concrete blocks, requiring different building skills, were used. He became a handyman (Buck et al 1993).
10 These operate firstly in training mode which builds the map using input examples and the "mapping" is then automatically able to classify any new input vector.

9

A methodological toolkit

From micro complexity to macro explanation

To be a realist requires a little faith and like all those who have faith, mine is often tested. There are two of me, not Jekyll and Hyde exactly, but two sometimes incompatible social science personalities. The first is the scientific realist who believes in a complex reality and wishes to discover methodological strategies to describe and explain that reality. The second is a practical social researcher, who is often frustrated at the over-theorisation and navel gazing of some social science. To paraphrase what is said in Wales and my native Cornwall, I like a "tidy" research project. A clear research question, an appropriate set of methods and a modest, but actionable conclusion. Especially when that conclusion has some puzzle solving or policy value.

My complex realist faith is tested when I see such a "tidy" piece of research, that does not wear its philosophical or theoretical credentials on its sleeve. Sometimes my students are surprised, knowing something of my methodological or philosophical work, when, in their dissertations, I advise them to ease up on the "epistemological positioning". And often when they do, they produce good realist research, not by accident, but because they have become instinctive realists in the way they do their research. This is rarely as a result of them wishing to please me, but more that they have read good realist research, often done by people who don't even know they are realists! I don't mean this to be patronising. Realist research does not need to wear its philosophical credentials on its sleeve, rather it's the way the research is conceived, executed and the results interpreted that makes it realist. One rarely hears of natural scientists pronouncing their philosophical position, each time they publish a paper!

The foregoing is by way of a preamble to a chapter that does not propose particular "realist" methods, but rather realist thinking about methods. Indeed, we might say there are no realist methods, just methods that realist might use. Some disagree with this. Some critical realists are either completely sceptical of quantitative methods, or allow them a limited role. Roy Bhaskar was sceptical, believing that quantitative methods, in social science, implied a degree of closure available only in controlled experimental conditions, in the natural sciences (Bhaskar 2008). The critical realist economist, Tony Lawson, (Lawson 1997), has been very sceptical about the success of aggregate models. His argument is that all statistical models must contain an error term, and the amount of variability in social life renders such models useless. He believes quantitative analysis should limit itself to the use of descriptive statistics. However, most critical realists nowadays take a more pluralist approach, seeing a role for combining quantitative and qualitative methods united in a triangulated strategy, underpinned by realist reasoning of abduction (see Chapter 6). Other realists, such as David Byrne (see Chapter 4) are sceptical of the assumptions of the general linear model (Byrne 2002, 2004), in its ability to capture the non-linearity of social complexity. Bhaskar, I think, was wrong because he saw social science quantitative methods as inevitably grounded in a Humean conception of causality as "constant conjunction". But, (a) this assumes we always wish to draw causal conclusions from quantitative data, which we don't and (b) when drawing causal conclusions, these can (and I'd say inevitably) must go beyond the statistical relationships produced. Lawson, is correct in his identification of the problem of the "error term", but that assumes (a) that quantitative methods are restricted to linear models and (b) that those models must claim a "real" representation of the world, when in fact we might treat them simply as heuristics.

Byrne, I think, is right *de jure*, but wrong, *de facto*, for a similar reason. A linear model is a statistical model, which is only a representation of a possible mechanism, it is not, nor never could be (as I argued in the last chapter) the "mechanism" itself, it must be moderated by the theoretical mechanism. I think the methodological pluralist approach is correct, though I do not necessarily believe this always implies mixed quantitative or qualitative methods, as the United States mixed methods advocates would suggest (Brewer and Hunter 2006, Tashakkori and Teddlie 1998). Pluralism puts practical necessity before methodological principle to provide valid and reliable results. In the end, realist reasoning is more important than method, though it doesn't follow that any method will do!

What are the realist methodological goals? In one sense they are the goals of science – description and explanation. This is simply because scientific realism supports these goals and proposes particular ways of achieving them. We must begin with description, before we can move to explanation. Initial descriptions, through both qualitative and quantitative approaches, will be descriptions of observable or measurable attributes, or the realities, as agents describe them through attitudes and beliefs. They will be descriptions of the contexts of these attributes, attitudes and beliefs and the extent of intransigent social objects (e.g. institutions, social attitudes, behaviours, etc.). But beyond these, realists require methodological approaches which can describe and explain underlying, perhaps hidden realties that are the social mechanisms.

Often such detailed description will lend itself to testable inferences, which may become explanations. We aim for explanations of complex processes that produce invariances and the complex mechanisms which sustain them. These are our "causal stories", that though based on the best evidence we have, will be testable inferences about extent, prevalence and direction. In social science, we also seek understandings, but these, as I have argued (Williams 2000a: 98) can be seen as a special form of explanation to perceive individual meaning in relation to the norms of a particular society (see Ruben 2009 for an argument that there is no logical difference between explanation and understanding).

I realise that the last two paragraphs are somewhat abstract and even prescriptive. Hopefully, in what follows, the abstract will become more concrete and more permissive that prescriptive!

Which brings me to the central message of this chapter. I have called it a "methodological toolkit", a concept incidentally suggested to me by David Byrne. The analogy of a toolkit is meant to suggest a range of methodological tools, with differing appropriateness for the methodological tasks we face. But I am not going to tip out the entire toolbox, but rather select a few tools and briefly discuss their methodological properties, more as exemplars than suggested methodological strategies. Very little of this chapter presents particular arguments, it is mostly illustrative and in places makes only the most superficial reference to methodological work, but my hope in doing this is to demonstrate the ecumenical possibilities of methods to complex realism.

Micro-complexity and macro explanation

Mostly we act and think at a micro level. Although a group of people may share many common characteristics, their "action space"[1] is bounded by the natural necessity of the physical world of time and physical laws, plus the actions they may take within the social contingencies that exist for them. In our thoughts and actions and interactions with other individuals, we at least accord ourselves that autonomy, and indeed for many aim beyond that "action space" in beliefs about their actions. Methodological individualism, holds that all social phenomena are reducible to individual characteristics. Explanations should make reference to individual beliefs, desires and actions. For example longitudinal analyses of how individuals answer questions about their ethnicity, in surveys, indicates a high level of consistency over time, but nevertheless (even when the measurement remains the same) a significant minority change their affiliation, indicating that whilst ethnicity is indeed a social phenomenon, it is mediated through individual beliefs and desires (Platt et al 2005. The problem of this position, from a complexity perspective, is individual beliefs, desires and actions are subject to complex interactions that create social objects that do not have a constant, or even similar relationship with the originating individual. So, whilst it is true that the measurement of ethnicity did not change, the decision to change one's ethnic identity varied between individuals, because the decision to do so was socially mediated differently.

The possibilities of those interactions appear, and are, complex. The constraints on individual autonomy, from the physical world and the conceptual necessity of the social world are also visible, so the micro-complexity we see is not stochastic, but partially ordered by those constraints (though these can also enable action). Analogously this is what we see through the microscope. The invariance sets in when the micro-actions create social objects, that have varying levels of intransigence. These, like Durkheim'social facts", have strong conceptual necessity and are capable of representation and measurement. They are things such as poverty, discrimination, social capital, but also ethnicity, social class and gender and they take specific manifestations in particular contexts. This is what we see through the macroscope. Except, we don't exactly. Just as the physicist does not "see" sub-atomic particles, she can, however, "see" and measure their macro effects. So, poverty in a society is represented and measured by a number of defined and abstract concepts are nevertheless experienced as specific and real manifestations by individuals.

We need the microscope and the macroscope to capture the complexity of social reality. However, if it were the case that the "microscope" could only permit inferences about the micro and the "macroscope" could only permit inference about the macro, then we could not capture the dynamic interactions between the micro and macro level that produce complexity. And even to talk of "micro" and "macro" seems to suggest a duality, or just two strata. But it is so much more than that and the foregoing description is itself a representation!

It is fashionable in methodological circles (and I think correctly so) to play down the idea of a methodological dichotomy between quantitative and qualitative methods. Indeed, I will say later, why this is correct, but for the moment it is worth preserving the distinction, perhaps as micro and macro methods, to say that they each have the property to behave as micro and macroscopes. The "invariances" of the social allows macro level generalisations from the micro-qualitative and case-based quantitative methods, permit micro level inference. It is these methodological properties that will help me structure the rest of the chapter.

I will begin at the micro level to explore how qualitative methods can provide micro level descriptions and understandings that allow inference at that level, but also inference to the macro level through generalisation and hypothetical explanation. At this level there are plenty of specific methods, but mostly they are either observational and/or interpretive in nature. However, at the macro level, to which I will then turn, the battery of methods can arise from very different forms of data, most are probabilistic, but some are only enumerative. My mention of particular methods is illustrative and not prescriptive, because it is the assumptions and inferences that matter. This is not to say there are no rules or limitations of method, so whilst all methods (I think) are potentially realist, the choice of method is not aesthetic, but based on methodological assumptions that exist apart from those of realism. For example, whilst experimental methods can be used in realist research (Cook 2002, Cook and Campbell 1979), there are methodological limitations, that produce violations of assumptions about (for example) randomisation, blinding and standardisation of treatments (Robson 2002: 123–146) and there are methodological practices to overcome these.

The methods I will refer too in these sections are each from the more "traditional" repertoire of qualitative and quantitative methods, but in the third section I will introduce some newer and innovative methods that blur the quantitative–qualitative divide and can be microscopically or macroscopically focussed.

The micro-method toolkit

In much of social science "micro methods" are qualitative and depend on interpretations by the researcher. Although many 20th-century sociologists, such as Herbert Blumer (Blumer 1969) saw interpretivism as "scientific", it bore little resemblance to what then counted and often still does, as "scientific" social science (Madge 1963). Indeed, the validation of findings as authentic or typical, is seen largely as a matter of judgement by the researcher. Though replicability is certainly possible in interpretive methods, this is not the same as the use of repeated measures or standardised questions in quantitative research.

For the vast majority of qualitative researchers using interpretive methods, scientific values such as reliability, replicability or standardisation, are beside the point, or as I suggested in Chapter 2, even an anathema in understandings of the social world. Interpretations are simply that, an individual matter of how situations or individual actions or utterance are understood. As I noted the arguments for scientific rejection, in social science, have been well rehearsed and rebutted and this is not my concern here. Rather, I want to show how "micro" methods, that do indeed depend on interpretation, can give us insights into how individuals, or small groups, create or are enabled or constrained by social objects. Furthermore, I want to show how micro-methods can demonstrate how social objects create intransigence at a meso and macro level and, in turn, how mechanisms might be discerned.

Interpretation can come through a range of methods and eclectic strategies of using those methods and analysing the ensuing data. The methodological rules are much more fluid and themselves are more subject to interpretation than those of data gathering and statistical analysis in quantitative research. *Inter alia,* they include: participant observation, in depth or "focussed" interviewing, focus groups, diaries, autoethnography, diaries, textual and content analysis. Any of these methods are suitable candidates for inclusion in a complex realist toolkit, but here I will focus on observational methods and interview methods, partly because their realist potential is more apparent, but also because they have a long history with many examples of "classic studies" in sociology and anthropology.

So, what is it we expect or want observational methods to do, in the current context?

Observational methods, broadly speaking, or those where a researcher(s) is partially, or wholly embedded in a social situation. Their role may be known to others in that situation and they may be relatively detached from it, or they may be full participants in that situation and their researcher role unknown or "partially" known to other participants (observer as participant – participant as observer) (Babchuk 1963). The degree of "participation" makes a difference, at one extreme as an "accepted" outsider observing and interpreting those observations, to the other where the researcher is part of, and part author of, that social situation. Even though the aims may be similar in both cases, they are dependent on the specific context and may be achieved through different levels of participation. Within observations, interviews may be conducted. These may be completely overt and even recorded, with participants answering specific questions, or they may be informal conversations, written up later by the observer. Let me flesh this out in respect of a realist approach: the observation, or interview, is seeking causes of beliefs and actions (or more properly descriptions of causes), in both directions, with the caveat that these are "causal stories" that, nonetheless, can be further corroborated, or falsified. What actions have causal efficacy and what might have caused actions taken, or beliefs held by participants? Is the interpretation of the researcher and thus the causal story an inference to the best explanation, or may there be rival and equally plausible explanations? As Aaron Cicourel remarked "Do our instruments capture the daily life, conditions, opinions, values, attitudes and knowledge base of those we study as expressed in their natural habitat?" (Cicourel 1982: 15). Secondly, how do participants understand their situation and their own beliefs and actions, in relation to the broader meso and macro context? Whilst the Thomas dictum "If men define situations as real, they are real in their consequences" (W. Thomas and Thomas 1928), is correct to an extent, what they act upon may not be a full or accurate assessment, of underlying social reality. For example, whilst it has become widely accepted that those who voted "leave" in the UK European Union referendum, of 2016, did so on an appraisal of their social reality, this was to a great extent based on false beliefs about how the European Union had/had not created that social reality (Bristow 2020). A realist analysis of observational data, may go beyond an interpretation of beliefs and actions, to seek underlying and perhaps not apparent causes.

But for such research to be possible, certain conditions must be fulfilled and limitations understood. To know the reality of others, even at a superficial level, implies – what I term – dependencies. I will summarise these only briefly, because they have been extensively discussed and debated in the literature of anthropology and philosophy of the social sciences and indeed, I introduced some of these in my discussion of anti-realism in Chapter 2.

Dependencies

Human action is both the building block of the social and the outcome of the social. But what do we mean by "action"? Action is not just behaviour, but rather it is intentional, that is it involves mental processes directed towards some object, person or state of affairs. It is the wink, rather than the blink. But the question is, can we always recognise intentionality and can we recognise it for what is, what is intended?

This question has been at the heart of interpretive research, at least since Weber Sociology was for him "… a science which attempts the interpretive understanding of social action in order thereby to arrive at a causal explanation of its course and effects" (Weber 1978 [1921]: 88). Although Weber identified different forms, or levels of understanding, he offered no methodological prescriptions. Both before and after Weber (roughly 1915–1950), "classical anthropologists", famously Malinowski, Radcliffe-Brown and Evans Pritchard conducted studies of (what was then known as) primitive societies. These anthropologists were clearly outsiders, yet nevertheless drew conclusions about the actions of those they observed. Often their conclusions offered functional explanations of what was going on (King 2011). Needless to say, they were criticised on "anti-colonial" grounds, but also criticisms were ontological and epistemological. That is, it was claimed, both the truths about the way things are and the way things should be, differs between "primitive" societies and Western societies, and there is an inevitable incommensurability between knowledge or morality in such radically different societies. Peter Winch, maintained that the task of social investigation is to elaborate the "forms of life" of a particular society (Winch 1990 [1958]: 42). These are embodied in rules which are expressed and known through language. To understand a form of life one must understand the language. As I described in Chapter 2, this is a radical version of the Sapir Whorf hypothesis, which holds that language is not just about communication, but also about developing and shaping the ideas themselves. These were ontological claims that led to epistemological conclusions, which might be summed up in Winch's work as "to know one you must be one" and a radical form of social constructivism.

I have mentioned this linguistic determinism for two reasons. The first is that (as I noted in Chapter 2) many still hold to this view in humanistic social science and this leads only to epistemological relativism. It is a blind alley, if we wish to understand and explain. Secondly, for a realist, it is important that we can overcome such conditions or limitations. If we are to say that there is a deeper reality underlying self-aware social action, that is either not understood or only partially understood by agents, then we need to know the meaning of actions, in order to move beyond them and to do this there must be shared understanding and communication.

An implication of the above-mentioned relativism must be that there can be no shared rationality, that is what is rational in one setting may not be the case in another. But also, that either there is no understanding, or very little understanding of other rationalities and that there is ontological equivalence of their referents. Put crudely, if there is an epistemological equivalence between witchcraft and physics, then because we cannot transcend that, we must assume an ontological equivalence. Rationality and relativism have often been juxtaposed in the literature (see e.g. Hollis and Lukes 1982). But rationality is not straightforward, even within one's own society. At a societal level, a moral panic is not rational, but at an individual level, the acts that contributed to the moral panic might be considered rational. And then what do we mean by "rational"? Weber distinguished four types of rationality, traditional habits, emotional acts, unreflective acts and calculated goal directed action (Weber 1978[1921]: 24–30). Each of these may be more important and dominate action in different contexts. Certainly, this will differ culturally and what an outsider may interpret as "irrational" may be done so when s/he expects one form of rational action, rather than another.

There have been attempts to provide a universal definition of rational action (see Rosenberg 1988: 25–26, but mostly these end up requiring *ceteris paribus* clauses to work in specific settings (see the belief–action definition from David Papineau in Chapter 4). Nevertheless, Weber's claim of different kinds of rationality is at least a testable proposition. Charles Taylor (1982) reflects on the classic study of witchcraft in the Azande people (and Winch's writings on it). In Azande society witchcraft was said to be hereditary, yet the Azande would nevertheless examine a person's intestines for signs of "witchcraft substance". As Taylor notes, a few post-mortem examinations should settle the hereditary question once and for all, but the Azande continued to examine intestines for signs of witchcraft (op cit: 88–89). Could we interpret this as irrational, such behaviour in Western society certainly would be, but is it just that a different form of rationality is being deployed and ends up with more reasoning "purchase" with its practitioners?

I think we can draw two conclusions. That, yes, rationality is a concept invented in Western society, but as tool of understanding, can provide insights beyond Western society – or indeed when different forms of rationality are deployed within our own society. Indeed, implicit in my argument for a situated objectivity, there is a dependence on a socially constructed form of rationality. To say that rationality is invented, or socially constructed, does not imply epistemological relativism, because there are points of ontological reference that exist independently of any particular beliefs. So, it might be rational for the Azande to examine entrails, but it is the case that they would never find evidence of witchcraft in doing so. A more contemporary example would be the Monte Carlo fallacy, the belief that if a particular event occurs more frequently than normal during the past it is less likely to happen in the future (or vice versa), in for example gambling. Whereas, the odds of the gambler's throw are the same (given a fair dice, etc.) at every throw. So, in interpreting gambling behaviour, we can understand the rationality of the gambler's action, but equally we can know the statistical reality that exists independently of the gambler. There is then, the reality of the individual perception (which drives beliefs and actions), but also an underlying and often ontologically contradictory reality.

The second conclusion is linguistic. Steven Lukes, has pointed out in order to begin to understand a society through its language, we must have some starting point, some referential categories upon which we can agree (Lukes 1994: 293). Yet as I have argued previously (in Chapters 2 and 5) the views of Winch, or Sapir and Whorf are much too pessimistic. Initial points of reference would always be possible, however different a society may be to that of the researcher. We do not live literally in different worlds, our physiology, our need to eat, sleep, defecate and procreate are little different. Shelter may take different forms, as might food, or the expressions of pain or joy. But these things are reference points which might allow the beginnings of understandings, despite apparent linguistically driven incommensurability.

Furthermore, the actions one can observe will have structure, they often will be repeated and discernible rules and norms often do not require linguistic knowledge. Although Clifford Geertz study of Balinese life in the 1950s, did partially rest on linguistic translation, much of it depended on the observation and interpretation of regularities (Geertz 1994).

The discussion of the Azande may well be important to some anthropologists, but for most social researchers, societies and settings that are so radically different to their own, are likely not to be encountered often. However, as I have suggested language and rationality are dependencies that must be negotiated. Rationality might be further decomposed into the relationship between beliefs, desires and actions. This is important, because causal consequences ensue, mostly and firstly at a micro level, but occasionally, directly at a macro level, and often eventually at a macro level, through multiple similar actions by many. The first might be exemplified by an individual terrorist act and the second through the aforementioned moral panics.

So far, in my discussion of dependencies, I have mentioned only those which have their origins in the mental or social, but an importance dependency, which is both social and physical, is the environment itself. It is social, because to a great extent, it embodies Popper's "third world", but it is also physical and enables and constrains actions, thereby creating and limiting action. It is also often overlooked in qualitative research. I do not necessarily mean the immediate environment of social action (though this is also important), but extended environment, both physically and historically. For example, to explain the fishing practices, the culture and political views of UK fishing communities, the migration or depletion of fish stocks is an important environmental consideration, and one which has a history (Reed et al 2013). Sue Fisher's ethnography of youth gaming practices, in an arcade (Fisher 1993) describes strategies and interactions of the young people as they played on the machines. But, although Fisher does not mention it, the young people's strategies were both enabled and constrained by the physical possibilities of the actual gaming machines and the gaming possibilities these allowed (Williams 2000b).

There is much more that could be said about dependencies, but my intention here was just to give a feel for those things that might help us towards, or inhibit the knowledge of micro level social reality. In the following example, research is primarily at a micro level, but this "microscope" provides the possibility to theorise to the "macro" and suggest some possible mechanisms.

Researching sexual practices in Thailand

This study, conducted by Russell Belk and colleagues, in the 1990s (Belk et al 1998), is typical of the genre of observational studies, that also utilise interviews. It is not intentionally realist in focus, but its assumptions and findings can be reinterpreted from a realist perspective. Although it is not beyond methodological criticism,[2] it does what one would ask of a realist research project and one can see how such research might be built upon, from a more overtly realist perspective.

The aim of the research was

> ... to provide a culturally embedded portrait of AIDS knowledge, attitudes, and risk-taking behaviors in prostitute patronage by students and tourists in the most heavily HIV-infected region of Thailand.
>
> Belk et al 1998: 197

The research did not explicitly test any theory and claimed to utilise grounded theory, to build subsequent theories (Charmaz 2006). Yet, implicit in the research is the concept of consumption and a comparison between Western ideas of consumption and those articulated by Thai and non-Thai (mainly Australian) respondents. A secondary assumption was that the risk-taking behaviour was grounded in a different rational framework to the standard western one.

The research was conducted in a provincial town and consisted of observations, in massage parlours and brothels. In-depth interviews were conducted with university students and sex tourists. There were also "key informants", such as a waiter and a local Red Cross worker. There were also conversations in situ with sex workers, clients, etc., in massage parlours and brothels. These were not explicitly reported.

Not surprisingly, the research did reveal a particular set of attitudes towards risky sexual behaviour, by young men and a number of conflicting cultural behaviours by the sex workers. Traditionally, in Thailand, young women were expected to be virgins at marriage, and "engaged" couples were not expected to have sex. Alongside this, though a practice now dying out, some men took concubines (in more westernised men these were now mistresses), this the opportunity of young Thai men to have sexual encounters, prior to marriage, was limited. Sex in brothels, or with prostitutes, was the norm and often continued into marriage. Indeed, the authors recount one example of a man being reported to his future wife as "gay", because he had not taken part in these practices.

Women expected men to do these things and expressed relatively mild disapproval. Indeed, the practice of *kheun khroo* (which means "first teacher") encouraged brothel attendance as a masculine rite of passage (op cit: 204). This particular form of masculinity eschewed the use of condoms. There were differing degrees of understanding of the AIDS risk, in particular sexual behaviours, amongst the Thai respondents, though there was an understanding that such behaviours were risky, but other reasoning seemed to prevail: that after a negative test, unprotected sex could be indulged in, that to use condoms was not masculine and more emphasis was placed upon the "cleanliness", of the women, which in practice often referred to their colour (op cit: 202).

The sex workers themselves were torn between conflicted demands. The cultural norm of virginity and traditional stigmatisation, versus the financial rewards which were often quite considerable and could assist their families to mitigate, or even escape poverty. Often, it was reported, girl children had become valued in rural areas, because of their money-earning potential in prostitution. According to Therevada Buddhism it is not dishonourable for women to work in prostitution, if it helps their family (op cit: 199).

Sex tourism, initially began during the Vietnam War, was a major part of the Thai economy, by the 1990s. Belk et al interviewed several (mainly Australian) men. Their reasoning, for unprotected sex, was that it was an "extreme sport", or like smoking, the pleasures outweighed the risks. Crudely, one might say, that the tourist reasoning was based on informal probabilistic reasoning, as opposed to the conflictual reasoning of the Thai men. Theirs was the same kind of consumer behaviour common in the west.

Partially, as a response to the growing AIDS epidemic at the time – where an estimate 600,000–700,000 Thais were HIV positive and around 40% of sex workers, the government had begun a campaign of education, encouraging the use of condoms. These campaigns resembled those undertaken in the west.

So how might we re-interpret the research, from a complex realist perspective? The point of the research was to explain how risky sexual behaviour persisted in Thailand and how this was fuelling the AIDS crisis. If this could be understood, in the Thai context, and an explanation provided, then effective measures to change behaviour might be taken.

From the findings, several interacting mechanisms can be hypothesised:

1. The traditional Thai emphasis of bridal virginity. Although less prevalent, though still present, the lack of opportunities for male sexual activity, produced a strong culture of premarital and extra-marital sex.
2. Thai masculinity, partially a response to the above, but developing its own taboos (condoms) and customs (kheun khroo).
3. The changing (but still conflictual) attitudes towards the practice of sex work as an economic imperative.

4. Western consumerism. The article describes the setting of the research "In addition to sex shows, touts, bar girls, and massage parlours, the street is anchored by a 7–11 at one end and a McDonald's on the other – just like a postmodern shopping mall with its anchor stores" (op cit: 199). Thus, although the setting is Thailand, the sex on offer is commodified, as would be the consumer products on sale, at each end of the street.
5. Sex tourism. This is an historical mechanism, that has changed from the exotic, during the Vietnam War period, to consumer behaviour now, though a particular kind of consumer behaviour that has its own taboos in originating countries.
6. The biological mechanism of the AIDS epidemic.

Each of these mechanisms is causal and some behave as contexts (though not all, 6 could not be a context for 1 and 2, because they predate 6). More broadly, one can see it as two conflicting understandings of reality, the Traditional Thai one and a western one, producing hybrid behaviours and conflicting rationalisations. The concern at the beginning of the paper, that we should not investigate through the lens of Western rationalism, is only partly right. Ethically and methodologically, an awareness of different reasonings is important, but the reasonings of the Thai participants, were hybrid and sometimes involved an attempt to resolve the cultural–rational imperatives (such as the toleration of sex work, because it brought material improvement). Each group of participants had a partial understanding of their realities (and the conflicts therein), but none had a complete or accurate insight, because they were agents only participating in one aspect of that overall reality, that produced the aids crisis. Although the researchers came from a different culture and spoke a different language, to the Thai respondents, from the findings it is reasonable to believe that there was enough of a cultural intersection for the researchers to be able to discern the underlying reality of the practices.

So, if one is a realist, where could this research go? In fairness to the researchers, their time in the field was limited, and their results impressive. So, what follows, is not intended as a criticism of what was achieved.

Firstly, realists should not fight shy of proposing middle range theory to explain what was going on (in this case a high number of AIDS/HIV cases in the general population and specifically amongst sex workers). Whilst grounded theory provides a means to build theory, to begin without a theory implies an epistemological vacuum, which can get filled with hunches and informal reasoning. No investigation begins tabula rasa. So a middle range theory might have tested the concepts of consumption and risk taking. But, one might object, is this not imposing a theoretical construct that incorporates a particular scientific rationality, that is not the same as that of the culture being studied.

I think the answer is twofold. Firstly, the culture studied in this case was not as "alien" as that of (say) the Azande, but was in fact cultural hybrid of traditional Thai culture that intersected and was being changed by a western consumerist and material culture. Secondly, research such as this, must rely on the tools of interpretation. It emphasises the importance not just of seeking a deeper more "authentic" interpretation of the social milieu researched, but turns a critical gaze on the researcher, her background and the context of the research. As I have argued there can be a meeting between critical gaze, at an individual level, and a fallibilist approach to testing theories. One's own assumptions, about theory and context can (and should) be tested by posing alternative explanations, that might falsify one's own assumptions. In this particular case, the starting assumption of an alternative rationality, was partially falsified by the self-aware conflict of risk taking in the respondents.

Secondly – the microscope and the macroscope. The combination of observation and interview provided, what Clifford Geertz (1973) called "thick" description, a funnelling and deepening description of the reality of the participants, within context. This, in turn, allows an understanding of reality, as experienced or articulated by participants, and possibly its antinomies with a deeper reality. Moreover, at this level the sexual practices can be seen to emerge from a trade-off between a knowledge of risk and a cultural imperative (amongst both the Thai men and the tourists) that can be viewed as a causal social object (see Chapter 4). The micro-complexity can only be grasped in principle, it is not measurable, but it can be explored through comparing participant accounts of beliefs and actions. In this example, the fieldwork would have been too short to do this rigorously, but with more time, more observations and interviews, such testing is certainly possible. Most sampling in such research is either theoretical (i.e. respondents are chosen on the basis of prior known characteristics consistent with the theory), snowball sampling, perhaps via a gatekeeper, or simply convenience sampling. But with enough resources and in amenable settings, techniques such as Respondent-Driven Sampling (RDS) (Heckathorn 1997) might be used. RDS is an adaptation of chain-referral sampling and often used to sample diverse hard-to-reach or hidden populations.

It combines "snowball sampling" (individuals refer those they know to the researcher and these individuals, in turn, refer those they know and so on). In RDS, this is done until sample saturation is achieved and a mathematical model is used to weigh the sample to compensate for the fact that the sample was collected in a non-random way. See http://www.respondentdrivensampling.org/reports/RDSsummary.htm.

In the example, some reference is made to AIDS/HIV prevalence and sexual tourism in Thailand, more generally, but also in other South East Asian countries, such as Cambodia. What I have termed moderatum generalisations, are testable propositions that begin from the micro level (Payne and Williams 2005, Williams 2000b). That is, one makes informal propositions about practices, conditions, contexts, etc., holding in one time, or place, to another. As King et al (1994) observed, the logic of inference can (and indeed should) be the same in qualitative research, as quantitative research, that is to provide descriptions or explanations on the base of empirical observation. But additionally, to do this in a publicly accountable way. For example, we might expect the practice of *kheun khroo* to have a purchase, not just through Thai culture, but maybe in a modified form in other South East Asian societies. We might also expect the characteristics and thus the causal efficacy in shaping the behaviour of the Thai sex workers, would be generalisable beyond Thailand. Assume, these things and possibly other characteristics and behaviours can be found more widely, and further assume that AIDS/HIV infection is lower in (say) Vietnam,[3] then one would be seeking those factors that differed between Thailand and Vietnam.[4] These are testable propositions, as much as any claims arising from survey data.

Observation and interviewing are as old as social science itself, there is nothing novel in the use of these methods and they are not in themselves realist. But what I have tried to do above, is to sketch out (and it can be little more than that in the space available) how we can look at a fairly typical observation study through a complex realist lens. I identified six possible mechanisms, each would possess dispositions (or "causal powers") to interact and change each of the others (given the logical limitation of time direction in some cases). Imagine a grid, with each cell representing a proposed mechanism, then imagine just one possible interaction between each cell and every other cell and imagine this grid changing over time, as the interactions change and you get a very simple notion of the complexity entailed.

Actually, something like this can be done in building a theoretical model, of the interaction of these mechanisms, where direction, cause and prevalence are specified. These proposed interactions might then be further tested qualitatively or quantitatively.

The macro-method toolkit

In the previous section I discussed only observation and interviewing, because these approaches provided an adequate illustration of how micro methods might be conceptualised from a realist perspective. The task with "macro", or quantitative methods, is more difficult, because the methodological reasoning differs more between them. For example, survey research mostly depends on the frequency theory of probability to infer from samples to populations, experiments depend on randomisation between experimental and control groups and compare results after an intervention with the first group. Big data research is often a-theoretical and seeks patterns in very large arrays of data.

In this section my main focus will be on the secondary analysis of longitudinal data.

I have spoken at length about the shortcomings and limitations of the general linear model and causal analysis. The first cannot account for the complexity of interactions and the second uses various modelling strategies to established probabilistic causality amongst measured variables. In these matters I am happy to agree with Byrne, Porpora, Freedman, etc. As I said in Chapter 4, I think their arguments are perfectly sound. However, if we accept the Cartwright dictum, that causality is one word, but many things, then a realist approach is to tell plausible causal stories. A lot hangs on the word plausible, it is a plausibility subject to both inference to the best explanation and Occam's Razor! But with these caveats suitably entered, I can see no reason why causal statements, arising from linear data cannot be part of our causal story, at least as falsifiable propositions.

I am wary of the term "gold standard", as often applied to Randomised Control Trials, but I do think that longitudinal, or panel data, from very large surveys, is the "gold standard" of survey research. Firstly, because sample sizes produce decent statistical significance, but mostly because this then assists us to measure change in characteristics, behaviours and beliefs over time. Causal direction (and thus spurious associations) can be shown (Elliot 2005: 101). This may be simply descriptive and suggest the beginning of a causal story, or it may give important clues to a causal mechanism. I and colleagues analysed England and Wales longitudinally linked Census data[5] to discover the proportion of people who continued to suffer from a limiting long term illness (LLTI) at two census dates (Collett et al 2006). The questions and respondent guidance remained the same from time T1 to time T2, so we argued that the measure was a reliable one. Given the simplicity of the wording, and census test procedures, we also argued had content validity. Thus no change/change between censuses is an accurate measure of the existence of LLTI in the study members. Simple cross-tabulations and logistic regression models were able to show the relationships and the strength of the relationships with LLTI. The intention was not to make causal claims, in these analyses, but to establish some parameters of the reality, upon which other research, that might explore causality, might be conducted.[6] The independent variables included sex, age, education, social class, housing, and location. These variables do not lend themselves to causal claims, in any simplistic way – for example living in private rented accommodation cannot "cause" illness, but poor quality housing (more likely in that sector) can produce, damp or insanitary conditions which can. But the variables, with exception of social class are not social constructs, but are properties of the physical world. The other possible exception is education and education qualifications, are social constructs, but one either has a qualification, or one does not.

Research by Alice Sullivan and colleagues (Sullivan et al 2018) explored whether attendance at faith, private or selective schools provided any advantage in terms of highest educational qualification, over those who attended comprehensive (state) schools. The dataset used was the British Cohort Survey, begun in 1970 (BCS70). It followed members through at ages at ages 5, 10, 16, 26, 30, 34, 38 and 42, so is able to measure change across a number of variables, in the same people, over time. Here the sample size, initially 17,000, (but 10,188 after excluding Scotland) mattered because 81% had attended comprehensive schools. The dependent variable was highest educational qualification, measured at age 42, but also earlier and the independent variables were school types. The models relied on a considerable number of control variables, including birth characteristics: sex, birth weight, as low birth weight is an indicator of prenatal disadvantage, occupation, social class, parents highest qualification, age of mother at first birth and frequency of reading to the child at age five, and on the type of newspapers regularly present in the home at age 16 (Sullivan et al 2018: 809–810).

The findings were that private schools did provide a residual advantage, in both the short- and long-term, but faith schools provided an advantage only in the shorter term.

As with the "micro" observation example, this research was not overtly realist, but the language of the discussion does suggest "causal stories". For example:

> We can speculate that the academic advantage of a religious upbringing may be due to cultural differences, such as stricter parenting practices or due to the protective influence of being part of a particular faith community.
>
> op cit: 818

The middle range theory being tested was that attendance at faith, private and selective schools conferred qualificational advantage later in life. This, in turn, might comprise a testable theory, within a wider theory of social capital. One limitation, as no doubt Dave Byrne would point out, that complexity of the relationships between the dependent, independent and control variables is "smoothed" and therefore only implicit. But given these findings, a realist researcher could focus in on the apparent micro level complexities, for example the biographies of individuals that took each educational pathway. In this way, the "macro" level of the statistical modelling of large datasets, shines a light on the micro by suggesting some possible explanatory trajectories of characteristics, behaviours and beliefs, which in turn can be explored through strategies, such as depth interviews.

Furthermore, the relationships explored in this kind of research are not simply statistical, though they are represented statistically. For example, as Jane Elliot describes (Elliot 2005: 103–106), causes may be direct or indirect, proximate and basic. She cites research by Balnaves and Caputi (2001) in which they found age to be an important predictor of academic performance at university and that mature students performed best of all. On further examination, it was found that such students had made a number of sacrifices to get to university, more likely to self-select their course, which in turn made them more motivated to succeed. Age did not "cause" academic success, but that was what was directly measured, but further analysis then revealed the indirect causes. Similarly, she cites research by Reskin (1988) on male-female wage disparity. The proximate cause could be seen to be occupational segregation, but the basic cause was that of an imbalance of male–female power relationships.

The "tools" in the various research projects described here are statistical and logical, rather than particular techniques. The Sullivan et al research used relatively straightforward regression models, but with longitudinal data. As I note in various places, in this book, a range of techniques, such, Structural Equation Modelling, Discriminant Analysis, Counterfactual Causality, etc., would be equally valuable in particular contexts of realist research, as long as we bear in mind they are statistical, or logical narratives, that help us to develop causal stories, but models are more than narratives, they make predictions and if one model has greater explanatory power, then it must add something in terms of prediction. One might translate this into realist terms, by saying that if one model describes a better and testable mechanism than another, then the second model is to be preferred, because it potentially gives a better description or explanation of reality. Not all narratives are therefore equal.

Very little research, using the more "traditional" quantitative methods described above, is overtly realist, though some can be interpreted in a realist way and, as I have said, for research to be realist, it does not have to announce itself in that way.

Case-based methods

In the previous sections I have described some more traditional research tools for exploring the micro and the macro. In a less catholic approach to realist method, I might have skipped these and moved straight to this section. I have not done so, because more traditional approaches still dominate in research (though this is changing fast) and training reflects this. Secondly, the case-based approaches I will describe here, though they often intentionally are grounded in a complex realist approach, are still only practised by a handful of researchers, some of whom have a computational, rather than social science, background. Nevertheless, this is to be applauded and augers well for a more interdisciplinary approach to social research.

As I noted earlier, in 2007 Mike Savage and Roger Burrows published, what became, a very influential paper, entitled "The Coming Crisis in Empirical Sociology" (Savage and Burrows 2007). In this paper they argued that sociology was likely to get left behind methodologically, if it continued to rely on the sample survey and depth interviews, as its primary source of data collection. Their argument was based upon (even then) the growing importance of big data, and what they termed "transactional data". This latter was the quotidian data that arises from our everyday lives, supermarket shopping, Amazon purchases, telecommunications, etc. Outside of sociology, organisations were routinely using transactional data, often combined with administrative data, to produce sophisticated predictive algorithms that can identify, sort and classify. I note Savage and Burrows, paper as an illustration of both the extent and sophistication of analyses of massive datasets, that could potentially be a basis of complex realist analysis, if only for the simple reason that to understand complexity at a societal level, to see how (e.g. "strange attractors" develop, where tipping points occur, very large data sets are highly advantageous.

An area in which the analysis of large-scale real-time data, has been in criminology. Twitter data, for example, can be used to predict extremism or hate crime, or large scale public disturbance. Matthew Williams and colleagues conducted an experiment, that used London as its "geography". They hypothesised that data collected from "online sources" could increase the amount of crime variance explained in statistical models, in excess of that explained by traditional "offline" sources (Williams et al 2016). They compared police recorded crime, with Twitter data. The latter is analysis of "sentiment" data – in this case words linked to social degeneration, or mention of crime – what criminologists call the "broken windows theory".[7] The number of observations was huge: $n = 8,417,438$, though given the technology to harvest these, in some ways an easier proposition that collecting data in more traditional ways!

This kind of work has largely been descriptive and predictive, though in much the same way as survey data does, it can establish where "invariances" may lie, that in turn can help us to hypothesise mechanisms. These are often geographical, as in the Williams et al research. Such research is case-based, and does not rely on samples. So, the observations are of real agents expressing their own sentiments and whilst these are "real" in the sense of the Thomas dictum, they can be predictors of action, which creates social objects – themselves real. In this way, something like the "broken windows" theory is a self-fulfilling prophecy.

As Savage et al noted, much "transactional data" research (which uses big data) is conducted by private companies, not social scientists and for the most part does not utilise traditional modelling techniques, but rather predictive algorithms. Indeed, quite a lot of big data research, conducted outside of social science, simply looks for "interesting" patterns in the data, it is neither theoretically or variable led, but really a type of data dredging (Hanan and Stuart 1966). Even though not many social scientists using big data, of various kinds, are locating this methodologically in realism, or even seeing it through the lens of complexity, nevertheless its methodological possibilities, in helping us to understand complex reality, are apparent. The possibilities of causal inference from big data was explored in a symposium in the journal *Political Science and Politics*, in 2015. In a paper exploring the possibilities of developing both theory and causal inference from big data, Monroe et al (2015), make a number of important observations. The first was "what do we mean by big data", do we mean just lots of data, or the kind of data it is? For example, what and how we can infer and theorise from GPS data, video data and transactional data, will be quite different. Furthermore, there are many new methods of capturing data, web scraping, natural language processing, statistical learning, machine learning, etc. None of these simply imply "data mining". Social data might actually be "small" but imply large numbers of interactions that can be captured through complex models. They conclude that this diversity means that, what we have labelled "big data" is far from incompatible with social scientific causal inference and theorising.

Social science case-based research has taken some other interesting directions in recent years. Some of the foundational work in this area is well documented in the collection of papers edited by David Byrne and Charles Ragin (Ragin and Byrne 2009). Indeed, these two researchers have invented some novel approaches to case-based methods.

Qualitative Comparative Analysis (QCA) was invented by Charles Ragin, but is now possibly the most utilised case-based method (Ragin 1987, Rihoux and Ragin 2009). The "qualitative" part is somewhat misleading, because it does not rely on traditional forms of interpretation (though as with all methods interpretation is always present). Though QCA can be used with large datasets, for the most part it is not and is mainly used for "meso" level analyses. It seeks patterns across multiple cases to understand why change occurs in some, but not others. It begins by specifying a theory of change – that is what is expected to change in the data. All types of cases are then listed and each type of case is defined by its unique combination of values of the independent and dependent variables that may attach to it. Logical inference is then used to reduce or simplify inferences. All the logically possible configurations are listed in a truth table. QCA takes two forms, that of "crisp set" where values are binary, or fuzzy set where they can take on intermediate values of QCA (Glaesser and Cooper 2014).

The analytic value of QCA to complex realism was explored in a paper by Lasse Gerrits and Stefan Verweij (2015).

> [QCA] allows for the examination of multiple causal configurations. The configurational approach implies that combinations of conditions (i.e. configurations) produce certain outcomes, different combinations may produce the outcome, and certain conditions can have different effects in different contexts. These characteristics are referred to respectively as conjunctural causation, equifinality and multifinality and summarized collectively as causal complexity or complex causation
>
> Gerrits and Verweij 2015: 175

Gerrits and Verweu show how the truth tables can show the necessary and sufficient conditions for something to happen, using the INUS conditions I described in Chapter 4. But as they note, though QCA is reductive in its method, that is it compresses reality and partial, it decomposes reality, it is nevertheless built on the notion of contingency (particularly in fuzzy set QCA) (op cit: 179). What makes it realist, is that it begins from "real" cases, rather than variables.

Other researchers, for example Byrne (2009), Uprichard (2009) Williams and Dyer (2004, 2009) have adopted a different approach to case-based analyses. These have used case-based cluster analyses to establish causal configurations or cluster analysis and discriminant function analysis, with longitudinal data, to establish case probabilities.

The latter research, conducted by Wendy Dyer, was a two stage analysis of referrals to a Custody Diversion Team (CDT) in the North East of England. In the first stage cluster analysis of data in a relational database was undertaken to identify a number of psychiatric and criminal "career types" experienced by mentally disordered offenders referred to a CDT. Critical events were measured in the lives of offenders, within the criminal justice/psychiatric system. In the second stage discriminant analysis was used to elucidate which variables best described the cases and the nature of the intervention interventions were operating as control parameters in determining the probabilistic trajectories of cases towards different future states. Discriminant analysis builds a linear discriminant function, which is used to classify observations. The overall fit is assessed by looking at the degree of difference in group means using Wilkes Lambda or by calculating the Mahalanobis distance.[8] The calculation of the Mahalanobis distance in the classification permits the derivation of the case probabilities within the trajectories (Williams and Dyer 2009).

The analyses in this research were an overt attempt to operationalise Popper's single case propensity theory of probability (see Chapters 3 and 4). The database was longitudinal and so, following the logic of single case probability, each "event" raised, or lowered, the probability of subsequent events, for that individual. The events themselves can be thought of as bifurcations, whereby a particular thing happens rather than any other thing and as with QCA, the cases themselves are "real" and the bifurcations in the clusters represent life events. This work is at a relatively early stage and has limitations, particularly that it requires longitudinal data with enough cases and data points to be able to model trajectories and "strange attractors". Though sample data could be used, datasets, such as the one described, contain records of all of the population of interest, allow for the calculation of the possibility space (Dyer and Williams 2020).

The work of Brian Castellani and colleagues, is perhaps the most sophisticated in complex realism in the social sciences, and might be an example of what Monroe et al meant by small data – implying networks, interdependencies or hierarchies (Monroe et al 2015: 71). Castellani and his colleague Frederic Hafferty building on the work of David Byrne have developed the SACS (Sociology And Complexity Science) toolkit (Castellani and Hafferty 2009). It is described as "a case-based, mixed-method, system-clustering, data-compressing, theoretically driven toolkit for modelling complex social systems" (Castellani and Rajaram 2012). The Toolkit has three main elements. Initially a theoretical model (what they call a theoretical blueprint) of what are seen as the major components of a complex system, are derived. The second element is a set of case-based instructions for modelling complex systems, what they call assemblage and possibly equivalent to operationalisation in more traditional research and finally, the third element (what they call the toolset) is a list of case-friendly computational modelling techniques.

The theoretical assumptions of SACS combine elements of various concepts and approaches discussed in this book so far and grounded in middle range theory, though specifically here this is referred to as "practice theory".[9] It can be thought of as a sophisticated variation on Pawson's CMO configuration, though here context is referred to as "environmental forces and case based analysis, that models case trajectories". Social practice is defined as "any pattern of social organization that emerges out of, and allows for, the intersection of symbolic interaction and social agency" (Castellani and Hafferty 2009: 38).

A specific example of the use of the SACS toolkit (Castellani et al 2018) is an exploration of co-morbid depression and physical health trajectories. Clinicians face a genuine problem of complexity, in that whilst poor physical health and depression are associated, this is presented in complex combinations of sociodemographic and clinical factors, which evolve along multiple and different trajectories. It is far from the case that these things are always coterminous and when they are, they may evolve differently. For example, in some chronic illnesses there may not be any relationship with depression. A key methodological challenge has been that, despite advances in other areas in computational methods and complex systems thinking, most research has employed traditional statistical methods, with cross-sectional data mapping discrete, rather than continuous change.

Castellani and his colleagues used a number of novel methods (these are described in the paper): case-based comparative method, vector quantisation, genetic algorithms, ordinary differential equations and partial differential equations. What these methods do is to transform complex trajectories into cases, clusters and densities. However, the important message for us, is that the methods begin from the assumption of case-based complexity, rather than variable analysis. The analyses were conducted in nine steps (op cit: 6)

Step 1 The modelling of multiple co-morbid trends through clustering case trajectories, treating each time instance as a measure and "the total of time instances/measures as the longitudinal k-dimensional vector profile for each case" (Ibid).
Step 2 Theoretical assumptions of expected number of clusters.
Step 3 The corroboration and optimisation of the clusters.
Step 4 The prior steps provide a topographical visualisation (see Figure 9.1) of types of physical health cases and comorbid depressive health cases most like one another are "graphically positioned as near neighbours with the most unlike cases placed further apart"(Ibid).
Step 5 Labelling of the cases according to their K means cluster membership.
Step 6 Expert corroboration of the visualisation by a panel.
Step 7 ANOVA and chi-square were used to determine how the identified 38 clinical and demographic variables accounted for 11 trends. However, tests of significance were not used, because the number of cases (259) was too small.
Step 8 This was the stage when computational modelling was used model the collective large scale dynamics. The model constructed 18 trajectories "upon which the 11 trends are based to construct a state-space of all possible trajectories for all seven years of the study" (Ibid).
Step 9 used the expert panel to construct a clinical narrative for each of the 11 trends.

Results are represented in Figures 9.1 and 9.2.

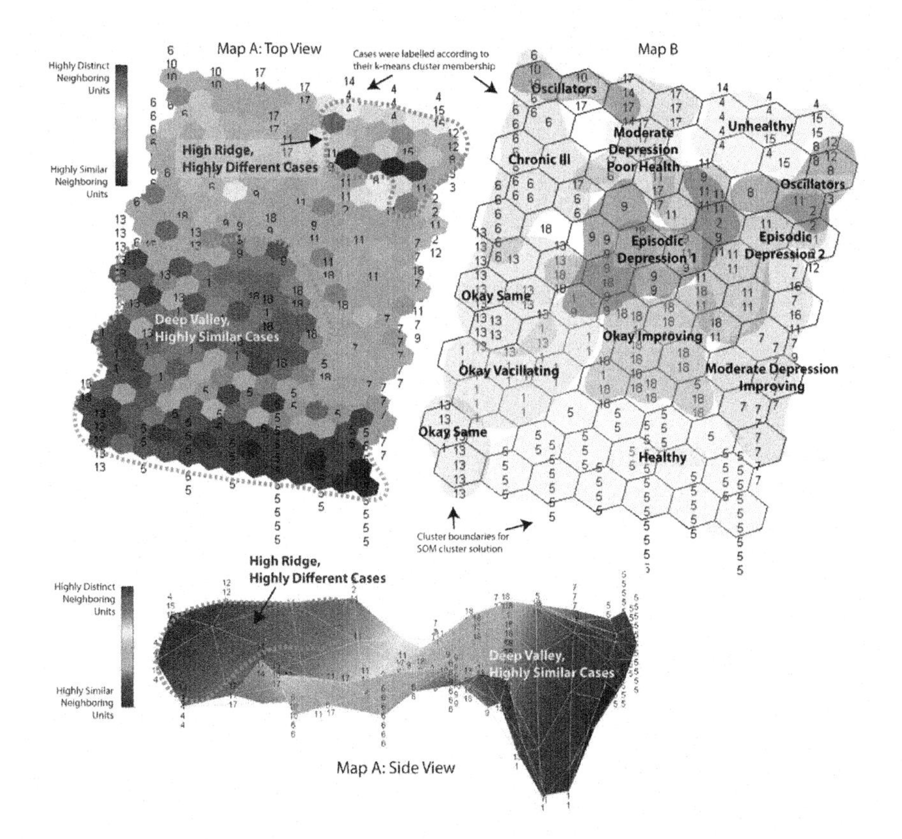

FIGURE 9.1 is a topographical representation of the 11 trends, mapped according to their K-means cluster membership. It graphically shows how the trends cluster into similarities and differences, by using vertical and horizontal visualisations of the topographies of different health states

As Castellani et al point out, this study was descriptive, rather than explanatory and was based on a relatively small cohort, but nevertheless there are a number of things that make it methodologically innovative.

Though conventional statistics were used in Step 7, for the most part a totally different approach is used. Cluster analysis and computational modelling demonstrate similarity and difference of cases and their trajectories over time, rather than fitting cases to variables.

Though the probabilities of single cases in comparison to other cases are not analysed, nevertheless the underlying logic of probability is that these cases themselves exhibit specific probabilities of outcomes, but that these can change through time. Some cases have relative stability (invariance), whereas others are very much more dynamic.

At Steps 2, 6 and 9 a degree of intersubjective interpretation is employed. Cluster analysis requires the research to a priori to theorise the nature and type of clusters expected, though a number of different solutions might be fitted. At steps

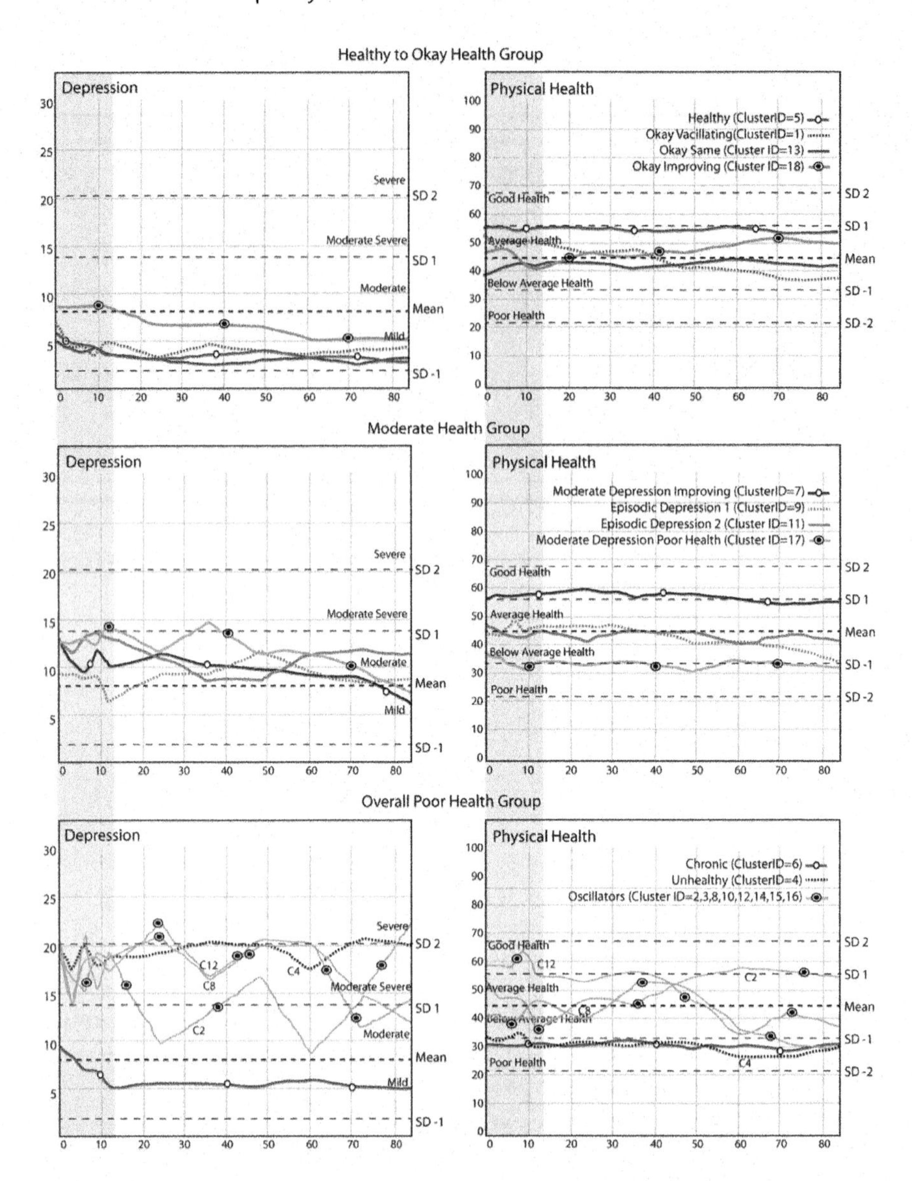

FIGURE 9.2 shows how the trends evolve through time, with depressive trends on the left side and the corresponding physical health trends on the right hand side. It shows that the most stable clusters were the Healthy to Okay Healthy clusters, but after these the dynamics intensify and diversify to finally the Overall Poor Health clusters

6 and 9 expert knowledge was used to interpret the data and at Step 9 construct a clinical narrative from the data.

Step 8 was methodologically the most sophisticated, but in modelling all possible trajectories, it allows us to empirically show variance and invariance and how this changes, over time.

More generally, in terms of complexity thinking, the clusters themselves represent attractors within the possibility space of socio demographic and clinical events. Their visual representation, in particular, demonstrates both the complexity, emergent properties (the ways comorbidity develops – or indeed fails to do so in particular groups) but also the relative intransigence in these patterns.

Castellani and colleagues' methods of analysis utilise a battery of modelling techniques and these will vary depending on the data and the questions asked. What, however, is important is that these approaches combine the micro and macroscope, in that they are dynamic and describe both trajectories and potentially mechanisms.

Simulation

Finally, I must mention a family of methods quite different in data and even starting assumptions to those above – that of simulation. Simulation the modelling of complexity in a miniature world, the results of which can then be compared with studies using real data. It can be wholly abstract and model only "toy worlds", it may be through artificial intelligence, or system dynamics (Grüne-Yanoff 2011: 612–615). In the social sciences, the commonest form of simulation is Agent-Based Modelling (ABM), sometimes referred to as Agent-Based Simulation. These models can be predictive, or explanatory, but for the most part they explore what happens when (artificial) agents begin interacting, given some usually quite simple rules. Models are often tested against those that use "real world" data from observations.

The predecessor of ABM was a very simple modelling application called Cellular Automata (CA) which provides a very simple picture of the logic of modelling. It consists of cells in regular grid, which may have one to three dimensions. Each cell has a number of states which change over time. One of the most famous CA model is Conway's "Game of Life", (Berkelcamp et al 1982) in which each cell, in the grid, is either "dead" or "alive", but dead cells with exactly three neighbours become "live", whereas "live" cells with less than two, or more than three neighbours, become "dead". These very simple rules lead to evolving systems, the future states of which cannot be known a priori, and are an excellent example of how complex patterns can emerge from simple systems.

There is controversy about to what extent simulation offers new philosophical challenges (Frigg and Reiss 2009), but three characteristics make it different to other kinds of models and may also be helpful in our understanding of emergence and thus complexity.

Firstly, they are epistemologically different in so far as they cannot be analytically broken down into components or readily expressed as a mathematical algorithms.

Secondly they incorporate a dynamic element of time. In a static (traditional model), elapsed time is represented only by variables measured at different time points. Simulation can help us to understand how complex systems change through time – not the least because we can use visualisation techniques.

Thirdly, and possibly more of a challenge, they cause us to question what we mean by an "agent" or the "social". In simulations agents are given characteristics and they interact, but they are (unlike agents in the real world) goal directed. Yet what emerges can often by artificial societies that have huge verisimilitude to "real" ones. So how important to the social is goal directed, or teleological behaviour to the creation of social entities and therefore to what extent are the social entities independent of particular agency?

What simulation and the case-based methods I describe above challenge, is the old quantitative–qualitative dichotomy. Obviously, simulation is neither of these things, but "case based" methods both concentrate on the "case", as in qualitative research, and on "counting" as in quantitative research. This provides interesting methodological possibilities, that can shift the microscope to the macroscope, by quantifying from case-based qualitative data, through analysis packages, such as NVivo and then conducting case-based cluster analysis, or QCA analyses. Conversely if one has case identifiers and subject to ethical constraints, it is possible to "open up" those cases through depth interviews and shift the macroscope to the microscope.

Realist closure and the changing nature of social research

The holy grail of realist research is "closure" and whilst possible, it is elusive. We can never capture reality in its completeness, not even locally, but we can capture data that is either direct measures of social reality, or proxies that can help us to theorise mechanisms. The direct measures can come from observations of real-time events, or micro level interactions or communications. These are analogous to natural scientists directly observing physical events at an atomic or sub-atomic level. But we also need to measure aggregates of events (such as Twitter postings), before we can visualise the patterns that indicate the existence of social objects, or mechanisms. In the latter case, observations of large numbers of events, will themselves not make that much sense unless interpreted in context.

Some case-based methods, such as those of Castellani and colleagues, or those used by Wendy Dyer, can demonstrate trajectories through time and the clustering of cases with particular characteristics can be demonstrated as occurring at points in time. We can examine both the trajectories and individual understandings of their "action space" and thus the creation of social objects. For example, in the Custody Diversion Team research, the mechanisms of referral can be examined in terms of their trajectories through time, but also how these exist within particular local settings (the contexts). The social object of the referral itself has a different meaning and consequence for the offender and for those in the criminal justice system, even though it arises from the same action. For the offender something happens to them that they must interpret and then "live", but for the criminal justice system, each individual referral is the result of an individual decision by a case worker. At the risk of drawing an analogy that might be considered a category mistake, or taken out of context, social objects are the electrons of the social world. By interacting with them, we change them, but they nevertheless coalesce into tangible things (for us mechanisms) that have causal properties. Thus, like the electron, to understand what is happening one must understand the behaviour at a quantum level, but also understand the macro-statistical patterning.

But most of the methods available to us, at the macro level, rely on sample surveys, panel data, official statistics, etc. Their analyses, for the most part, relies on the assumptions of the general linear model and the modelling techniques have been part of the social scientists toolkit for decades. But, this kind of research, more than any demonstrates that it is not the tools themselves that are important (with the caveat I mentioned about appropriateness) but the way we theorise the questions we asked of the data and the models we build. This is more analogous to natural scientists indirectly observing evidence for phenomena, rather than the actual phenomena, what Byrne described as "variate traces" (Byrne 2002: 29–42). In a paper I wrote, a little while ago (Williams 2018), I used an example of a "classic" study utilising causal analysis, Blau and Duncan's research on social stratification (Blau and Duncan 1978), to illustrate how realists might re-imagine, or even re-purpose such research.

In the1950s and 1960s, Marxists believed that the United States was a highly stratified society, with status determined by family background and transmitted through the school system, yet nevertheless the system was permeable to an extent and individuals could transcend their stratum. Blau and Duncan produced a correlation matrix of Son's occupation; Son's first job; Son's education; Father's Occupation; Father's Education, as measured in the 1962 Current Population Survey. The measurements themselves were standardised, for example: education in number of years and occupation on a prestige scale of 0. A path analysis was then conducted (reproduced on page 131 of the Freedman paper) which indicates causality between (for example) father's and son's education, between father's occupation and son's occupation. The standard deviations indicated the level of permeability in the causal paths. Although crude is a nice example of a proposed mechanism. The Outcome (O) is the *relatively* fixed strata and the mechanism proposed is one of a superstructure of education and family type, themselves the outcome of an economic "base". In this research only the superstructure mechanism is explored. The contexts are the United States itself, because presumably a similar mechanism could exist elsewhere, but also local contexts, which may be cultural or socio-economic. A modern day realist would want to improve on the mechanism, to better titrate the permeability by exploring, perhaps at a meso or micro level, what socio economic and cultural differences might exist to change the chances of mobility through education or occupation. In other words, construct other "mini mechanisms" and test them on a subset of this sample (or a sample emulating it). However, I cite this example, not to defend causal analysis, on its own terms, but rather to show what a realist might *do* with causal analyses.

In this chapter I have used the analogy of the "microscope" and the "macroscope" to contextualise the value of methodological approaches to theorise upwards to mechanisms and downwards to suggest profitable lines of enquiry to look for the causal foundations of those mechanisms. What, we might call, "traditional methods" are legitimate tools in this enterprise. Uniquely, complex case-based approaches allow, within one methodological space, the ability to focus the theoretical gaze in each direction, but whichever methods one uses, rarely is closure a matter of "gotcha" – incontrovertible empirical proof, be that a confirmation or falsification, because we can only ever know reality through its representations – never grasping the "noumena" of the social. Rather, closure is an inference to the best explanation, that arises from the most rigorous methodological testing of our theories, that in turn can be modified and re-tested. In that sense, methodologically, complex realism is a dialectical approach that searches for truth, but on that journey settles for greater insight and the elimination of error.

Notes

1 I differentiate "action space" here from my earlier discussion of possibility space. Action space consists of those actions that are possible for an individual, where possibility space encompasses these plus things that could possibly happen to them, subject to the social contingencies in that particular case.
2 Realists have conflicting views about the value of grounded theory. It might be seen as a form of "abstracted empiricism" in which there is a temptation to interpret data along common sense or a priori understandings, but some realists (e.g. Kempster and Parry 2014) have argued that "retroductive" strategy, which seeks the "causal powers" (dispositions) in the data can assist in contextualisation and generalisation.
3 In 2018 (some years after the study reported here, 9% of the Thai population were HIV positive and 03% of the Vietnamese population https://www.unaids.org/en/regionscountries/countries. Accessed 01/05/20.
4 "If an instance in which the phenomenon under investigation occurs, and an instance in which it does not occur, have every circumstance in common save one, that one occurring in the former; the circumstance in which alone the two instances differ is the effect, or the cause, or an indispensable part of the cause of the phenomenon". This is John Stuart Mill's "method of difference" (cited in Hage and Foley-Meeker 1988: 47–48). There are five "methods" in which he attempted to codify causal relations. However, like INUS conditions, discussed inn Chapter 4, they at least suffer from the need for ceteris paribus clauses. However the "method of difference" can have empirical value as an analytic strategy, even if it does not permit us to identify a specific cause.
5 The United Kingdom Office for National Statistics (ONS) Longitudinal Study (LS) is a continuous linked s sample of records from each census, in England and Wales, from 1971 to 2011. https://www.ons.gov.uk/aboutus/whatwedo/paidservices/longitudinalstudyls. Accessed 24/06/20.
6 In Chapter 5, I noted how this could be extended to "explain" higher levels of LLTI in Welsh males.
7 The Broken Windows theory (Wilson and Kelling 1982) proposes that disorder ("broken windows" is a metaphor) within a neighbourhood is linked to higher levels of crime and civil disorder. (Wilson and Kelling 1982)

8 The Mahalanobis distance (MD) is the distance between two points in multivariate space. It is a multi-dimensional generalisation of the idea of measuring how many standard deviations away P is from the mean of D https://www.statisticshowto.com/mahalanobis-distance/. Accessed 21/04/20.
9 Practice Theory is a broad concept, though often most associated with Pierre Bourdieu and his theory of Habitus (Bourdieu 1977). It is implicit in a number of theoretical positions which stress the dynamic and dialectical interplay between agent motives and intentions and how they maintain or change the social world. Castellani and Rajaram (2012) define it as being "comprised of five key components: interaction, social agents, communication, coupling and social knowing".

10

A manifesto for complex realism

Manifestos are issued by political parties prior to elections and are statements of the policies that party would like to implement, should it be elected. Manifestos are debated by opponents and supporters alike and in practice what is finally implemented may be rather different to the original document. It is in this spirit that I offer this conclusion. I want to say what I think Complex Realism should look like in social science, but as I said in the Introduction, it is a hypothesis, an invitation to test and perhaps falsify, either logically, or methodologically, what I have argued and proposed in this book.

This chapter, though derived from the arguments, claims and propositions of the previous chapters, is nevertheless something of a polemic and a summary of what I am advocating. Except where I introduce new materials, I have eschewed further referencing.

In this concluding chapter I want to summarise my argument in the three key domains of realism: ontology, epistemology and methodology.

Ontology

I have suggested, in a number of places in this book, that to be a realist requires taking something on trust, perhaps a leap of faith. That is, we begin from the premise that there is a real world, beyond that which we can observe. Empiricism, does not need to do this, because it is sceptical about unobservables, though as I have said, in practice empiricist social research, particularly that in the causal analysis tradition is not quite so evangelical. Idealists, in social research, deny we can say anything beyond the "realities" we can see that are created by language and interaction. Neither deny the existence of reality, or a social reality, but they do deny that we can know beyond measurement or social construction.

Things depend less on trust, once we begin to say what we mean by a reality beyond observation, because that then becomes a proposition about what it is like, that might be tested and here we find some common ground with the empiricists around the basic character of scientific investigation. It is the shift to testable propositions that turns metaphysical realism into scientific realism. But more of that in the next section. Here I want to outline some manifesto claims about the nature of social reality:

The social world is real, but it is socially constructed

What we call social reality is an ontological "mix". It is the socially interpreted and created aspects of the physical world – in the first case, a naturally existing object, such as a "mountain" and in the second a created physical object with social meaning, such as a computer, or a bowl of soup!. Then there are social creations that do not have direct physical referents, such as ceremonies, customs, laws, habits. These are created, observed, changed and abandoned through time and space. They are social constructions, often linguistic, often codified and preserved in a "third world" of knowledge, the things of human creation that stand separately from us, music, works of art, books, scientific evidence. But they are, as Durkheim insisted, social facts. They are as real as the physical effects of those things we did not create, or physical effects of those physical things we did create. They are real, because they have causal consequences that enable and constrain future action.

There is no natural necessity, only conceptual necessity

The social world is not determined and there is no natural necessity, other than that which supervenes on physical properties. That is, the social world always contains the potential to be different, however unlikely that might be. In the physical world, there is natural necessity, because all of the properties of the physical world are grounded in fundamental laws, even though they may operate *ceteris paribus*. I acknowledge that Nancy Cartwright does not take this view, but for the purposes of the contrast between the social and physical world, the invariances in the latter are very much more determined and mostly cannot be changed by human will. Crudely put, gravity and thermodynamics will ultimately trump our efforts to subvert them. Not so the social world, where any necessity is conceptual. That is, something is what it is by virtue of social convention: criminal law, the role of a president, the money economy, the game of ice hockey, etc. But it does not follow from this that anything goes. Some things are so improbable as to be all but impossible. But, in these cases, we can always tell a story that shows the possibility, however slight, of a different possibility. So if there is no natural necessity then....

The social world is probabilistic

There is nothing new about probability in the natural and social sciences. In the latter, however, it has almost exclusively been an epistemological or statistical matter. What I propose, and following Karl Popper, is that the real nature of the world, and most especially the social world, is that it is probabilistic. This does not mean that there are no things that just "are", but these things in the social world are either down to their being grounded in the physical world, or they are past tense. They are realised probabilities – they are equivalent to 1. For example, on 12 December, 2019, the Conservative government was re-elected, in the UK. Right up until the votes were cast, this was only a probability, but one that changed over time, up until the election, as a result of voters changing their minds, either for or against, the Conservatives. Up until the votes were cast the probabilities were between 0 and 1. Analysts pore over why Labour lost, so spectacularly and whatever the conclusions, the result was the outcome of a nesting of probabilities derived from prior events, earlier "1"s (e.g. the Conservative slogan "Get Brexit Done", the election of Jeremy Corbyn, as Labour leader, the adoption of particular policies by one or other party).

I have proposed that the statistical basis of complex realism, is that of the single case propensity interpretation of probability. This is an ontological theory of probability, unlike the frequency theory of probability, which is epistemological and the basis of most statistical reasoning, in the social sciences. The single case theory (or interpretation) of probability is that probability lies in the single case and in each case there are differing propensities to achieve particular outcomes. Though each case is potentially unique, in respect of a characteristic or trajectory, because the antecedent conditions may be similar, there are convergences of similar probabilities. This version of probability, I have argued, is entirely compatible with a complexity approach. Complexity is not stochastic, it is fluid and new states emerge, but patterns and stability exist. Indeed, if such stability did not exist, there would be no order in the social world. Complexity is about the dynamics of both change and order in the world.

The vocabulary of complexity evolved, as I noted in Chapter 3, in the natural sciences. Sometimes I think its use in the social sciences is a kind of natural science envy, but more than that it never is quite up to capturing the specific kind of complexity, that arises from self-aware agents in the social world. Somewhat ironically, some of the empirical work I described in the previous chapter, does a better job without the vocabulary. But let us revisit some of the complexity neologisms and see how they might be compatible with the claim that the social reality is probabilistic.

The first is possibility space, also described as phase space. In a closed system, we could think of it as a multiplication of all possible states and trajectories, but because the social world is the quintessential open system, theoretically the possibility space is the whole social world. But if we deploy the concept of conceptual necessity, as a limit on local space-time possibilities, then it remains useful. For example, we can model educational attainment with identified variables, for much of the population and get good predictive models. This is because of the conceptual necessity of things like parental education, household composition, parental occupation, income, school type, etc. Let me stress, these are not determinates, but possibilities that get closer to "1" if we multiply up the cases in the population. It is this kind of reasoning that Qualitative Comparative Analysis (QCA), or case-based cluster analysis, described in the previous chapter, that relies on the logic of necessary and sufficient conditions (QCA) or bifurcations (cluster analysis).

The second is the concept of the "strange attractor". These are relatively stable patterns, in systems, for example the looping orbit of a planet around the sun, or stable patterns in turbulence flows. In the social world, we can see these in stable patterns of behaviour that are reinforced by sanction, or cultural norms, but in their turn, they produce relative invariance, that is they are invariant whilst certain conditions hold. These conditions may well be path dependencies, perhaps embodied in law, custom or particular effective individual behaviours (such as assassinations!). So, even though there is a "world of propensities" (Popper 1995) these coalesce, locally and at aggregate levels into measurable patterns and identifiable trajectories.

All of these things are ontologically probable. As I write this, the world is experiencing the pandemic of Covid-19, Coronavirus. In its inception, spread and the reactions to it, we can see the ontology of complex reality played out before us. Moreover, it is a complexity that has both physical and social dimensions. Consider the story:

A virus "jumps" from an animal host, in a Chinese "wet market" to human being and an initial unknowing infection begins. But the infection does not spread evenly across the world. As a result of particular social behaviours (travel, dense interaction in crowds) "strange attractors" appear. These are not just the obvious ones of clusters of infections, but the social arrangements of hospitals and health care. We see the emergence of sanctioned or directed forms of behaviour, such as social distancing, which themselves are variants of social objects. From the turbulence of disease, emerge invariances, new mechanisms of control or financial intervention. But in all of this, we see nested "possibility spaces", where some things are very likely to happen (e.g. shortages of materials, such as ventilators or therapeutics) and many things that are very unlikely, such as a country completely escaping infection. Certain path dependencies, resulting from specific decisions by politicians, or supply chains, can be seen to have greater probabilities of occurring than other things. And at an individual level, whilst the prevalence of the virus, would not yield a zero infection in most individuals, the existence of social sanctions and behaviour patterns and the individual interaction with them, changes the probability of infection.

In other words, its probability all the way down!

There are causes in the social world

If we define causality as B would not have happened if not for A and A was prior in time, to be B, then there is causality in the social world. Unfortunately, defining A and B and the processes that link them, is far from straightforward and it led Nancy Cartwright to say that a cause is one word, but many things. Yet, to abandon causality would be to abandon a key tenet of realism and in David Lewis's words all there would be to the world "is a vast mosaic of local matters of particular fact, just one little thing then another" (Lewis 1986: ix–x). This would also emasculate the possibilities of social research to description only.

In Chapter 4, I discussed several approaches to causality, and I concluded that we should take a pluralist approach to causality and methodologically aim to tell plausible causal stories. But I also suggested that ontologically causality is a matter of probability, but not as an epistemological question, where we aim to reduce error within statistical association, but rather as a property of ontological probability. This is the way Popper saw it. Causes are the realisation of propensities – the outcome with a probability of 1 (or their impossibility, therefore 0). Causality is, then, a special case of probability. If we consider this, it unsurprising that causes at a macro and meso level are so slippery. The realisation of 1 – certainty, is the product of earlier realisations of 1 and the 1 in a specific case is causally unique, right up until the moment other cases are realised as "1"s. When many cases are realised, in the same way, invariance is created as social objects, or mechanisms. But every single outcome is nested in matrix of earlier probabilities. Metaphysically, we should perhaps abandon our push–pull view of causality and think of it as events realised through time. Time is important: in the succinct phrase, attributed to John Wheele it is "what keeps everything from happening at once" (Williams 2016: 225).[1]

This was probably what Bertrand Russell was getting at, when he denied the value of causal thinking in physics (see Chapter 4). Atomic decay is not "caused", but is a property of the thing, in itself, over time. However, atomic decay and educational attainment are very different concepts. The first depends on known and regular properties, the second on changing propensities through time.

But what about the question of free will, or specifically beliefs as causes? In this respect, what I suggest sounds like a passive theory of causality, where things just happen through time, but I do not think this is the case. Mental propensities, just as much as physical ones do "play out" over time, but this is because new information and processing of that information, changes our beliefs about the world and these too are nested in the beliefs and actions of others. Our beliefs, just as much as our physical characteristics and social positioning or constraints, are dispositional. Both A and B may hold the same belief (and indeed share other dispositions), but A may act on such a belief and B does not. However, and finally, an observed individual action (my example of Denzil hitting Garfield) may look like and may be treated as "push–pull" cause–effect; the same probabilistic matrix of beliefs desires and dispositions, underlay the singular action. Prior to the striking of the blow, there was merely a changing propensity for Denzil to hit Garfield. Denzil and Garfield's pugilism was a one off, but bifurcations, where A and not B happens, in aggregate patterns of behaviour, are at the micro level the same thing as those things we think of as singular causality.

There are social objects and mechanisms in the social world

Throughout this book I have deployed the notion of invariance. Invariance is a property or relationship that is invariant under appropriate transformations. These transformations will be the realisation of dispositions, perhaps repeatedly, through time. Queen Elizabeth II, of Britain, had both the disposition to be a monarch, which has been realised over time, or she had the disposition to abdicate, as did her uncle. Because properties or relationships exist through time, whilst they exist, they are invariant. That does not mean they do not change, but they do not change sufficiently to become something else quite different. I have suggested that these invariances can be thought of as social objects. Social objects are dynamic and may be fleeting, say the exchange of a greeting, or long lasting, such as the monarchy. They are causal, because to a varying degree they change or reinforce our beliefs or behaviours. A particular greeting may have produced only the slightest change in beliefs or actions, but forms of greeting (salutations, handshakes, etc.) can become customs and social objects, in themselves.

But what of mechanisms? Let me be candid: there is no sharp divide between social objects and mechanisms. Both are merely linguistic placeholders, for the "real". But mechanisms certainly imply something bigger and a connectivity, or coalescence, between social objects. Moreover, social objects are often the local or apparent evidence for mechanisms. They are often the "effects" that imply broader and deeper mechanisms. As, I have suggested, social objects can have considerable invariance, but most social objects are less enabling or constraining as mechanisms. We can, for example, think of criminal law as both a social object, but also a mechanism. We can break particular laws, and possibly get away with it, but the mechanism of the corpus of many criminal laws, the judiciary and the police cannot be "broken" or even much subverted, by an individual. Some mechanisms, may not be coercive, in the way criminal law is, but they can be economically or socially constraining, for example my earlier discussion of counter urbanisation as a complex mechanism that can provide economic and social advantage to some, but not to others.

The ontological idea of a mechanism is, perhaps, an ideal type, that we can understand but for all the reasons of the complexity and dynamism of social life, we cannot grasp in actuality. Ray Pawson quite rightly stresses the important of context. Mechanisms, like individuals, are dispositional and similar mechanisms may behave differently in different contexts. Moreover, those contexts may themselves be mechanisms.

The ontology of social complexity can be further distilled into one sentence. Social reality at any given time is the product of the historic realisation of a matrix of contingent outcomes that have the properties of relative invariance, emergence and dynamic change.

Epistemology

Realists emphasise ontology, which is why any complex realist manifesto will have the most to say about ontology. But the test for realists, is to move from metaphysical positions on what the world is like, to how we can know it. Thus, epistemology is the bridge between the ontological position and the means to provide adequate empirical closure, through method.

We can only know the social world under a description

I have mentioned Roy Bhaskar's separation between the intransitive world of nature and the transitive world of science, in Chapter 4. Science (and social science) are human social endeavours that can only partially describe and explain the world. It is an epistemological version of Gödel's paradox. To know the whole of reality, we would need a meta-reality as a standpoint outside of it, Thomas Nagel's "view from nowhere" (Nagel 1986). This leads us, as realists, to have to infer beyond what we can know with our senses or instruments, to what empiricists call "non observables". For the purists amongst them, this is a sin, but as we know they got into epistemological trouble when they tried to separate out an observation language from a theory language. In social science empiricism – or positivism, is less dogmatic and will often make informal inferences about unobservables, even though, as I noted, in Blalock's words this is "pious opinion"!

Realists do not deny the existence of unobservables, and indeed it is an article of faith is that there is more to the world than we can sense or measure. So, it follows from that, that what we measure or understand, is rarely the thing in itself, but a representation of the thing in itself. And representations can be multi-layered, or multi-faceted. Though, as I have said, we have an intuitive grasp of social class, but knowing social class, requires a knowing of relative economic worth, of work practices and work relationships, different kinds of social relations, cultural attributes and varying amounts and types of social capital. These are not manifest and are often hidden in a matrix of antecedent characteristics. A research project that had social class as an independent variable, could if it was explored in depth, be solely concerned with the identification, operationalisation and measurement of these many characteristics, to the exclusion of all else. So, in practice researchers represent social class through a handful of occupational categories. This is not reality we are representing, but it might just (with other things) allow us to infer. And when we infer, often we have things we can choose between to infer too. We do this all the time, in everyday life. A car grinds to a halt and the fuel gauge is on empty. Now, we could reason that the car stopped, because of an electrical fault, but given the other evidence, this seems unlikely and the absence of fuel is deemed to be the culprit. It is an inference to the best explanation.

We may of course be wrong in our inference and I have advocated earlier an informal version of Popper's falsification principle, what I have called reflexive fallibilism. With Popper, I agree we should subject our theories to the most stringent tests we can, rather than seeking evidence to corroborate them. What might be the counterfactual story? Is this more plausible, equally plausible or less so? So, our representations and inferences operate in a context of agnosticism, but this does not mean we cannot provide sufficient knowledge of the social world. That is, our research, should provide descriptions and explanations, that we believe are a better representation of reality, than the one we had prior to our research, but equally maybe not so good as those provided by future research.

Whilst formal logic and statistical inference are indispensable tools in the natural and social sciences, it is because science is a social enterprise, perhaps a competition to seek truth, rarely are there definitive moments where a theory is completely falsified or corroborated. This is "heroic science" and it is the exception, not the rule. In social science, because most of our useful theories are middle range theories, limited by time and place, what we can take from these theories to elsewhere is also limited. So, the social sciences are enterprises of the longue durée, they are Lakatos's positive and negative heuristics, or even Popper's evolutionary epistemology.[2]

There can be objective knowledge

If we agree there are objects and we can have knowledge of those objects, perhaps mediated through representations, then we can have objective knowledge. But what is objective knowledge? Because our knowledge is representational it is not direct. And the representations themselves are derived socially. For example, we have many ways of measuring social class. But it is more than even the social basis of measurement. What and why we choose to measure, or know through ideographic means, is also a social product.

My argument, then, has been that objectivity is "situated": that is the questions we ask and the way we ask them, in the sciences, is the product of social concern or interest. But, it does not follow that once we set out to investigate the problems we have set ourselves, that our prejudices and preferences will infuse our investigations. The reason for this is that precisely because science is a social enterprise, it has social rules that constitute that enterprise, rather like ice hockey or tennis. For example, the values of science, such as parsimony, accuracy, etc. In respect of objectivity I have proposed that there are three values, or to continue my analogy, "rules", that transcend any particular situation, they are rules of the game.

First is that of truth as a correspondence with the facts. Truth, for the scientist, is not a state of grace. It is a state or a destination, at which one rarely arrives. Truths, when captured, are usually in the negative, where we find error. Perhaps by eliminating error we move closer to the truth. This was Popper's concept of verisimilitude and like inference to the best explanation, it is an informal concept (Popper 1979: 134–138). In the social world it is even more slippery, because what is a truth at *t1* and in a particular place, may not be at *t2* and in a different place. Methodologically, that should bother us, but it does not affect the logic of correspondence. At a given time and place truth A and truth B, that make logical claims about the same matter cannot both be right. Moreover, although we are in the business of testing middle range theories to find specific truths and hold at a time and place, these are captured in a meta-truth, which although he never expressed it in such a way, was Merton's ultimate goal for generalising beyond middle range theory.

The second is that there are objects in the world. This sounds trivial, but it is as opposed to an epistemological relativist view that there are just ideas about things in the world, that all have epistemological equivalence. So, objectivity is a search for the truth about those objects.

Finally, there will be purpose. Even the most abstract investigation will have purpose or motivation. This value is important for two reasons. Firstly, because it will drive the investigation and will be its rationale. Secondly because purpose itself can and should be subject to the same investigative scrutiny as the phenomenon itself.[3] Science itself has its historical origins in "purpose" (Williams 2000a), medicines, engineering solutions, weapons and so on. As I have said, science is a social construction and the manifestation of a particular set of historical circumstances. It could have been otherwise. But, nevertheless, it has developed the characteristics to transcend particular purposes in its quest for truth.

However, for there to be objectivity, there must be objects in the world. I have suggested that Popper's "third world" is a grounding for objective knowledge. If I publish a paper that makes certain scientific claims, then these claims stand apart from me. If they are "good science", they are testable claims, which might be falsified, or perhaps corroborated. They are certainly social objects and though they have a physical existence, they are socially constructed. But they can also be the arbiters of truth, in that scientific objects in that third world are testable propositions and the ontological basis of objectivity.

Methodology

There are no realist methods, but there are realist methodologies. In this respect I am guided by Merton's notion of middle range theory that tests a theory in one time and place and then cautiously proposes that it may be generalised to another time and place. Thus, with Maki and Little, I advocate a *local* realism, that may propose features generalisable to other places or times. This is a good principle, but as we saw in Chapter 8, with the example of Zetterberg's axioms of social mobility, such theories may predict, but they do not explain. Pawson described this as a "flat ontology", it does not capture the depth of social reality. For Pawson this is captured through the mechanism. Mechanisms, as I have said, cannot be isolated as a kind of social "naked singularity",[4] they can only be captured as representations, or models, but equally they are not fantasies and such representations and models can provide enough empirical insight to test or modify a theory. So, the realist goal of "empirical closure" must be achieved through methods which can, inference to the best explanation, capture the salient features of ontological depth.

To this end I have advocated a methodological pluralism, which can embrace many methods. In Chapter 9, I used two analogies: the toolkit and the "microscope-macroscope". The first suggesting that different methodological tools are suitable for different jobs, but sometimes we may have to use the tools at hand. The micro/macroscope, though an analogy, was meant to indicate that we can look at – or into, social reality from the micro or macro perspectives and this suggests different tools in the kit. The microscopic approaches can capture single instances, beliefs, actions and even causes at singular instances, but then through testable "*moderatum* generalisations", we can see how these things may create, maintain or destroy social objects, how they may uncover mechanisms, or the contexts in which they operate.

Following Goldthorpe, I agree that sociology is a population science that social objects cohere into identifiable and measurable social aggregates. This is the macroscope, necessarily descriptive at a population level, but permitted interpretations of data that indicate complex mechanisms. In this respect, I have expressed support, indeed with caveats, for the methods based on the general linear model. Though, as I have suggested through examples such as ethnicity, social class or homelessness, the variables as operationalised are not even direct representations of social reality, but "stand in" for complexity.

But although I have expressed support for these "traditional" methods, there are new methods that are truly realist, because they shift the emphasis from representation through variables, to following case trajectories. They are often longitudinal and within them, often use the battery of tried and tested methods, such as regression or cluster analyses. Indeed, they also must use variables, but the emphasis is what happens to the case. These methods are in their infancy and they are limited in scope, because certain data conditions must be met, for example the need for population, rather than sample data.

An afterword

Complex realism is not meant to be a doctrine, but more a way of looking at the social world from a particular philosophical and methodological perspective. This book is simply my attempt to say what I think it might look like. I think it could lead to a different way of doing social science that can transcend the antinomies of interpretivism and positivism. Though it does share some of the characteristics of these. With interpretivism, it is the acceptance that what we know is inevitably interpreted and with positivism, it shares the objective of a scientific study of the social world. But what is different to these is the position that there is a social reality, that may be known by social science, but that reality is indeterminate and probabilistic in character. And this shapes our thinking about investigation.

But do we need a different way of doing social science? Difference does not mean destruction of what is already good, but a questioning of how we think about the social world and consequently, how we investigate it.

In the introduction I briefly reviewed the changes within and the challenges to social science that have developed over the past 20 years. As I write the final words of this book we face two major global challenges. The first of these is the pandemic of Covid-19 and the second is the growth of authoritarianism in many countries. Both are challenges to social science. The first, because pandemics are not respecters of the niceties of the divide between the natural and social worlds and the second, because it challenges the very foundation of science – the search for truth. Is social science up to these challenges?

Because complex realism emphasises the interaction between the natural and social worlds in multiple interlocking mechanisms this, I think, implies a trans-disciplinary approach to investigation, that as Karl Popper once remarked, makes us students of a problem, not a discipline. Secondly, science in very broadest sense, is the great legacy of the Enlightenment and can be a force for good that we should defend.

Notes

1 Though usually attributed to Wheeler, he may have only repeated the phrase. The earliest use of it may have been, in 1919, in a story entitled "The Girl in the Golden Atom" by Ray Cummings in the magazine *All-Story Weekly*.
2 Popper applied this idea equally to scientific theories and social/ moral ideas and practices. Whilst I think the evolution of theories in science is a valuable framework, as I said in Chapter 7, I am much less comfortable in applying evolutionary epistemology to a moral dimension. Though I confess, consistent with my argument for a value continuum, this may be a difficult distinction to make.
3 The Strong Programme, in the sociology of knowledge advocated an exploration of, what might be thought of as, the causes of knowledge. So it was that they believed that the sociology of knowledge itself should be subject to the same investigative standards (Barnes 1977, Bloor 1991 [1976]).
4 A naked singularity is a hypothetical construct in general relativity theory. If it existed it would be a visible gravitational singularity that would indicate the existence of a black hole. Our current understanding of black holes is that gravitational forces are so strong that even light cannot escape them.

REFERENCES

Abdel-Khalek, A. (2006) Measuring happiness with a single item scale, *Social Behavior and Personality: An International Journal*, 34(2), 139–150.

Albrow, M. (1990) *Max Weber's Construction of Social Theory*. London: Macmillan.

Anderson, K. (2017) *Fantasyland: How America Went Haywire*. London: Penguin Random House.

Anderson, S.F. (2019). Misinterpreting p: The discrepancy between p values and the probability the null hypothesis is true, the influence of multiple testing, and implications for the replication crisis, *Psychological Methods*. Advance online publication. https://doi.org/10.1037/met0000248.

Archer, M. (1995) *Realist Social Theory: The Morphogenetic Approach*. Cambridge: Cambridge University Press.

Archer, M. (2007) *Making Our Way Through the World*. Cambridge: Cambridge University Press.

Archer, M. (2012) *The Reflexive Imperative*. Cambridge: Cambridge University Press.

Archer, M., Bhaskar, R., Collier, A., Lawson, T. and Norrie, A. (eds.) (1998) *Critical Realism: Essential Readings*. London: Routledge.

Ardrey, R. (1970) *The Social Contract: A Personal Inquiry Into the Evolutionary Sources of Order and Disorder*. London: Atheneum.

Arendt, H. (1958) *The Human Condition*. Chicago: University of Chicago Press.

Ariel, B., Bland, M. and Sutherland, A. (2021 – in press) *Experimental Design*. London: Sage (*The Sage Quantitative Methods Kit*) Williams, M., Wiggins, D. and McCoach, B. (eds.).

Aull Davies, C (1999) *Reflexive Ethnography* London: Routledge.

Babchuk, N. (1963) The role of the researcher as participant observer and participant-as-observer in the Field Situation, *Human Organization*, 21(3), 225–228.

Balnaves, M. and Caputi, P. (2001) *Introduction to Quantitative Research Methods: Am Investigative Approach*. London: Sage.

Barnes, B. (1977) *Interests and the Growth of Knowledge*. London: Routledge & Kegan Paul.

Barnes, B. and Bloor, D. (2002). Relativism, rationalism and knowledge sociology in: Daniel Rothbart, (ed.) *Science Reason and Reality—Issues in the Philosophy of Science*. Beijing: Peking University Press, p 14, 328.

Barringer, S., Eliason, S. and Leahey, E. (2013) A history of causal analysis in the social Sciences in Morgan, S. (ed.) *Handbook of Causal Analysis for Social Research.* Dordrecht: Springer. pp 9 26.

Bateson, N. (1984) *Data Construction in Social Surveys.* London: Allen and Unwin.

Baudrillard, J. (1983) *Simulations.* New York: Semiotext.

Beebee, H. (2006) *Hume on Causation.* London: Routledge.

Bekoff, M. (2002) Animal Reflections, *Nature,* 419, 255. doi:10.1038/419255a.

Belk, R., Østergaard, P. and Groves, R. (1998) Sexual consumption in the time of AIDS: A study of prostitute patronage in Thailand, *Journal of Public Policy and Marketing,* 17(2), 197–214.

Berg, J. and Barker, J. (1854) *Great Discussion on the Origin, Authority, & Tendency of the Bible, between Rev. J. F. Berg and Joseph Barker.* Boston, MA: J.B. Yerrington & Son.

Berkelcamp, E., Conway, J. and Guy, R. (1982) *Winning Ways for Your Mathematical Play. Volume 2: Games in Particular.* London: Academic Press.

Berry, B.J.L. (1976) The counterurbanisation process: Urban America since 1970, *Urban Affairs Annual Review,* 11, 17.

Bhaskar, R (1989) *Reclaiming reality: a critical introduction to contemporary philosophy.* London: Verso.

Bhaskar, R. (1998) *The Possibility of Naturalism.* 3rd edn. London: Routledge.

Bhaskar, R. (2008) *A Realist Theory of Science.* 3rd edn. London: Routledge.

Bird, A. (1998) *Philosophy of Science.* London: UCL Press.

Blalock, H. (1961) *Causal Inference in Nonexperimental Research.* Chapel Hill, NCA: University of North Carolina Press.

Blastland, M. and Spiegelhalter, D. (2013) *The Norm Chronicles.* London: Profile Books.

Blau, P. and Duncan, O. (1978) *The American Occupational Structure.* New York: Free Press.

Bloor, D. (1991[1976]) *Knowledge and Social Imagery.* 2nd edn. Chicago: University of Chicago Press.

Blumer, H. (1969) *Symbolic Interactionism: Perspective and Method.* Englewood Cliffs, NJ: Prentice-Hall.

Bohm, D. (1984[1957]) *Causality and Chance in Modern Physics.* London: Routledge & Kegan Paul.

Boudon, R. (1974) *The Logic of Sociological Explanation.* Harmondsworth: Penguin.

Boudon, R. (2004) *The Poverty of Relativism.* Oxford: Bardwell Press.

Bourdieu, P. (1977) *Outline of a Theory of Practice.* Cambridge: Cambridge University Press.

Bourdieu, P. and Wacquant, L. (1992) *An Invitation to Reflexive Sociology.* Chicago: University of Chicago Press.

Bradley, W. and Schaefer, K. (1998) *The Uses and Misuses of Data and Models: The Mathematization of the Human Sciences.* Thousand Oaks, CA: Sage.

Bramley, G. (1988) 'The Definition and Measurement of Homelessness' in Bramley, G (ed.) *Homelessness and the London Housing Market.* Bristol: SAUS.

Brewer, J. and Hunter, A. (2006) *Foundations of Multi-Method Research.* Thousand Oaks, CA: Sage.

Bridgeman, P. (1954 [1927]) *The Logic of Modern Physics.* New York: Macmillan.

Bristow, J. (2020) Post-Brexit boomer blaming: The contradictions of generational grievance, *The Sociological Review.* https://doi.org/10.1177/0038026119899882.

Brookfield, C. (2017) *"Quantification is the root of all evil in sociology" What does it add up to? The place of quantitative research methods in British sociology.* Unpublished PhD thesis. Cardiff: Cardiff University.

Brown, R. (1973) *Rules and Laws in Sociology.* London: Routledge.

Bryman, A. (1988) *Quantity and Quality in Social Research.* London: Routledge.

Bryman, A. (1998). Quantitative and qualitative research strategies in May, T. and Williams, M. (eds.) *Knowing the Social World. Buckingham:* Open University Press.

Buck, M., Bryant, L. and Williams, M. (1993) *Housing and Households in Cornwall: A Pilot Study of Cornish Families*. Plymouth: University of Plymouth.

Bunge, M. (1961) Causality, chance and law, *American Scientist*, 49, 432.

Bunge, M. (1996) *Finding Philosophy in Social Science*. New Have: Yale University Press.

Bunge, M. (1997) Mechanism and Explanation, *Philosophy of the Social Sciences*, 27(4), 410–465.

Bunge, M. (2004) Clarifying some misunderstandings about social systems and their Mechanisms, *Philosophy of the Social Sciences*, 34(3), 371–381.

Burley, S. (2007) *Migration and Economy in Cornwall*. PhD thesis. Plymouth: University of Plymouth. https://pearl.plymouth.ac.uk/handle/10026.1/2160. Accessed 22/06/20.

Byrne, D. (1998) *Complexity Theory and the Social Sciences:* An Introduction. London: Routledge.

Byrne, D. (2002) *Interpreting Quantitative* Data. London: Sage.

Byrne, D. (2004) Complex and contingent causation – The implications of complex realism for quantitative modelling: The case of housing and health in Carter, B. and New, C. (eds.) *Making Realism Work*. London: Routledge. pp 50–66.

Byrne, D. (2020) Understanding class in the Post-industrial era – thoughts on modes of Investigation, *Frontiers in Sociology*. May. | https://doi.org/10.3389/fsoc.2020.00039.

Byrne, D. and Callaghan, G. (2013) *Complexity Theory and the Social Sciences: the State of the Art*. London: Routledge.

Calhoun, C. (2017) Populism, nationalism and Brexit in Outhwaite, W. (ed.) *Brexit Sociological Responses*. London: Anthem. pp 57–76.

Callon, M. (1999) Some elements of a sociology of Translation: Domestication of the scallops and fishermen of St. Brieuc Bay in Biagioli, M. (ed.) *The Science Studies Reader*. New York: Routledge. pp 67–83.

Campbell, D. (1973) The social scientist as methodological servant of the experimenting society, *Policy Studies Journal*, 1, 72–75.

Campbell, D. (1984) Can we be scientific in applied science in Connor, R., Altman, D. and Jackson, C. (eds.) *Evaluation Studies Review Annual*. Newbury Park Cal.: Sage.

Campbell, D. (1991) Methods for the experimenting Society, *Evaluation Practice*, 12, 223–260.

Carnap, R. (2000 [1966]) 'theoretical laws and theoretical concepts' in McErlean, J. (ed.) *Philosophies of Science: from Foundations to Contemporary Issues*. Belmont CA: Wadsworth. 35–46.

Cartwright, N. (1983) *How the Laws of Physics Lie*. Oxford: Clarendon Press.

Cartwright, N. (1989) *Nature's Capacities and Their Measurement*. Oxford: Oxford University Press.

Cartwright, N. (1999) *The Dappled World – Studies at the Boundaries of Science*. Cambridge: Cambridge University Press.

Cartwright, N. (2004) Causation: One word, many things, *Proceedings of the Biennial Meeting of the Philosophy of Science Association*, 71, 805–819.

Cartwright, N. (2007) What makes a capacity a disposition? in Kistler, M. and Gnassounou, B. (eds.) *Dispositions and Causal Powers*. Aldershot: Ashgate. pp 195–205.

Carver, R. (1978) The case against statistical significance Testing, *Harvard Educational Review*, 48(3), 378–399.

Castellani, B (2014). 'FOCUS: Complexity and the failure of quantitative social science'. *Discover Society* 12: 12. https://discoversociety.org/2014/11/04/focus-complexity-and-the-failure-of-quantitative-social-science/

Castellani, B. and Hafferty, F. (2009) *Sociology and Complexity Science: A New Field of Inquiry*. New York: Springer.

Castellani, B. and Rajaram, R. (2012) Case-based modeling and the SACS toolkit: A mathematical outline, *Computational and Mathematical Organization Theory*, 18(2), 153–174.

Castellani, B., Griffiths, F., Rajaram, R. and Gunn, J. (2018) Exploring comorbid depression and physical health trajectories: A case-based computational modelling approach, *Journal of Evaluation in Clinical Practice*. https://doi.org/10.1111/jep.13042.

Casti, J. (1991) *Searching for Certainty: What Scientists Can Know About the Future.* London: Abacus.

Champion, T. (2001) Urbanisation, suburbanisation, counterurbanisation and reurbanisation in Paddison, R. and Lever, W. (eds.) *Handbook of Urban Studies.* London: Sage Publications Ltd. pp 143–161.

Charmaz, K. (2006) *Constructing Grounded Theory.* London: SAGE Publications.

Cicourel, A. (1964) *Method and Measurement in Sociology.* New York: Free Press.

Cicourel, A. (1982) Interviews, surveys and the problem of ecological validity, *American Sociologist*, 17(1), 11–20.

Cilliers, P. (1998) *Complexity and Postmodernism: Understanding Complex Systems.* London: Routledge.

Clifford, J. and Marcus, G.E. (1986) *Writing Culture: The Poetics and Politics of Ethnography.* Berkeley: University of California Press.

Cohen, J. and Stewart, I. (1994) *The Collapse of Chaos: Discovering Simplicity in a Complex World.* Harmondsworth: Penguin.

Cohen, M. (1918) Mechanism and causality in physics, *The Journal of Philosophy, Psychology and Scientific Methods*, 15(14), 365–386.

Cole, S. (1992) *Making Science: Between Nature and Society.* Cambridge, MA: Harvard University Press.

Collett, T., Williams, M., Maconachie, M., Chandler, J. and Dodgeon, B. (2006) Long-termness with regards to sickness and disability: An example of the value of longitudinal data for testing reliability and validity, *International Journal of Social Research Methodology, Theory and Practice*, 9(3), 224–243.

Collier, A. (1998) Explanation and Emancipation in Archer, M., Bhaskar, R., Collier, A., Lawson, T. and Norrie, A. (eds.) *Critical Realism: Essential Readings.* London: Routledge. pp 444–471.

Collins, H. (2010) *Tacit and Explicit Knowledge.* London: University of Chicago Press.

Consoli, M. and Pluchino, A. (2018) *Michelson–Morley Experiments an Enigma for Physics and the History of Science.* Singapore: World Scientific.

Cook, T. (2002) Randomized experiments in educational policy research: A critical examination of the reasons the educational evaluation community has offered for not doing them, *Educational Evaluation and Policy Analysis*, 24(3), 175–199.

Cook, T. and Campbell, D. (1979) *Quasi-Experimentation: Design and Analysis Issues for Field Settings.* Chicago: Rand McNally.

Coombes, M, Dalla Longga and Raybould, S (1989) 'Counterurbanisation in Britain and Italy: A comparative critique of the concept, causation and evidence' *Progress in Planning* 32 Part 1 1–70.

Couvalis, G. (1997) *The Philosophy of Science: Science and Objectivity.* London: Sage.

Cox, D. (1992) Causality: Some statistical aspects, *Journal of the Royal Statistical Society Series A*, 155, 291–301.

d'Onise, K., Wang, Y. and McDermott, R. (2007) The importance of numbers: Using capture-recapture to make the homeless count in Adelaide, *Australian Journal of Primary Health*, 13(1), 89–96.

de Vaus, D. (1996) *Surveys in Social Research.* 2nd edn. London: UCL Press.

Deacon, B. (1997) The hollow jarring of the distant steam engine: Images of Cornwall between West barbary and delectable duchy in Westland, E. (ed.) *Cornwall the Cultural Construction of Place.* Penzance: Patten Press. pp 7–24.

Deacon, B., Perry, R. and George, A. (1988) *Cornwall at the Crossroads?* Redruth: The Cornish Social and Economic Research Group.

Derrida, J. (1978) *Writing and Difference.* London: Routledge.

Dodd, S. (1942) *Dimensions of Society*. New York: Macmillan.

Dodd, S. (1963[1947]) Developing demoscopes for social Research, *American Sociological Review*, 13, 310–319.

Doppelt, G. (1978) Kuhn's epistemological relativism: An interpretation and Defense, *Inquiry: An Interdisciplinary Journal of Philosophy*, 21(1–4), 33–86.

Durkheim, E. (1970[1952]) *Suicide*. London: Routledge and Kegan Paul.

Durkheim, E. (1972) *Selected Writings* (Giddens, A. (ed.)). Cambridge: Cambridge University Press.

Dyer, W. and Williams, M. (2020-in press) Toward a complex realist approach in social research, *International Journal of Social Research Methodology*.

Edwards, A., Housley, W., Williams, M., Sloan, L. and Williams, M. (2013) Digital social research, social media and the sociological imagination: Surrogacy, augmentation and re-orientation, *International Journal of Social Research Methodology*, 16(3), 245–260.

Elliot, J (1999) 'Modela Are Stories Are Not Real Life' in Dorling, D and Simpson, S (eds), *Statistics in Society*. London: Arnold 95–102.

Elliot, J. (2005) *Using Narrative in Social Research: Qualitative and Quantitative Approaches*. London: Sage.

Elster, J. (1998) A plea for Mechanisms in Hedström, P. and Swedberg, R. (eds.) *Social Mechanisms: An Analytical Approach to Social Theory*. pp 45–73.

Elster, J. (2007) *Explaining Social Behavior*. Cambridge: Cambridge University Press.

Elzey, R. (1998) In-migration to Newquay: Migrants' lifestyles and perspectives on Environments, *Cornish Studies*, 6(1), 127–42.

Feyerabend, P. (1975) *Against Method*. London: New Left Books.

Feynman, R., Leighton, R. and Sands, M. (1963). The Brownian movement in Feynman, R, Leighton, R and Sands, M (eds) *The Feynman Lectures of Physics*, Vol I. Reading, MA: Addison-Wesley Pub. Co. pp. 41–45.

Fielding, A (1992) 'Migration and Social Mobility: South East England as an Escalator Region' *Regional Studies* Vol 26, No 1, pp 1–15.

Fielding, A. (1982) *Counterurbanisation in Western Europe*. Progress in Planning Vol 17. London: Pergamon.

Fisher, S. (1993) The pull of the fruit machine: A sociological typology of young players, *Sociological Review*, 3, 41.

Francot, L.M.A. (2014) Dealing with complexity, facing uncertainty: Morality and ethics in a complex society, *Archiv für Rechts- und Sozialphilosophie*, 2014(2), 201–218..

Freedman, D. (2011) Statistical models and shoe leather in Vayda, A. and Walters, B. (eds.) *Causal Explanation for Social Scientists*. Lanham ML: Rowan and Littlefield. pp 151–167.

Freese, J. and Peterson, D. (2017) Replication in social science, *Annual Review of Sociology*, 43, 147–165.

Fricker, R. (2016) Sampling methods for online surveys in Fielding, N., Lee, R. and Blank, G. (eds.) *The SAGE Handbook of Online Research Methods*. London: Sage pp 162–183.

Frigg, R. and Reiss, J. (2009) The philosophy of simulation: Hot new issues or same old stew, *Synthese*, 169, 593–613.

Fuller, S. (1997) *Science*. Buckingham: Open University Press.

Geertz, C. (1973) *The Interpretation of Cultures*. New York: Basic Books.

Geertz, C. (1994) Thick description: Toward an interpretive theory of culture in Martin, M. and McIntrye, C. (eds.) *Readings in the Philosophy of Social Science*. Cambridge MA: MIT Press. pp 213–232.

Gergen, K. (2001) *Social Construction in Context*. London: Sage.

Gerrits, L. and Verweij, S. (2015) Critical realism as a meta-framework for understanding the relationships between complexity and qualitative comparative Analysis, *Journal of Critical Realism*, Vol 12 166–182.

Gigerenzer, G. (2008) Why heuristics work, *Perspectives on Psychological Science*. January. https://doi.org/10.1111/j.1745-6916.2008.00058.x.

Gigerenzer, G., Krauss, S. and Vitouch, O. (2004) The null ritual what you always wanted to know about significance testing but were afraid to ask in D. Kaplan (ed.) *The Sage Handbook of Quantitative Methodology for the Social Sciences*. Thousand Oaks, CA: Sage.

Gillies, D. (2000) *Philosophical Theories of Probability*. London: Routledge.

Glaesser, J. and Cooper, B. (2014) Exploring the consequences of a recalibration of causal conditions when assessing sufficiency with fuzzy set QCA, *International Journal of Social Research Methodology*, 17(4), 387–401.

Gleick, J. (1987) *Chaos: Making a New Science*. Harmondsworth: Viking Penguin.

Godfrey, B., Williams, C. and Lawrence, P. (2008) *History and Crime*. London: Sage.

Goldthorpe, J. (2016) *Sociology as a Population Science*. Cambridge: Cambridge University Press.

Goodman, N. (1973[1955]) *Fact, Fiction and Forecast*. Indianapolis: Bobbs Merrill.

Gorard, S. (2012) Who is eligible for free school meals? Characterising free school meals as a measure of disadvantage in England, *British Educational Research Journal*, 38(6), 1003–1017.

Gouldner, A. (1973) *For Sociology: Renewal and Critique in Sociology Today*. Harmondsworth: Penguin.

Grüne-Yanoff, T. (2011) Artificial worlds and agent based simulation in Jarvie, I. and Zamora-Bonilla, J. (eds.) *The Sage Handbook of the Philosophy of the Social Sciences*. Los Angeles: Sage. pp 613–631.

Guba, E. and Lincoln, Y. (1994) Competing paradigms in qualitative research in Guba, E. and Lincoln, Y. (eds.) *Handbook of Qualitative Research*. Thousand Oaks, CA: Sage. pp 105–117.

Hacking, I. (1983) *Representing and Intervening: Introductory Topics in the Philosophy of Natural Science*. Cambridge: Cambridge University Press.

Hacking, I. (1990) *The Taming of Chance*. Cambridge: Cambridge University Press.

Hacking, I. (2002 [1983]) Making up people in I Hacking, *Historical Ontology*. Cambridge MA: Harvard University Press. pp 99–114.

Hage, J. and Foley-Meeker, B. (1988) *Social Causality*. London: Unwin Hyman.

Haig, B. (2016) *Realist Inquiry in Social Science*. London: Sage.

Hall, N. and Paul, L. (2008) Causation and pre-emption in Clark, P. and Hawley, K. (eds.) *Philosophy of Science Today*. Oxford: Clarendon.

Hammersley, M. (2002) Research as emancipatory: The case of Bhaskar's realism, *Journal of Critical Realism*, 1(1), 33–48.

Hammersley, M. (2008) *Questioning Qualitative Research: Critical Essays*. London, UK: Sage.

Hampshire, S. (1972) Dispositions in Hampshire, S. (ed.) *Freedom of Mind and Other Essays*. Oxford: Clarendon Press. pp 37–38.

Hanan, C. and Stuart, A. (1966) Data-dredging procedures in survey analysis, The *American Statistician*, 20(3), 20–23.

Hanson, N.-R. (1981[1958]) *Patterns of Discovery*. Cambridge: Cambridge University Press.

Harding, S. (1996) Rethinking standpoint epistemology: What is "Strong objectivity"? in Keller, E.F. and Longino, H. (eds.) *Feminism and Science*. Oxford: Oxford University Press. pp 235–248.

Harré, R. (1986) *Varieties of Realism: a Rationale for the Natural Sciences*. Oxford: Blackwell.

Harré, R. (2002) social reality and the myth of social structure, *European Journal of Social Theory*, 5(1), 111–123.

Harré, R. and Madden, E. (1975) *Causal Powers*. Oxford: Blackwell.

Hartsock, N. (1998) *The Feminist Standpoint Revisited and Other Essays*. Boulder CO: Westview.

Hartwig, M. (ed.) (2007) *Dictionary of Critical Realism*. London: Routledge.

Hatton, Z. and Williams, M. (2002) *Sure Start Lescudjack Interim Evaluation Report The Process and the Outcomes So Far*. Plymouth. University of Plymouth, Department of Sociology.

Hayek, F. (1944) *The Road to Serfdom*. Chicago: University of Chicago Press.

Healey, R. (1993) Measurement and quantum indeterminateness, *Foundations of Physics Letters*, 6, 307–316.

Healy, M. (1988) *GLIM: an Introduction*. Oxford: Clarendon Press.

Heckathorn, D. (1997) Respondent-driven sampling: A new approach to the study of hidden populations, *Social Problems*, 44(2), 174–199.

Hedström, P. and Swedberg, R. (1998b) Social mechanisms: An introductory essay in Hedström, and Swedberg, P. (eds.) *Social Mechanisms: An Analytical Approach to Social Theory*. pp 1–32.

Hedström, P. and Swedberg, R. (eds.) (1998a) *Social Mechanisms: An Analytical Approach to Social Theory*. Cambridge: Cambridge University Press.

Hempel, C. (1965) *Aspects of Scientific Explanation*. New York: Free Press.

Herrnstein, R. and Murray, C. (1994) *The Bell Curve: Intelligence and Class Structure in American Life*. New York: The Free Press.

Hoefer, C. (2008) Introducing Nancy Cartwright's philosophy of science, in Hartman, S; Hoefer, C. and Bovens, L. (eds.) *Nancy Cartwright's Philosophy of Science*. London: Routledge.

Holland, J. (2014) *Complexity – A Very Short Introduction*. Oxford: Oxford University Press.

Hollis, M. (1977) *Models of Man: Philosophical Thoughts on Social Action*. Cambridge: Cambridge University Press.

Hollis, M. and Lukes, S. (1982) *Rationality and Relativism*. Oxford: Oxford University Press.

Holton, G. (1993) *Science and Anti-Science*. Cambridge, MA: Harvard University Press.

Hooper, D., Coughlan, J. and Mullen, M. (2008) Structural equation modelling: Guidelines for determining model fit, *Electronic Journal of Business Research Methods*, 6(1), 53–60.

Hubble, E. (1929) A relation between distance and radial velocity among extra-galactic nebulae, *Proceedings of the National Academy of Sciences*, 15(3), 168–173.

Hurrell, S. (2014) Critical realism and mixed methods research: Combining the intensive and extensive at multiple levels in Edwards, P., O'Mahoney, J. and Vincent, S. (eds.) *Studying Organisations Using Critical Realism*. Oxford: Oxford University Press. pp 241–263.

International Committee for Weights and Measures [ICWM] (2011) *Mise en pratique for the definition of the kelvin*. Consultative Committee for Thermometry. Sevres (France). https://www.bipm.org/utils/en/pdf/MeP_K.pdf.

Isaacs, J. and Downing, T. (2008) *Cold War*. London: Abacus- Little Brown.

Janack, M. (2002) Dilemmas of Objectivity, *Social Epistemology*, 16(3), 267–281.

Jones, T. (1998) Interpretive social science and the "Native's" point of view, *Philosophy of the Social Sciences*, 28(1), 32–68.

Jose, P.E. (2013) *Doing Statistical Mediation and Moderation*. New York: Guilford Press.

Jung, M., Sprott, J. and Greene, C. (2019) Immigrant perceptions of the police: The role of country of origin and length of settlement, *The British Journal of Criminology*, 59(6), 1370–1389.

Kahneman, D. and Tversky, A. (1972) Subjective probability: A judgement of Representativeness, *Cognitive Psychology*, 3, 430–454.

Keat, R. and Urry, J. (1982[1975]) *Social Theory as Science*. 2nd edn. London: Routledge & Kegan Paul.

Kempster, S. and Parry, K. (2014) Critical realism and grounded theory in Edwards, P., O'Mahoney, J. and Vincent, S. (eds.) *Studying Organisations Using Critical Realism*. Oxford: Oxford University. pp 86–108.

Kennedy, N. and Kingcome, N. (2007) Disneyfication of Cornwall — Developing a poldark heritage complex, *International Journal of Heritage Studies*, 4(1), 45–59.

Kincaid, H. (1996) *Philosophical Foundations of the Social Sciences: Analyzing Controversies in Social Research*. Cambridge: Cambridge University Press.

King, A. (2011) Functionalism and structuralism in Jarvie, I. and Zamora-Bonilla, J. (eds.) *The Sage Handbook of the Philosophy of the Social Sciences*. Los Angeles: Sage. pp 429–446.

King, A. and Smith, D. (2017) The Jack Wills crowd: Towards a sociology of an elite subculture, *British Journal of Sociology*, 69(1), 44–66.

King, G., Keohane, R.O. and Verba, S. (1994) *Designing Social Inquiry: Scientific Inference in Qualitative Research*. Princeton: Princeton University Press.

Kitcher, P. (2001) *Science, Truth and Democracy*. Oxford: Oxford University Press.

Knafo, S. (2015) Bourdieu and the dead end of reflexivity: On the impossible task of locating the subject, *Review of International Studies*, 42, 25–47.

Körner, S. (1955) *Kant*. Harmondsworth: Penguin.

Kowalczuk, K. (2011) *Population Growth in a High Amenity Area: Migration and Socio-Economic Change in Cornwall*. PhD Thesis Plymouth: University of Plymouth. https://pearl.plymouth.ac.uk/handle/10026.1/323 Accessed 20/06/20.

Kreft, I., de Leeuw, J. and Aiken, L. (1995) The effect of different forms of centering in hierarchical linear models, *Multivariate Behavioral Research*, 30(1), 1–21.

Kuhn, T.S. (1970[1962]) *The Structure of Scientific Revolutions*. 2nd edn. Chicago: Chicago University Press.

Lacey, L. (1999) *Is Science Value Free? Values and Scientific Understanding*. London: Routledge.

Lakatos, I. (1978) *The Methodology of Scientific Research Programmes. Philosophical Papers*, J. Worrall and G. Curry (eds.).Vol 1. Cambridge: Cambridge University Press.

Lather, P. and St. Pierre, E. (2013) Introduction to Special issue-post qualitative research, *International Journal of Qualitative Studies in Education*, 26(6), 629–633.

Latour, B. (1986) *Laboratory Life: The Construction of Scientific Facts*. Princeton, N.J.: Princeton University Press.

Latour, B. (2005) *Reassembling the Social: An Introduction to Actor-Network-Theory*. Oxford: Oxford University Press.

Lauder, H., Brown, P. and Cheung, S.-Y. (2018) Fractures in The education-economy relationship: The end of the skill bias technological change research programme? *Oxford Review of Economic Policy*, 34(3), 495–515.

Lawson, T. (1997) *Economics and Reality*. London: Routledge.

Lawson, T. (2019) *The Nature of Social Reality*. London: Routledge.

Lazarsfeld, P. (1993) *On Social Research and It's Language*. London: University of Chicago Press.

Le Boutillier, S. (2001) Theorising social constraint: The concept of supervenience, *Sociology*, 35(1), 155–179.

Le Boutillier, S. (2003) Emergence and analytic dualism, *Philosophica*, 71, 59–80.

Lederman, L. and Hill, C. (2013) *Beyond the God Particle*. Buffalo, NY: Prometheus Books.

Letherby, G., Scott, J. and Williams, M. (2013) *Objectivity and Subjectivity in Social Research*. London: Sage. (Chapters 4 and 6.)

Lewis, D. (1973) *Counterfactuals*. Oxford: Blackwell.

Lewis, D. (1986) *Philosophical Papers II*. Oxford: Oxford University Press.

Little, D. (1991) *Varieties of Social Explanation*. Boulder, CO: Westview.

Little, D. (2009) The heterogeneous social: New thinking about the foundations of the social sciences in Mantzavinos, C. (ed.) *Philosophy of the Social Sciences, Philosophical Theory and Scientific Practice*. Cambridge: Cambridge University Press. pp 154–178.

Longino, H. (1990) *Science as Social Knowledge: Values and Objectivity in Scientific Enquiry*. Princeton NJ: Princeton University Press.

Lukes, S. (1994) Some problems about rationality in Martin, M. and McIntyre, L. (eds.) *Readings in the Philosophy of Social Science*. Cambridge, MA: MIT Press. pp 285–298.

Lundberg, G. (1963[1947]) *Can Science Save Us?* New York: Longmans Green.

Lynch, M. (2000) Against reflexivity as an academic virtue and source of privileged Knowledge, *Theory, Culture and Society*, 17(3), 26–54.

Lyotard, J.-F. (1984) *The Postmodern Condition: A Report on Knowledge*, translated byGeoff Bennington and Brian Massumi. Minneapolis, MN: Minnesota University Press.

MacInnes, J. (2009) *ESRC Initiative on Undergraduate Teaching of Quantitative Methods. Interim Report of the Strategic Advisor.* Available from: http://www.esrc.ac.uk/_images/Undergraduate_quantitative_research_ methods_tcm8-2722.pdf.

Mackie, J. (1965) Causes and conditions, *American Philosophical Quarterly*, 2(4), 245–264.

Madge, J. (1963) *The Origins of Scientific Sociology*. London: Tavistock.

Mahoney, J (2000) 'Path Dependence in Historical Sociology' *Theory and Society* 29 4 507–548.

Maki, U. (2005) Reglobalizing realism by going local, or (how) should our formulations of scientific realism be informed about the sciences? *Erkenntnis*, 63, 231–251.

Mandelbrot, B. (1982) *The Fractal Geometry of Nature*. London: Times Books Collins.

Manicas, P. (1987) *A History and Philosophy of the Social Sciences*. Oxford: Blackwell.

Marcuse, H. (1964) *One-Dimensional Man: Studies in the Ideology of Advanced Industrial Society*. Boston: Beacon Press.

Margolis, J. (2005) *Introduction to Philosophical Problems*. London: Bloomsbury.

Marsh, C. (1982) *The Survey Method: The Contribution of Surveys to Sociological Explanation*. London: George Allen and Unwin.

Maxwell, J. (2012) *A Realist Approach to Qualitative Research*. Thousand Oaks, CA: Sage.

May, T. (1999) Reflexivity and sociological practice, *Sociological Research Online*, 4(3). http://www.socresonline.org.uk/4/3/may.htlm.

May, T. and Williams, M. (1998) *Knowing the Social World*. Buckingham: Open University Press.

McCarthy, L. (2013) Homelessness and identity: A critical review of the literature and theory, *People, Place and Policy Online*, 7(1), 46–58.

Mead, G.H. (1910) What social objects must psychology presuppose? *The Journal of Philosophy, Psychology and Scientific Methods*, 7(7), 174–180.

Medvedev, Z. (1969) *The Rise and Fall of T.D. Lysenko*. New York: Columbia University Press.

Mellor, D. (1971) *The Matter of Chance*. Cambridge: Cambridge University Press.

Mellor, D. (1995) *The Facts of Causation*. London: Routledge.

Mennell, S. (1974) *Sociological Theory: Uses and Utilities*. New York: Praeger.

Merton, R. (1967) *On Theoretical Sociology*. New York: Free Press.

Merton, R. (1968) *Social Theory and Social Structure*. New York: Free Press.

Merton, R.K. (1973) *The Sociology of Science: Theoretical and Empirical Investigations*. Chicago: University of Chicago Press.

Mill, J.S. (1987[1872]) *On the Logic of the Moral Sciences*. London: Duckworth.

Miller, G. (1921) The history of science as an error Breeder, *The Scientific Monthly*, 12(5), (May, 1921), pp. 439–443.

Mills, C.W. (1959) *The Sociological Imagination*. Oxford: Oxford University Press.

Mills, K. (2017) What are the threats and potentials of big data for qualitative research? *Qualitative Research*, 18(6), 591–603.

Mitchell, P. (1993) The demographic revolution in Payton, P. (ed.) *Cornwall Since the War*. Redruth: Institute of Cornish Studies/Dyllansow Truran. pp 135–156.

Monroe, B., Pan, J., Roberts, M. and Sen, M. (2015) No! Formal theory, causal inference, and big data are not contradictory trends in political science, *Political Science and Politics*, 48(1), 71–74.

Morning, A. (2008) Reconstructing race in science and society: Biology textbooks, 1952–2002, *American Journal of Sociology*, 114(Suppl), S106–137.

Mulkay, M. (1991) *Sociology of Science: A Sociological Pilgrimage*. Buckingham: Open University Press.

Mumford, S. (2007) Filled in space in Kistler, M. and Gnassounou, B. (eds.) *Dispositions and Causal Powers*. Aldershot: Ashgate. pp 67–80.

Musgrove, F (1963) *The Migratory Elite:* London: Heinemann.

Nagel, T. (1986) *The View from Nowhere*. Oxford: Oxford University Press.

Needham, J. (1976) *Science and Civilisation in China*. Cambridge: Cambridge University Press.

NESS (2008) *The Impact of Sure Start Local Programmes on Three Year Olds and Their Families*. London: National Evaluation of Sure Start.

NESS (2010) *The Impact of Sure Start Local Programmes on Five-Year-Olds and Their Families*. London: National Evaluation of Sure Start.

Neugebauer, R. and Wittes, J. (1994) Voluntary and involuntary capture-recapture, *American Journal of Public Health*, 84(7), 1068–1069.

Nguendo Yongsi, H.-B. (2010) Suffering for water, suffering from water: Access to drinking-water and associated health risks in Cameroon, *Journal of Health Population and Nutrition*, (5), 424–435.

Ninness, C., Rumph, M., Clary, L., Lawson, D., Lacy, J.-T., Halle, S., McAdams, R., Parker, S. and Forney, D. (2013) Neural network and multivariate analyses: Pattern recognition in academic and social research, *Behavior and Social Issues*, 22, 49–63.

Norrie, S. (2011) Reality and probability: Contra Williams, *Social Epistemology*, 25(1), 57–66.

Nozick, R. (2001) *Invariances: The Structure of the Objective World*. Cambridge, MA: Harvard University Press.

Nuffield Foundation. (2014) *Aims and Activities of the Q-Step Centres*. London: Nuffield Foundation.

Nye, D. and Ashworth, C. (1971) Emile Durkheim: Was he a nominalist or a realist?, *The British Journal of Sociology*, 22(2), 133–148.

O'Mahoney, J. and Vincent, S. (2014) Critical realism as an empirical project: A beginner's guide in Edwards, P., O'Mahoney, J. and Vincent, S. (eds.) *Studying Organisations Using Critical Realism*. Oxford: Oxford University Press. pp 1–20.

Office For National Statistics (ONS). (2014) *2011 Census: Methods and Quality Report*. London: ONS. https://www.ons.gov.uk/census/2011censusqualitysurveyreport25feb_tcm77-352932.pdf Accessed 16/06/20.

Outhwaite, W. (1987) *New Philosophies of Social Science* London: Macmillan.

Papineau, D. (1978) *For Science in the Social Sciences*. London: Macmillan.

Papineau, D. (2001) Metaphysics over methodology – or, why infidelity provides no grounds to divorce causes from probabilities in Galavotti, M., Suppes, P. and Costantini, D. (eds.) *Stochastic Causality*. Stanford, CA: CSLI Publications. pp 15–38.

Parker, T.S. and Chua, L.O. (1989) Poincaré maps in Parker, T.S. and Chua, L.O. *Practical Numerical Algorithms for Chaotic Systems*. New York: Springer. 31–56.

Parsons, T. (1954) The incest taboo in relation to social structure and the socialization of the child, *The British Journal of Sociology*, 5(2), 101–117.

Parsons, T. (1968) *The Structure of Social Action*. 3rd edn. New York: Free Press.

Parsons, T. and Shils, E.A. (1951) *Toward a General Theory of Action*. New York: Harper & Row.

Pawson, R (2000) 'Middle-Range Realism' *Archive Européenes de Sociologie*, Vol. XLI pp 283–325.

Pawson, R. (2006) *Evidence Based Policy*. London: Sage.

Pawson, R. (2013) *The Science of Evaluation: a Realist Manifesto*. London: Sage.

Pawson, R. and Tilley, N. (1997) *Realistic Evaluation*. London: Sage.

Payne, G. (2014) Survey, statisticians and sociology: A history of (a lack of) quantitative methods, *Enhancing Learning in the Social Sciences*, 6(2), 74–89.

Payne, G. and Williams, M. (2005) Generalisation in qualitative research, *Sociology*, 39(2), 295–314.

Payne, G., Williams, M. and Chamberlain, S. (2004) Methodological pluralism in British sociology, *Sociology*, 38(1), 153–164.

Pearl, J. (2000) *Causality*. Cambridge: Cambridge University Press.

Peirce, C. (1931) *Collected Papers*. Hartshorne, C. and Weiss, P. (eds.). Vol 2. Cambridge MA: Harvard University Press.

Perry, R., Dean, K. and Brown, B. (1986) *Counterurbanisation: Case Studies in Urban to Rural Movement*. Norwich, England: Geo Books.

Phillips, D. (1987) *Philosophy, Science and Social Inquiry: Contemporary Methodological Controversies in Social Science and Related Applied Fields of Research*. Oxford: Pergamon.

Platt, J. (1996) *A History of Sociological Research Methods in America 1920–1960*. Cambridge: Cambridge University Press.

Platt, J. (2004) Women's and men's careers in British sociology. *British Journal of Sociology*, 55(2), 187–210.

Platt, J. (2012) Making them count: How effective has official encouragement of quantitative methods been in British sociology?, *Current Sociology*, 60(5), 690–704.

Platt, L., Simpson, L. and Akinwale, B. (2005) Stability and change in ethnic groups in England and Wales, *Population Trends*, 125, 31–46.

Polanyi, M. (1973) *Personal Knowledge*. London: Routledge and Kegan Paul.

Ponchaud, F. (1978) *Cambodia Year Zero*. Harmondsworth: Penguin.

Popper, K. (1959a) *The Logic of Scientific Discovery*. London: Routledge.

Popper, K. (1966) *The Open Society and Its Enemies, Volume II, The High Tide of Prophecy: Hegel, Marx and the Aftermath*. London: Routledge and Kegan Paul.

Popper, K. (1976) *Unended Quest: An Intellectual Autobiography*. Glasgow: Fontana.

Popper, K. (1979) *Objective Knowledge: An Evolutionary Approach*. Oxford: Oxford University Press.

Popper, K. (1989 [1963]) *Conjectures and Refutations – The Growth of Scientific Knowledge*. 5th edn. London: Routledge.

Popper, K. (1994) *Knowledge and the Body Mind Problem: In Defence on Interaction*. London: Routledge.

Popper, K. (1995) *A World of Propensities*. Bristol: Thoemmes.

Popper, K. (1999) *All Life Is Problem Solving*. London: Routledge.

Popper, K.R. (1957) The propensity interpretation of the calculus of probability, and the quantum theory, in S. Körner (ed.) *Observation and Interpretation*. London: Butterworth Scientific.

Popper, K.R. (1959b) The propensity interpretation of probability, *British Journal for the Philosophy of Science*, 10, 25–42.

Popper, K.R. (1982) *Quantum Theory and the Schism in Physics*. London: Routledge.

Popper, K.R. (1983) *Realism and the Aim of Science* (from the Postscript to the Logic of Scientific Discovery). London: Routledge.

Porpora, D. (2008) Sociology's causal confusion in Groff, R. (ed.) *Revitalizing Causality: Realism about Causality in Philosophy and the Social Sciences*. London: Routledge. pp 195–204.

Portes, A. (1998) Social capital: Its origins and applications in modern sociology, *Annual Review of Sociology*, 24, 1–24.

Psillos, S. (1999) Abduction: Between conceptual richness and computational complexity in Kakas, A.K. and Flach, P. (eds.) *Abduction and Induction: Essays on Their Relation and Integration*. Dordrecht: Kluwer. pp 59–74.

Puri, R. (2001) Quantum theory of damping *Mathematical Methods of Quantum Optics*. Berlin: Springer Verlag.

Ragin, C. (1987) *The Comparative Method: Moving Beyond Qualitative and Quantitative Strategies*. Berkeley: University of California Press.

Ragin, C. and Byrne, D. (eds.) (2009) *Case Based Methods*. London: Sage.

Reed, M. and Harvey, D. (1992) The new science and the old: Complexity and realism in the social sciences, *Journal for the Theory of Social Behavior*, 22, 353–380.

Reed, M., Courtney, P., Urquhart, J. and Ross, N. (2013) Beyond fish as commodities: Understanding the socio-cultural role of inshore fisheries in England, *Marine Policy*, 37, 62–68.

Reskin, B. (1988) Bringing the men back in: Sex differentiation and the devaluation of women's work, *Gender and Society*, 2, 58–81.

Rihoux, B. and Ragin, C. (2009) *Configurational Comparative Methods: Qualitative Comparative Analysis (QCA)*. Thousand Oaks, CA: Sage.

Riker, W. (1982) The two-party system and Duverger's law: An essay on the history of political science, *American Political Science Review*, 76, 753–766.

Robert, S and Randolph, W (1983) 'Beyond decentralization: the evolution of population distribution in England and Wales, 1961–1981' *Geoforum* 14 1 75–102.

Robson, C (2002) *Real World Research* 2nd Edition. Oxford: Blackwell.

Rock, P. (1973) Phenomenalism and essentialism in the sociology of deviance, *Sociology*, 7(1), 17–29.

Root, M. (2007) Social problems in Kincaid, H, Dupré, J and Wylie, A (eds.) *Value Free Science? Ideals and Illusions*. Oxford: Oxford University Press.

Rosenberg, A. (1988) *Philosophy of Social Science*. Oxford: Clarendon.

Rowe, F., Bell, M., Bernard, A., Charles-Edwards, E. and Ueffing, P. (2019) Impact of internal migration on population redistribution in Europe: Urbanisation, counterurbanisation or spatial equilibrium? *Comparative Population Studies*, [S.l.], 44, November.

Ruben, D.-H.((2009) Comment: Going in circles in Mantzavinos, C. (ed.) *Philosophy of the Social Sciences, Philosophical Theory and Scientific Practice*. Cambridge: Cambridge University Press. pp 312–324.

Rubin, D.B. (2005) Causal inference using potential outcomes: Design, modeling, decisions, *Journal of the American Statistical Association*, 100(469), 322–331.

Ruelle, D. (1991) *Chance and Chaos*. Harmonsworth: Penguin.

Russell, B. (1991) Einstein's law of Gravitation in T. Ferris (ed.) *The World Treasury of Physics, Astronomy and Mathematics*: Boston: Little Brown.

Russell, B. (1992) On the notion of cause, orig. 1912, in Slater, J. (ed.) *The Collected Papers of Bertrand Russell v6: Logical and Philosophical Papers 1909–1913*. London: Routledge Press. pp 193–210.

Russell, B. (2009[1912]) *The Problems of Philosophy*. Gutenberg Project. https://www.gutenberg.org/files/5827/5827-h/5827-h.htm. Accessed 26/06/20.

Salmon, W. (1971) *Statistical Explanation and Statistical Relevance*. Pittsburgh: University of Pittsburgh Press.

Salmon, W. (1989) *Four Decades of Scientific Explanation*. Pittsburgh: University of Pittsburgh Press.

Sapperstein, A. (1995) War and chaos, *American Scientist*, 83, 548–557.

Savage, M. and Burrows, R. (2007) The coming crisis of empirical sociology, *Sociology*, 41(5), 885–889.

Savage, M., Barlow, J., Dickens, P. and Fielding, T. (1992) *Property, Bureaucracy and Culture: Middle Class Formation in Contemporary Britain*. London: Routledge.

Savage, M., Devine, F., Cunningham, N., Taylor, M., Li, Y. and Hjellbrekke, J., et al. (2013). A new model of social class: Findings from the great British class survey. *Sociology*, 47, 219–250.

Sayer, A. (1992) *Method in Social Science: A Realist Approach*. 2nd edn. London: Routledge.

Sayer, A. (2000) *Realism and Social Science*. London: Sage.

Schleiermacher, F. (1998) *Hermeneutics and Criticism, and Other Writings*. Translated and edited by Bowie, A. Cambridge: Cambridge University Press.

Seager, W. (2000) Supervenience and determinism in Newton-Smith, W. (ed.) *A Companion to the Philosophy of Science*. Oxford: Blackwell.

Searle, J. (1995) *The Social Construction of Reality*. Harmondsworth: Penguin.

Senior, M. (1998) Area variations in self-perceived limiting long term illness in Britain, 1991: Is the Welsh experience exceptional? *Regional Studies*, 32(3), 265–280.

Shapiro, S. (1987) The social control of impersonal trust, *The American Journal of Sociology*, 93(3), 623–658.

Sharif, S., Mostafiz, I. and Guptan, V. (2018) A systematic review of structural equation modelling in nursing research, *Nurse Researcher*, 26(2), 28–31.

Skvoretz, J. (1998) Theoretical models: Sociology's missing links in Sica, A. (ed.) *What Is Social Theory: the Philosophical Debates*. Malden, MA: Blackwell. pp 238–252.

Sleigh, J., Harvey, M., Voss, L. and Denny, B. (2014) Ketamine more mechanisms of action than just NMDA blockade, *Trends in Anaesthesia and Critical Care*, 4, 76–81.

Smelser, N. (1997) *The Problems of Sociology. The Georg Simmel Lectures 1995*. Berkeley, CA: University of California Press.

Sokal, A. and Bricmont, J. (1998) *Intellectual Impostures*. London: Profile Books.

Soloman, R. (1995) *A Passion for Justice: Emotions and the Origins of the Social Contract*. New York: Rowman and Littlefield.

Sullivan, A., Parsons, S., Green, F., Wiggins, R., Ploubidis, G. and Huynh, T. (2018) Educational attainment in the short and long term: Was there an advantage to attending faith, private, and selective schools for pupils in the 1980s? *Oxford Review of Education*, 44(6), 802–822.

Suppes, P. (1984) *Probabilistic Metaphysics*. Oxford: Blackwell.

Tallis, R. (1995) *Newton's Sleep: Two Cultures and Two Kingdoms*. London: Macmillan.

Tashakkori, A. and Teddlie, C. (1998) *Mixed Methodology: Combining Qualitative and Quantitative Approaches*. Thousand Oaks, CA: Sage.

Tauber, A (1997) 'Introduction' in Tauber, A (Ed.) *Science and the Quest for Reality*. London: Macmillan. 1–49.

Taylor, C. (1982) Rationality in Hollis, M. and Lukes, S. (eds.) *Rationality and Relativism*. Cambridge, MA: MIT Press. pp 87–105.

Taylor, C. (2018) The reliability of free school meal eligibility as a measure of socio-economic disadvantage: Evidence from the millennium cohort study in Wales, *British Journal of Educational Studies*, 66(1), 29–51.

Thomas, W. and Thomas, D. (1928) *The Child in America: Behavior Problems and Programs*. New York: Knopf.

Tiple, G. and Speak, S. (2005) Definitions of homelessness in developing countries, *Habitat International*, 29(2), 337–352.

Titmuss, R. (1971) *The Gift Relationship*. New York: Pantheon Books.

Uprichard, E. (2009) Introducing cluster analysis: What can it teach us about the case? in Ragin, C. and Byrne, D. (eds.) *Case Based Methods*. London: Sage.

van Bouwel, J. and Erik Weber, E. (2011) Explanation in the social sciences in Jarvie, I. and Zamora-Bonilla, J. (eds.) *The SAGE Handbook of the Philosophy of Social Sciences*. pp 632–646.

van Fraassen, B (1985) 'Empiricism in the Philosophy of Science,' in P. Churchland and C. Hooker (eds.), *Images of Science*, Chicago IL: University of Chicago Press, pp. 245–308.

van Fraassen, B. (1980) *The Scientific Image*. Oxford: Oxford University Press.

van Witteloostuijn, A. (2020) New-day statistical thinking: A bold proposal for a radical change in practices, *Journal of International Business Studies*, 51, 274–278.

Vincent, S. and Wapshott, R. (2014) Critical realism and the organisational case study: A Guide to discovering institutional mechanisms in Edwards, P, O'Mahoney, J and Vincent, S (eds) *Studying Organisations using Critical Realism*. Oxford: Oxford University Press

Vining, D and Kontuly, T (1978) 'Population Dispersal from Major Metropolitan Regions: An International Comparison' *International Regional Science Review* 3 (1) 49–73.

von Wright, G. (1993) Two Traditions in Hammersley, M. (ed.) *Social Research: Philosophy, Politics, Practice.* London: Sage.

Wakefield A, Murch S, Linnell, A, Casson DM, Malik M (1998) 'Ileal lymphoid nodular hyperplasia, non-specific colitis, and pervasive developmental disorder in children [retracted].' *Lancet* 351, 637–41.

Ware, L., Maconachie, M., Williams, M., Chandler, J. and Dodgeon, B. (2007) Gender life course transitions from the nuclear family in England and Wales 1981–2001, *Sociological Research Online*, 12(4). http://www.socresonline.org.uk/12/4/6.html.

Watts, C. and Gilbert, N. (2014) *Simulating Innovation: Computer-Based Tools for Rethinking Innovation.* Cheltenham: Elgar.

Weaver, W. (1948) Science and complexity, *American Scientist*, 36(4), 536–544.

Weber, M. (1974) "Objectivity" in social science and social policy in G. Riley (ed.) *Values, Objectivity and the Social Sciences.* Reading, MA: Adison-Wesley.

Weber, M. (1978[1921]) *Economy and Society.* Oakland, CA: University of California Press.

Webster, D. (2002) "Unemployment: how official statistics distort analysis and policy, and why", *Radical Statistics.* https://www.radstats.org.uk/conf2002/webster.htm.

Whorf, B. (1956) *Language, Thought and Reality* J. Carroll (ed.). New York: Wiley.

Willet, J. (2011) National identity and regional development: Cornwall and the campaign for objective 1 funding, *National Identities*, 15(3), 297–311.

Williams, C. (1997) *Counter-Urbanisation: Housing and Households in Cornwall.* PhD Thesis. Plymouth: University of Plymouth. https://pearl.plymouth.ac.uk/handle/10026.1/420. Accessed 22/06/20.

Williams, M. (1998) The social world as knowable in May, T. and Williams, M. (eds.) *Knowing the Social World.* Buckingham: Open University Press. pp 5–21.

Williams, M. (1999) Single case probabilities and the social world: The application of Popper's propensity interpretation, *Journal for the Theory of Social Behavior*, 29(2), 187–201.

Williams, M. (2000a) *Science and Social Science: An Introduction.* London: Routledge.

Williams, M. (2000b) Interpretivism and generalisation, *Sociology*, 34(2), 209–244.

Williams, M. (2001) Complexity, probability and causation: Implications for homelessness research, *Journal of Social Issues*, 1(2). http://www.whb.co.uk/socialissues/. Accessed 09/07/20.

Williams, M. (2002) The Status of generalisation in interpretive research in May, T. (ed.) *Qualitative Research in Action.* London: Sage. pp 125–143.

Williams, M. (2003a) The problem of representation: Realism and operationalism in survey research, *Sociological Research On Line,* 8(1). http://www.socresonline.org.uk/8/1/williams .html.

Williams, M. (2003b) Why is Cornwall poor? Poverty and migration since the 1960s, *Journal of Contemporary History*, 17(3), 55–70.

Williams, M. (2005a) Situated objectivity, *Journal for the Theory of Social Behavior*, 35(1), 99–120.

Williams, M. (2005b) Definition, measurement and legitimacy in studies of homelessness in Romero, M. and Margolis, E. (eds.) *Social Inequalities* (Blackwell Companion to Sociology Series). Malden, MA: Blackwell. pp 190–210.

Williams, M. (2006) Can scientists be objective? *Social Epistemology*, 20(2), 163–180.

Williams, M. (2009) Social objects, causality and contingent realism, *Journal for the theory of Social Behavior*, 39(1), 1–18.

Williams, M. (2011) Contingent realism – Abandoning necessity, *Social Epistemology*, 25(1), 37–56.

Williams, M. (2014) Probability and models in Edwards, P O'Mahoney, J and Vincent, S(eds.) *Studying Organisations Using Critical Realism.* Oxford: Oxford University Press. pp 282–299.

Williams, M. (2015) Situated objectivity, values and realism, *European Journal of Social Theory*, 18(1), 76–92.

Williams, M. (2016) *Key Concepts in the Philosophy of Social Research*. London: Sage.

Williams, M. (2017) Making up mechanisms in realist research in Emmel, N., Greenhalgh, J., Manzano, A., Monaghan, M. and Dalkin, S. (eds.) *Doing Realist Research*. London: Sage. pp 25–40.

Williams, M. and Champion, T. (1998) Cornwall, poverty and in migration, *Cornish Studies 2nd Series*, 6, 118–126.

Williams, M. and Cheal, B. (2001) Is there any such thing as homelessness? Measurement, explanation and process in "homelessness" research, *European Journal of Social Research-Innovation*, 11(3), 239–254.

Williams, M. and Cheal, B. (2002) Can we measure homelessness? A critical evaluation of the method of capture-recapture, *International Journal of Social Research Methodology*, 4(3), 313–332.

Williams, M. and Dyer, W. (2004) Realism and probability in Carter, B. and New, C. (eds.) *Making Realism Work*. London: Routledge. pp 67–86.

Williams, M. and Dyer, W. (2009) Single case probabilities in Ragin, C. and Byrne, D. (eds.) *Case Based Methods*. London: Sage.

Williams, M. and Dyer, W. (2017) Complex realism in social research, *Methodological Innovations Online*. https://journals.sagepub.com/doi/full/10.1177/2059799116683564

Williams, M. and Husk, K. (2013) Can we, should we, measure ethnicity? *International Journal of Social Research Methodology*, 16(4), 285–300.

Williams, M., Cheal, B. and Gomez, S. (1995) *Homelessness in Plymouth: Stage Two*. Plymouth City Council/Shelter UK.

Williams, M., Payne, G., Hodgkinson, L. and Poade, D. (2008) Does British sociology count?: Sociology students' attitudes toward quantitative methods, *Sociology*, 42(5), 1003–1021.

Williams, M., Sloan, L. and Brookfield, C. (2017) A tale of Two sociologies: Analysis versus critique in UK Sociology, *Sociological Research Online*, 22(4). https://journals.sagepub.com/doi/10.1177/1360780417734146.

Williams, M.L., Burnap, P. and Sloan, L. (2016) Crime sensing with big data: The affordances and limitations of using open source communications to estimate crime patterns, *British Journal of Criminology*, 57(2), 320–334.

Willis, P. (1977) *Learning to Labour How Working Class Kids Get Working Class Jobs*. Farnborough: Saxon House.

Wilson, J. and Kelling, G. (1982) "Broken windows the police and neighborhood safety" *Atlantic Monthly*. March. http://illinois-online.org/krassa/ps410/Readings/Wilson%20and%20Kelling%20Broken%20Windows.pdf Accessed 24/06/20.

Winch, P. (1990 [1958]) *The Idea of a Social Science and Its Relation to Philosophy*. London: Routledge.

Wittgenstein, L. (1953) *Philosophical Investigations*. Oxford: Blackwell.

Wolpert, L. (1992) *The Unnatural Nature of Science*. London: Faber.

Woolf, R. (2009) Truth as a value in Plato's republic, *Phronesis*, 54(1), 6–30.

Woolgar, S. (1988) *Knowledge and Reflexivity: New Frontiers in the Sociology of Knowledge*. London: Sage.

World Health Organisation (WHO). (2018) *International Classification of Diseases (ICD)*. https://www.who.int/classifications/icd/en/.

Worrall, J. (1990) Scientific revolutions and scientific rationality: The case of the elderly holdout in Wade Savage, C. (ed.) *Scientific Theories*. Minneapolis: University of Minnesota Press. pp 319-337.

Wu, Y., Sun, I. Y. and Cao, L. (2017), 'Immigrant Perceptions of the Police: Theoretical Explanations', *International Journal of Police Science and Management*, 19: 171–86.

INDEX

Note: Page numbers in *italics* indicate figures and numbers with "n" indicate end note in the text

"abstracted empiricism" 27, 31, 115, 194n2
"accidental laws" 50
"action space" 170, 192, 194n1
Actor Network Theory 101n1, 145n12
actuality 70, 104, 123n4, 201
administrative data 184; *see also* data
Agent-Based Modelling (ABM) 191
Agent-Based Simulation 191
agnosticism 112, 203
"Aim of Science, The" (Popper) 104
alternative rationality 180; *see also* rationality
analysis *see* causal analysis
ANOVA 138–139, 188
anthropology/ anthropologists 91, "classic studies" 173; functionalism 110; philosophy and 174, 176; sociology and 110, 173
anti-causal thinking 59
"anti-colonial" 174
"anti-positivism" 30, 129; *see also* positivism
anti-realism in social science 24–25; 27–35; causal analysis 27–29; language 29–35; mythology 29–35; quantitative methods 27–29
anti-science 30
Arab Spring 45–46, 57
Archer, M. 38
Arendt, H. 30
Aristotle 22, 30, 104
artificial intelligence 140, 191
atomic hypothesis 18
attitudes: behaviour and 99; beliefs and 74, 85, 115, 169; measurement 85, 87; migrants and non-migrants 161; multi-dimensional 82; negative 138; positive 138; risky sexual behaviour 177; scales 139
authoritarianism 32, 45, 206
autonomy: behavioural 72; cognitive values 129; individual 52, 171; internal 140; neutrality and 129; physical dispositions 72; social objects 75
Azande 175–176, 179

"bad science" 143
Balnaves, M. 183
Bateson, N. 85
Baudrillard, J. 32
Bayesian approaches 131
Bayesian probability 39
behaviour 16; action and 24; attitudes and 99; autonomy 72; beliefs 16, 182–183, 201; collective 151; consumer 178–179; divergent 44; emotions and 84; gambling 175; human 74, 151; hybrid 179; large social matrix 70; mechanisms 165; "negative" 153; research 99; risk-taking 177; sexual 177–178; sex workers 177, 181; social 17, 52, 90, 199; stable 51; teleological 192
beliefs 16; actions and 35, 56, 70, 75, 156, 165–166, 170, 173, 176, 180, 201, 205; attitudes and 74, 85, 115, 169;

behaviour 16, 182–183, 201; causes 19; desires and 73–74, 200; dispositions 70; false 78, 173; inter-relationships of mental states 17; measurement 85; social and religious 129; social objects 73–74
Belk, R. 177–178
Berkeley, G. 21
Berry, B. J. L. 103
Bhaskar, R. 7–8, 33–35, 75, 95, 127, 135, 169, 202
big data 4, 110, 181, 184–185; *see also* data
biological mechanism 179; *see also* mechanism
Bird, A. 18
Blalock, H. 29, 86–88, 202
Blastland, M. 40
Blau, P. 60, 193
Blumer, H. 172
Bohm, D. 56–57
Bouazizi, M. 45–46, 57
Bourdieu, P. 114, 195n9
Boyle's Law 49
"bracketing" 112
Bramley, G. 82, 88–89, 127
Brewer, J. 28
Brexit (2016) 51
bridal virginity 178
Bridgeman, P. 85–86
British Cohort Survey (BCS70)182
British Sociological Association (BSA) 120
Broken Windows theory 185, 194n7
Brookfield, C. 12n2, 120
Brown, R. 50
Brownian motion 37, 130
Bryman, A. 33
Bunge, M. 29
Burrows, R. 110, 184
Butterfly Effect 42, 45, 67, 70
Byrne, D. 5, 8, 42–43, 65, 79, 82, 85, 93, 112, 169–170, 181, 183, 185–186, 193

Callaghan, G. 42–43, 79
Callon, M. 54n9
Cambodian revolution (1970) 52
Cameroon 90
Campbell, D. 6–7
Canada 90, 138
Caputi, P. 183
Cartwright, N. 8, 25–27, 49, 54n10, 55, 79, 80n14, 181, 197, 200
Carver, R. 111
case-based complexity 188; *see also* complexity
case-based methods, methodological toolkit 184–192
Castellani, B. 8, 58, 70, 110, 187–188, 191–192, 195n9
Castro, F. 52
causal analysis 20; apotheosis 3; linear model and 181; practice and application 64; quantitative methods and 27–29; sociologists 59; statistical inference 66; tradition 29, 61, 150, 196; variants of path analysis 62, 80n9
causal efficacy 26, 77–78
causal inference 64, 66, 185; *see also* inference
causality/cause 55–79, 80n1; complexity and 78–79; denial of 58–59; determination 56–58; empiricism 58–59; operationalising 56–66; probabilistic 59–70; social objects 70–78; in social world 199–201
"causal powers" 19, 36n4, 194n2
"causal stories" 26, 170, 183
cause–effect relationships 19, 57, 59, 67, 70, 74
Cellular Automata (CA) 191
ceteris paribus 26, 49, 50–51, 72–73, 94, 175, 197
challenges: complex biology 16; complexity 188; empirical 118; empiricism 14; logical positivism 103; mathematicians 44; methodological 5, 44, 110; philosophical 4, 191; rationality 21; realism 18, 22–27; social organisation 4; social research 44; social science 206
Chamberlain, S. 119
Champion, T. 99
Chaos Theory 37, 42
Cheal, B. 83
Cheney, D. 42
Chicago School 28
Cicourel, A. 2, 173
Cilliers, P. 5
"classical anthropologists" 174
Clifford, J. 32–33, 113
cloud systems 43
cluster analysis 189, *190*, 205
Cogito (Descartes) 48
Cold War 42, 45
collective behaviour 151; *see also* behaviour
collectivisation 143
Collin, H. 105

complexity/complex 5–6, 37–38, 53; case-based 188; causality and 78–79; contingency and 41–46; mechanisms 165–166, 170; neologisms 198; policy intervention 44; probability causality and 66–70; problem 188; reality 168; real representation 81–83; social life 3, 89; *see also* causality/cause
complex realism 6–8, 25, 39, 194, 196–206; conceptual necessity 197; defined 1; developement 5; epistemology 202–204; methodology 204–205; natural necessity 197; ontology 196–201; social world 197–201; *see also* realism
computer simulation 46
conceptual necessity 48, 51, 57, 171, 197–198
consciousness 126, 134, 140
constant conjunction 20, 80n9, 169
constructivism 31, 75
constructive empiricism 25; *see also* empiricism
constructivism 21, 34–35, 75, 174
consumer behaviour 179; *see also* behaviour
"contextual realism" 12n1
"contextual values" 144
contingency: complexity and 26, 41–46; concept 38; ontological 26; social world 51
"contingent realism" 12n1
conventional values 137
Conway, J. 191
Corbyn, J. 198
Cornish language 33
Coronavirus 199
correspondence theory of truth 36n6
counterfactual causality 63, 183 *see also* causality/cause
counterurbanisation: mechanisms 159–163; process 103; theory representation 97–100
Couvalis, G. 104
"covering law" model 81
Covid-19 51, 143, 199
creating social objects 74–78; *see also* social objects
criminology 131, 137–138, 166n6, 184
critical realism 6–8, 34, 37–38
"critical stance" 7
Cuban missile crisis 42, 52
cultural–rational imperatives 179
"the culture of analysis" 3
Cummings, R. 206n1
Current Population Survey (1962) 193
Custody Diversion Team (CDT) 186

Dale, A. 105
Dalton, J. 18
"dappled world" 79, 25–27
Darwin, C. 106
Darwinism 142
data: administrative 184; availability 4; big 4, 110, 181, 184–185; cluster analysis of 186; collection 3–4, 172, 184–185; GPS 185; longitudinal 181; quantitative 38; science 19; social media 4; transactional 4, 110, 184–185; video 185
"data mining" 185
"data scientists" 4
Davies, C. A. 113
"decision bifurcations" 70
decision-making 52, 150
deductive nomological (DN) 47–48, 81, 102, 121
denial of causality 58–59; *see also* causality/cause
dependencies, methodological toolkit 174–177
dependent variables 3, 62, 64, 83, 138, 149, 182, 186; *see also* variables
Derrida, J. 32–33
Descartes, R. 48
desires: actions and 124, 176; beliefs and 11, 17, 70, 73–74, 150, 154, 200; social objects 73–74; social sciences and 30
determination, causality 56–58
determinism 68
"deterministic causality" 56–57
"deterministic chaos" 42–43
de Vaus, D. 84
digital revolution 4
Discriminant Analysis 183, 186–187
Discriminant Function Analysis 92
discrimination 171
disorganised complexity 37; *see also* complexity
dispositions, social objects 71–73
Dodd, S. 27, 59
duck-rabbit illusion 103
dummy variables 64
Duncan, O. 60, 193
Durkheim, E. 6, 48, 52, 197
Duverger's Law 50
Dyer, W. 8, 186

economic(s): "base" 193; decline in Cornwall 159–163; "laws" 50; liberalism 143

Economic and Social Research Council (ESRC) 3
Eddington, A. 106
Einsteinian physics 104
Einsteinian relativity 107
Einstein's concept of simultaneity 85
Einstein's theory of general relativity 106–107
Einstein's theory of special relativity 22
"elderly holdouts" 109, 122n3
electro-chemical stimulus 15
Elliot, J. 92–93, 112, 117, 183
emergence 45; complex 37, 191; dynamic change 201; probabilistic causality 68–70; properties and relations 45; second wave feminism 30; stable patterns 52; strange attractors and 38; weak 46
empirical adequacy 25
"empirical closure" 205
empirical realist 6
empiricism: causality 58–59; logical 30, 92; realism 19–20; social science 202; *see also* "abstracted empiricism"
empiricist principle of experience 25
English 33, 51
Enlightenment critique 7
"epistemological positioning" 168
epistemological relativism 21, 32, 139–140, 143, 174–175
epistemological thesis, objective knowledge 128–139
epistemology 38–41, 202–204
"error term" 169
ethnicity 3, 60–61, 87, 95, 97, 170–171
ethnography 113, 176
ethnomethodology 112
European Union 33, 51, 173
Evers, C. W. 38, 98
evolutionary epistemology 203
"experimenting society" 7
explanans, explanandum 47

face-to-face interviews 3
"fact value" continuum 85
false beliefs 78, 173
falsification/falsificationism 115
falsification: reflexivity and 119; theory choice 105–108
feedback 17
feminism 7
Feyerabend, P. 30
Fisher, S. 176
"fixed points" 53
"flat ontology" 97, 109–110, 204
"forms of life" 31
"fractal structure" 44
Francot, L. M. A 142
Freedman, D. 63–65, 181
"free floating" probabilities 47
frequency theory 38–39, 59, 67, 181
functionalism 110
fundamentally probabilistic 80n2

Galilean physics 104
Galilean traditions 30
"Game of Life" 191
Geertz, C. 176, 180
General Linear Model (GLM) 61, 136, 145n10
Gergen, K. 34
Gerrits, L. 186
Gigerenzer, G. 111, 116–117
Gilbert, N. 39
Gleick, J. 42
GLIM (statistical software) 3, 13n7
Gödel's paradox 202
"god particle" 23
"gold standard" 182
Goldthorpe, J. 8, 52–53, 65, 74, 96, 205
Gouldner, A. 133, 137
GPS data 185; *see also* data
Great Britain 97–98, 107, 120, 131; Brexit (2016) 51; causal analysis in 64; censuses 85; economically and socially deprived communities 44; Office for National Statistics (ONS) 88, 194n5; quantitative social science 29; referendum 33; Sure Start project 44

Hacking, I. 8, 22, 80n3
Hafferty, F. 187
Haig, B. 38, 90
Hall, N. 55–56
Hammersley, M. 7
Hanson, N. R. 103
"hard cores of theoretical assumptions" 122
Harré, R. 17, 23, 47–49
Hartwig, M. 38
Harvey, D. 5
Hayek, F. 143
Heidegger, M. 31
Hempel, C. 81
hermeneutics 31
"heroic" physics 104
"heroic science" 106, 203
Herrnstein, R. 135
"heuristics" 109, 116
Higgs boson 23

historical mechanism 179; *see also* mechanism
homelessness/"homeless" 82–83, 85, 91–92, 127–128
Hopkins, G. M. 79
Hoyle, F. 108–109
Hubble, E. 108, 122n2
human behaviour 74, 151; *see also* behaviour
humanism 4
Hume, D. 20, 48, 58–59, 105
Humean proof 20
"Hume's Problem" 23, 30, 115
Hunter, A. 28
hybrid behaviour 179
hypothesis: alternative 111; Dalton's atomic 18; null 111, 116, 136; research 64; Sapir Whorf 31, 174; statistical 111; synthesis and 8–9; testing 80n7, 111, 116

idealism, realism 20–22
immigrants 137–139
"incredulity toward meta-narratives" 32
independent variable 3, 62, 138, 186, 202; *see also* variables
individual action 52
individualism, methodological 90, 150, 170
inference: causal 64, 66, 185; logical 186; statistical 66; theory choice 115–119
inference to the best explanation (IBE) 117–119
instrumentalism, constructive empiricism 25
instrumentation 20
interacting mechanisms 178–179
Internet research 4
interpretation: assessment 114; "authentic" 113, 180; beliefs and actions 173; data 205; frequency 131; historical 32; human 140; misunderstanding 113; quantification 22; regularities 176; relative 32; social constructs 91
interpretive sociology 112
interpretivism 172
"intransitive object" 75, 95
INUS (Insufficient but Necessary part of a complex of Unnecessary but Sufficient conditions). 58, 186
invariance 51–52, 70, 74–75, 125, 142, 170–171, 185, 201
investigation, realism 35–36

Jung, M. 137–139, 141

Kant, I. 15, 21, 48
Kennedy, J. F. 42, 66–67
keow 33
"key informants" 177
kheun khroo 181
Khmer Rouge 143
Khrushchev, N. 52
King, S. 66
Knafo, S. 114
knowledge *see* objective knowledge
"knowledge of knowledge" 124, 129
Kreft, I. 116
Kuhn, T. 30, 103–105
Kuhn's paradigms 109

Lakatos, I. 102, 108–109, 116, 122
Lamarckian principle 142
Lancet 143
language 29–35
Laplace, P. 41, 68
large-scale real-time data 184
laws and regularities, mechanisms 148–151
Lawson, T. 45, 169
Lazarsfeld, P. 27, 59
Lewis, D. 63
Limiting Long Term Illness (LLTI) 94, 182
linear dependency 41
linear regression 138–139
linguistic dexterity 33
linguistic philosophy 32
"lingustic turn" 31
literary criticism 31
Little, D. 8, 90, 204
"living alone" 93
local realism 90–92, 204; *see also* realism
local to global, operationalism 93–96
Locke, J. 58
"logical atomism" 36n5
logical empiricism 30, 92; *see also* empiricism
logical inference 186; *see also* inference
logical necessity 47
logical positivism 20, 30, 58, 85, 102–103, 106
Longino, H. 8, 132, 139, 144
longitudinal data 181; *see also* data
Lorentz, E. 42
Lundberg, G. 27–28, 59, 87
Lynch, M. 113
Lysenkian genetics 129, 142–143

Mackie, J. L. 57–58

MacLure, M. 32
macro explanation, methodological toolkit 170–172
macro-level analyses 69
macro-method toolkit 181–184
Macron, E. 46–47
macro social relationships 16
Madden, E. 47–49
Mahalanobis distance (MD) 187, 195n8
Mahoney, J. 54n4, 54n9
Maki, U. 8, 90, 204
making up, mechanisms 147–157
Marcus, G. E. 32–33, 113
Marcuse, H. 30
Markov Chain 69
Marsh, C. 65
Marx, G. 58
Marx, K. 6
Marxism 7, 96, 101n10, 106, 109, 123n4
materialism 21, 35
material–mental relationship 15
May, T. 1
mean velocity 22
Measles, Mumps, Rubella (MMR) vaccine 143
measurement: attitudes 85, 87; beliefs 85; ethnicity 87; operationalism 89–93; rubric 86; social reality 3
mechanisms 146–166; biological 179; complexity 165–166, 170; contexts and 151–156; counterurbanisation 159–163; economic decline in Cornwall 159–163; hypothesise 185; interacting 178–179; laws and regularities 148–151; making up 147–157; modelling 157–165; principal 163–165; reality 156–157, 165–166; theoretical 169; theory and models 157–159
Mellor, D. H. 59
mental objectivity 134
mental processes 126, 174
mental propensities 200
Merton, R. 54n3, 96–97, 100, 204
"Meso" 36n2
meso social relationships 16
"meta-narrrative" 31
metaphysical realism 197; *see also* realism
metaphysics 58
methodenstreit 2, 30
"method of difference" 194n4
methodological criticism 177
methodological framework, theory choice 112–121
methodological individualism 90, 150, 170
"methodological self consciousness" 113
methodological thinking 5
methodological toolkit 168–194; case-based methods 184–192; dependencies 174–177; macro explanation 170–172; macro-method toolkit 181–184; micro-complexity 170–172; micro-method toolkit 172–181; overview 168–170; realist closure 192–194; sexual practices in Thailand 177–181; simulation 191–192; social research 192–194
methodology: complex realism 204–205; values 131, 136
"metric-mania" 4
Michelson–Morley experiment 22
micro-complexity 170–172, 180
micro-method toolkit 172–181
micro social relationships 16
middle range theory 96–97, 100, 183, 204
migration 98
Mill, J. S. 29, 129, 194n4
Millennium Cohort Study (MCS) 3
Miller, G. A. 15
Mills, C. W. 27, 115
mind-dependency 17
"mini mechanisms" 193
"minor theories" 97
modelling mechanisms 157–165
"moderatum generalisations" 205
modus ponens / modus tollens 119
"money economy" 141
Monroe, B. 185
Monte Carlo fallacy 175
"moral sciences" 129
moral values 131–132
Morning, A. 54n9
motivation 98–99, 115, 154, 161, 204
multiple regression 24
Murray, C. 135
mythology, anti-realism 29–35

Nagel, T. 202
naïve falsificationism 108; *see also* falsification
naked singularity 204, 206n4
natural necessity 8, 48–51, 69, 87, 197
natural sciences 87, 90, 96, 101n1, 111, 129, 132, 197–198
natural scientists 168
necessity 46–53; *see also* conceptual necessity
negative attitudes 138
negative heuristic 109
"neo-positivist" 4

"nested probabilities" 70
neutrality 129, 133
Newton, I. 67, 68–69, 104, 107, 134
Newtonian laws of gravity 67, 107
Newtonian physics 104
Newtonian space 31
Newton's laws of motion 41
New Zealand Census 96
Neyman–Rubin causal model 63
Nietzsche, F. 31
nihilism 31
"non observables" 202
"non realists" 8
non-zero probabilities 40
"normal science" 104
"noumena" 15, 21, 194
Nozick, R. 8, 51, 53, 54n11
null hypothesis 111; *see also* hypothesis
NVivo 192

objective knowledge 124–144, 203; epistemological thesis 128–139; ontological thesis 125–128; physical reality 125–128; situated objectivity 128–139, 144; social objects 125–128; social reality 125–128; values and morality in third world 142–143
objective theories 38
objectivity 129, 137; operationalisation 136; situated 133, 139; "situatedness" 138; social value 136; value 136–139; as a value 132–136
"observational language" 30
Occam's Razor 25, 118, 182
Office for National Statistics (ONS) 88, 194n5
ontological equivalence 175
"ontological naturalism" 17, 126
ontological probability 41, 200
ontological theory 78, 198
ontological thesis, objective knowledge 125–128
ontology 38–41; complex realism 196–201; realists 202; social complexity 201
"open society" 142
operationalism/operationalisation 21, 28, 85–96; causality 56–66; local realism 90–92; local to global 93–96; measurement 89–93; objectivity 136; realist representation 93–96; representation 85–96; social or historical narrative 92–93
optical illusion 103
organised complexity 37; *see also* complexity
Oswald, L. H. 42
Outhwaite, W. 35

Pakistan 57
Papineau, D. 58–59, 62, 73–74
"paradigms" 4, 104
Parsons, T. 30, 52, 54n3, 54n12, 74
particle-wave duality 122n3
"passive" anti-realism 27
Paul, L. 55–56
Pawson, R. 7–8, 97, 100, 109–110, 187, 201, 204
Payne, G. 119
Pearl, J. 63
Pearson, K. 59, 80n3
Peirce, C. S. 117
perceptions: affluence and opportunity 163; awareness 113; dependent 21; immigrant 137; independent 125; poverty 132; reasons and 4; sense 48; student 121; of things 134
"phase space" 43
phenomenalism/phenomenology 112, 115
philosophical challenges 4
philosophy and anthropology 174
Phlogiston genetics 129
physical electro-chemical stimulus 126
physical laws 50, 67, 81
physical objects 77, 130, 197
physical reality 15–16, 17–18, 125–128
physical structures 17
physical systems 53
Planning for Real methods 44, 54n7
Plato 136
Platt, J. 59, 119–120
pluralism 169
Polanyi, M. 103
political pollsters 24
Popper, K. 8–9, 30, 38–39, 43, 67–68, 70–71, 102, 104, 106, 108–109, 112–113, 115, 119, 122n1, 123n4, 198, 206n2; "all life is problem solving" 142; concept of verisimilitude 203; evolutionary epistemology 203; open society 143; single case propensity theory of probability 187; "third world" of knowledge 124, 140, 142, 145n12, 176, 204
Porpora, D. 64–65, 181
Portes, A. 54n9
"positioning" 29
positive attitudes 138
"positive" heuristic 109
positivism 2, 4, 202; critique of 8; logical 20, 30, 58, 102–103, 106

"possibility spaces" 43–45, 199
post-modernism 31–32
Practice Theory 195n9
pragmatism 28
pre-scientific thinking 104
principal of mechanisms 163–165
a priori mode of necessity 47–48
Pritchard, E. 174
"private language" 31
probability(ies) 38–41; causality 57, 59–70, 78; ontological 41; range 49; realism and 38; space 69; theory 53
"propensities" 39, 41, 53, 67–68; *see also* frequency theory
"protective belt" 109
"proxy" variable 86
pseudo-scientific, social science 2
psychoanalysis 106
psychological illness 16
Puri, R. 36n8
"push–pull" cause–effect 200
"puzzle solving" 104

Q-Step 3, 121
Qualitative Comparative Analysis (QCA) 65, 186–187, 192, 199
qualitative research 4
quantitative analysis 28
quantitative crisis 121–122
quantitative data 38
quantitative methods 27–29
quantitative research 3, 172
quantum damping 26, 36n8
quantum gravity 2
quantum physics 56–57

R (application) 3
Ragin, C. 185–186
Rajaram, R. 195n9
Randomised Control Trials 182
rationalism, Western 179
rationality: alternative 180; relativism and 175
"reactionary" science 30
real but contingent, social objects as 75–76
realism 14–36; anti-realism in social science 27–35; challenges 22–27; complex realism 6–8, 53; critical 6–8, 34, 37–38; empirical forms 6; empiricism 19–20; entities 22; idealism 20–22; investigation 35–36; local 204; metaphysical claim 18, 125; physical reality 15–16, 17–18; probability and 38; reality 35–36; rivals of 18–22; self-aware 6; social reality 16–18; theories 22; transcendental forms 6
realist(s) 54n9; about entities 24; closure 192–194; "closure" 93, 95; objectivity 128, 142; ontology 202; operationalisation 89–96, 100; philosophy 6; representation 93–96; research 168, 172; science 6; "scientific" 23; theory of language 34
"realist evaluation" movement 7
reality: complex 168; mechanisms 156–157, 165–166; realism 35–36; *see also* representation
"red shift" 108
Reed, M. 5
reflective self-awareness 126
"reflexive fallibilism" 118–122, 141
reflexive falsification 120
"reflexive turn" 112
reflexivity: falsification and 119; problem of 115; theory choice 112–115
relationships *see* cause–effect relationships; macro social relationships
relative invariance 51
relative propensity 53
relative stability *see* invariance
relativism 30, 128; epistemological 32, 139–140, 143, 174–175; problem of 141; rationality and 175
relativity theory 21, 81
reliability 81, 172
replicability 172
representation 81–101; complex real 81–83; counterurbanisation theory 97–100; operationalism 85–96; social survey 84–96; theories 96–100; theory choice 121–122
research programmes, theory choice 108–111
Reskin, B. 183
Respondent-Driven Sampling (RDS) 180
"retroductive" strategy 194n2
"revolutions in science" 104
"rhetorics of persuasion" 33
risk-taking behaviour 177; *see also* behaviour
rivals of realism 18–22
Rock, P. 115
Roman Catholic Church 48, 50
romanticism 31
Rubin, D. 63
Rubin causal model (RCM) 63
Ruelle, D. 44
Russell, B. 6, 15, 36n5, 56, 68, 200

Salmon, W. 62
Santa Fe Institute 37
Sapir, E. 31
Sapir Whorf hypothesis 31, 174
Sapperstein, A. 69
Savage, M. 110, 184–185
Sayer, A. 45–46, 49–50, 71, 73
scepticism 2, 20, 25–26, 28, 31, 59
Schleiermacher, F. 113
science realism 49
scientific knowledge 102, 134
"scientific method" 30
scientific realism 18, 21, 23, 168, 169, 197
Searle, J. 90
second law of thermodynamics 47
"second order" reflexivity 114
self-awareness 16, 126
self-aware realism 6
self-consciousness 113
"self organisation" 52
self-reflection 113
self-similarity 44
Senior, M. 94–95
"sentiment" data 185
sexual practices in Thailand 177–181
simple attractors 54n5
simulation, methodological toolkit 191–192
singular causality 57
"situatedness" 138
situated objectivity 128–139, 133, 144
Sloan, L. 12n2
"smart heuristics" 116
"snowball sampling" 180
social action 74
social and psychological basis of theory choice 102–111
social capital 171, 202
social class 17, 61–62, 85, 149, 171, 202–203
social complexity 54n3, 169, 201
social construction 105, 129, 196
social constructivism 34
social data 185
social degeneration 185
"social facts" 48
social knowledge 143
social laws 50–51
social life 3
socially constructed and real social objects 75
social media data 4
social morality 142
social objects 35, 36n2, 49, 54n9, 70–78, 71, 138, 139, 172; autonomy 75; beliefs 73–74; causal efficacy of 77–78; creating 74–78, 192; desires 73–74; dispositions 71–73; dynamics 76, 201; mechanisms in social world 201; micro-actions 171; moral dimension 128; objective knowledge 125–128; physical objects 77; as real but contingent 75–76; relationship to other social objects 77–78; socially constructed and real 75; thought objects 77
social or historical narrative, operationalism 92–93
social progress 7
social reality 5, 34, 110, 125, 177, 192, 196–197, 204; measurement 3; objective knowledge 125–128; realism 16–18
social relations, illness 16
social research 2, 4, 7, 44, 192–194, 196
social sciences 101n1, 129–130, 132, 135, 168–169, 197; anti-realism in 27–35; empiricism 202; laws 142; methodologists 6; models 26; opposition 2–3; pseudo-scientific 2; success 2
social stratification 193
social survey 3, 84–96
social systems 43–44
social values 131–132, 136
social world: complex realism 197–201; probabilistic 197–199
Socio-Economic Classification (SEC) 88
"sociological" variables 85
Sociology And Complexity Science (SACS) 187–188
Sokal, A. 2
Spiegelhalter, D. 40
SPSS 3
Stalin, J. 142
standardisation 172
STATA 3
statistical analysis 172
statistical hypothesis 111
Statistics Canada 138
"steady state" theory 108
stochastic change 125
"strange attractors" 43–44, 52–53, 75, 83, 184, 199
"strong emergence" 46
Strong Programme 206n3
Structural Equation Modelling (SEM) 62–63, 92, 183
Structure of Scientific Revolutions, The (Kuhn) 104

subjective probability 39
subject–object separation 130
suicide 52
sui generis 131
Sullivan, A. 182
Sure Start project (Great Britain) 44, 54n6
synthesis and hypothesis 8–9
system dynamics 191
systems theory 54n3

tabula rasa 46, 103, 134, 179
"tacit knowledge" 105
Tarski, A. 36n6
tautology 136
Taylor, C. 175
teleological behaviour 192; *see also* behaviour
testing, theory choice 121–122
Thailand: culture 181; masculinity 178; sexual practices in 177–181; sex workers 181
"theoretical language" 30
theoretical mechanism 169; *see also* mechanisms
theories: mechanisms 157–159; representation 96–100
theory choice 102–122; falsification 105–108; inference 115–119; methodological framework 112–121; "reflexive fallibilism" 119–121; reflexivity 112–115; representation 121–122; research programmes 108–111; social and psychological basis 102–111; testing 121–122
Therevada Buddhism 178
"third world" of knowledge 124, 140, 142, 145n12, 176, 204
Thomas, D. 34
Thomas, W. I. 34, 173
thought objects 77
Tilley, N. 7
tout court 17, 54n10, 79
"toy worlds" 191
transactional data 4, 110, 184–185; *see also* data
"transcendental idealism" 21
transcendental necessity 47–48, 69
transcendental realist 6
transitive objects 75, 95
Trump, D. 32
"truth content" 23
"truth value" 28
Turing, A. 140
Twitter 4, 184, 192
"Two Traditions" (von Wright) 29–30

ubiquity 4, 39
UK Censuses 88
United States 42, 52, 92, 98, 131, 193; causal analysis in 64; imports 29; industrialisation 132; quantitative social science 29; sociologists 128; sociology 30
universal realism 90
"unknown, unknowns" 42
un-measured variables 64; *see also* variables
Uprichard, E. 186

validity 81, 84–85, 90, 95–96, 182
value(s): continuum in science 130–132; conventional values 137; freedom and values 129–130; methodological 131, 139; moral 131–132; morality in third world 142–143; objectivity 136–139; objectivity as 132–136; social 131–132
"value free" social science 128
"value free sociology" 130
van Bouwel, J. 82
van Fraassen, B. 8, 25, 27, 117–118
variability 62, 169
variables: dependent 3, 62, 64, 83, 138, 149, 182, 186; dummy 64; independent 3, 62, 138, 186, 202; "proxy" 86; "sociological" 85; un-measured 64
variance 63, 66, 125, 149, 185, 190
"variate traces" 193
verisimilitude 203
Verweij, S. 186
"vibrating strings" 36n1
video data 185
Vienna circle 106
Vietnam 181
Vietnam War 178–179
"view from nowhere" 202
virginity 178
"voluntary code" 76
von Wright, G. H. 29–30

Wakefield, A. 143
Wales 182
Watts, C. 39
Weaver, W. 37
Weber, E. 82
Weber, M. 8, 21, 130, 132, 141, 174
western consumerism 179
Western Europe 99
Western rationalism 179

Wheele, J. 200, 206n1
Whorf, B. 31
Wilkes Lambda 187
Williams, M. D. 1–3, 69
Williams, M. L184–186
Willis, P. 60
Winch, P. 2, 31, 33
Wittgenstein, L. 21, 31–32, 104
Wolpert, L. 113
Woolgar, S. 114
Work, Employment and Society (WES) 120
"world of propensities" 199
Worrall, J. 109, 122n3
Wu, Y. 138

Zetterberg, H. 204